In Search of the Lost Ark:
The Quest for the Ark of the
Covenant

by
Don Stewart

In Search of the Lost Ark:
The Quest for the Ark of the Covenant

by
Don Stewart

TABLE OF CONTENTS

Introduction

SECTION 3   "ARKEOLOGY:" IN SEARCH OF THE LOST ARK

Was the Ark Taken By Foreign Invaders?

Has The Ark Been Found?

INTRODUCTION

One of the most fascinating subjects that a person can study concerns the most sacred object of Israel's past—the Ark of the Covenant. The story of the Ark parallels the story of a nation who was called by God to be His witness to the world. The Bible records that Israel was supernaturally led by God from a land of slavery to a land of promise. At the center of their journey was the Ark of the Covenant. Though the Ark has been lost for over 2,500 years the mystique that surrounds this ancient artifact is still with us today. Explorers are continuing to look in various spots around the world for this elusive object.

The Entire Story

The approach in this book will be to examine the Ark of the Covenant in its overall Biblical context. Consequently attention will be paid to its construction, history, and meaning as well as its possible location. Our desire is to be thorough in our consideration of this subject, therefore extensive end notes will be at the end of each chapter for those who wish to pursue any matters further. Future editions of this book will update any new information that comes to the author's attention.

Reverence

When God spoke to Moses out of the burning bush He said:

Do not draw near this place. Take your sandals off your feet, for the place where you stand is holy ground (Exodus 3:7).

We must remember that the Ark was the most holy object that God has ever commanded mankind to build. Hence we should approach the subject with reverence and respect. With this attitude in mind, let us now examine one of the most important issues we could ever consider; the true story of the Ark of the Covenant.

Acknowledgment:

The cover concept and layout as well as all the original
drawings were done by Kim Stewart—
the best wife in the world.

SECTION ONE

THE MOST SACRED OBJECT
EVER CONSTRUCTED-
THE ARK OF THE COVENANT

CHAPTER 1

RAIDERS OF THE LOST ARK

The summer of 1981 saw the release of the blockbuster movie *Raiders of the Lost Ark*. The fanciful plot, set in the 1930's, depicted the search for the long lost Ark[1] of the Covenant—the container that held the Ten Commandments which were given to Moses by God. The searchers included a corrupt French archaeologist, treacherous Nazi's, and a dashing American archaeologist named Indiana Jones, portrayed by Harrison Ford. In the end Indiana got both the Ark and the girl. It was a marvelous adventure film.

The film raised the consciousness of the world to the subject of the Ark of the Covenant. This ancient artifact, constructed so long ago, became a topic of interest to the general public. Questions abounded concerning this sacred relic. What was the Ark of the Covenant? Did it have some secret power? Does it still exist? What would happen if the lost Ark were found? Would the discovery of the Ark have anything to do with end-time Bible prophecy?

These questions, along with many others, will be the focus of this book.

Where is the Ark?

The Ark of the Covenant was constructed some 3,500 years ago on Mt. Sinai under God-given directions to the prophet Moses. After forty years of leading the children of

Israel through the wilderness, the Ark was brought to the Promised Land. Eventually the Ark of the Covenant was placed in a permanent home in Solomon's Temple in Jerusalem.

The last historical reference we have to the Ark is in 621 B.C. For some unknown reason the Ark had been removed from the Temple. King Josiah ordered it returned:

> Then he said to the Levites who taught all Israel, who were holy to the Lord: 'Put the holy ark in the house which Solomon the son of David, king of Israel built. It shall no longer be a burden on your shoulders. Now serve the Lord your God and His people Israel' (2 Chronicles 35:3).

In 587 B. C. the armies of the Babylonian Empire under the command of King Nebuchadnezzar, came down and burned the Temple at Jerusalem and took captive some of the holy vessels.

About seventy-one years after this destruction there was a Second Temple[2] built by a man named Zerubbabel. According to Jewish tradition, five things that were in the First Temple were missing from the Second Temple: the Spirit of Prophecy, the Holy Fire, the Shekinah Glory, the Urim and Thummin[3] and the Ark of the Covenant. Since the time of the Babylonian captivity the fate of the Ark has been a mystery. The most sacred object to the nation of Israel vanished without a trace. The Bible is silent as to the Ark's fate. What happened to the Ark of the Covenant remains a mystery to this day. Historian Joan Comay, writes:

> The Ark of the Covenant installed by King Solomon had apparently disappeared before the destruction of the Temple in 587 B.C. It is surmised that the Ark may have been removed and hidden; there is no mention of it among the sacred vessels carried off by the Babylonian conquerors and restored by King Cyrus at the time of the return. In this mysterious fashion the most sacred . . . object of the Hebrew faith and nation vanished from history, never to reappear.[4]

The Most Important Treasure

The Ark of the Covenant is the most treasured object humanity could ever expect to find. It's importance can hardly be overstated. An ancient Jewish saying states that:

Palestine is the center of the world.
Jerusalem is the center of Palestine.
The Temple is the center of Jerusalem.
The Holy of Holies is the center of the Temple.
The Ark is the center of the Holy of Holies.
In the center of the Ark rests the stone called "The Foundation Stone of the World."

The Ark of the Covenant was the central object of the Old Testament.

The Possibility of Discovery

The ramifications of the Ark's discovery could not be calculated. Rabbi Leibel Reznick, who believes the Ark may still exist under the Temple Mount in Jerusalem, writes:

Of all the treasures yet to be discovered, what could be more important, more fascinating and more awe-inspiring than the Tablets of the Ten Commandments? No other archeological find would have greater impact on the destiny of man. These Tablets are the foundation of the three major religions. What a religious resurgence their discovery would cause. How it would cause scholars and laymen to reevaluate the past, examine the present, and speculate on the future cannot be imagined. Is it possible that such a sacred treasure lies but a few feet beneath what our eyes can see? Jewish tradition has always maintained that the treasures would remain until the coming of the Messiah. Muslim tradition forbids the site from being explored. Curiosity is nature's most powerful force. Tradition is God's immovable object of faith. Here on the Temple Mount we find the answer to that ancient conundrum, "What happens when an irresistible force meets an immovable object?" for the treasures are yet to be discovered.[5]

The Lost Ark Found?

Since the release of *Raiders of the Lost Ark* in 1981, there have been three well-publicized claims that the Ark of the Covenant has been found.[6]
There is an ancient tradition that the prophet Jeremiah buried the Ark on Mt. Nebo which lies in present-day Jordan.
On October 31, 1981, an American named Tom Crotser found a golden box-shaped object while he was digging on nearby Mt. Pisgah in Jordan. He later announced to the world that he had discovered the Ark of the Covenant.

Though he and his companions took over two hundred pictures of the "Ark," Crotser has never publicly released his photographs; only showing them to certain select people.

Moved to Ethiopia?

In March of 1992, a book was written by British journalist Graham Hancock titled *The Sign and the Seal: The Search for the Lost Ark of the Covenant*. The back cover of the book reads:

> THE SUBJECT OF THIS BOOK
> COULD CONSTITUTE THE
> SINGLE MOST SHATTERING
> SECRET OF THE LAST
> THREE THOUSAND YEARS

Hancock revives an ancient theory that the Ark was brought to Ethiopia. He, however, rejects the traditional Ethiopian story that the Ark was brought by Menelik, the supposed son of Solomon and the Queen of Sheba. He alleges that it was brought out of Israel in about 650 B.C. during the reign of the evil King Manasseh where it eventually made its way to Ethiopia. The Ark, he contends, now resides in a chapel in Axum, Ethiopia.

Under the Temple Mount?

In April of 1992, a show aired on CBS television where Rabbi Yehuda Goetz, chief Rabbi of the Western Wall in Jerusalem, claimed that the Ark had recently been discovered in a secret chamber underneath the Temple Mount in Jerusalem. He claims it is in a safe place waiting to be revealed at the proper time. Others have given a similar account.

Earlier in 1992, at the First Annual Temple Conference in Jerusalem, co-hosted by the author, Rabbi Chaim Richman of the Temple Institute[7] told a similar story.

None of these claims, however, have yet proven to be true.[8]

We will examine these three claims as well as other possible theories as to the mysterious fate of the Ark.

Bible Prophecy

The author has documented in another book, *The Coming Temple: Center Stage for the Final Countdown*,[9] why he believes a Third Temple will someday be built in Jerusalem, and the place that it has in Bible prophecy. The Ark of the Covenant may play a significant role in this future Temple.

Though the Ark was the centerpiece of the First Temple, it vanished before the Second Temple was built. If the Ark of the Covenant were to be found, it would provide unimagined motivation toward the Jewish goal of building a Third Temple.

We do not know if the genuine Ark still exists or if it will someday be found. If, however, the Ark is discovered, it is possible that it may figure into end-time Bible prophecy. There are several Bible passages, that we will consider later in the book, that may hint at the Ark's future discovery.

The Ever Unfolding Story

As we examine the history of the Ark, the present state of the search, and it's possible role in the future, we will embark on a journey that will span over four thousand years. It is the story of a people, the nation of Israel, and their special calling by God. Their story continues to this day, as the God of Abraham, Isaac and Jacob still works His plan in our modern world.

The movie *Raiders of the Lost Ark*, which brought worldwide interest to this subject, may be the preliminary act in an even greater drama—the actual discovery of the Ark of the Covenant.

Endnotes for Chapter 1

1. The word Ark is derived from the Latin term *arca*. It refers to a chest or a box. Other English translations render the term "chest" or "Covenant Box." The Hebrew noun *aron* is used 195 times in the Old Testament for the Ark of the Covenant.

2. Zerubbabel built the Second Temple which was eventually enlarged by Herod. Herod's enlargement is also referred to as the "Second Temple" though some writers call it the "Third Temple." In this book the term "Second Temple" will apply to both Zerubbabel's and Herod's structures.

3. The Spirit of Prophecy was the gift of prophecy. This gift, however, was operating during the Second Temple period (Haggai, Zechariah, Malachi). Upon their death (all in the same year say the Rabbi's) the gift of prophecy ceased. The Holy Fire came down from heaven on the altar. It descended first upon the altar of the Tabernacle when the sons of Aaron were consecrated to the priesthood. It descended a second time when the First Temple was inaugurated. It was continually kept lit by the priests. The Shekinah glory was the visible glory of God. The Urim and Thummin (lights and perfections) were the stones in the breastplate of the High Priest. They were used to help discern the will of God. All of these, including the Ark, were lacking in the Second Temple.

4. Joan Comay, *The Temple of Jerusalem*, New York, Holt, Rhinehart, and Winston, 1975, p. 134.

5. Leibel Reiznik, *The Holy Temple Revisited*, Northvale, New Jersey, Jason Aronson, Inc, 1990, pp.146,147.

6. The author is aware of other claims to the Ark's location. On other theories see Appendix 2.

7. The Temple Institute, headquartered in Jerusalem, is in the process of making implements that they believe will be used in a soon to be built Third Temple.

8. For years, unsubstantiated claims have been made that the Israeli government has the Ark and are keeping it under lock and key.

9. Don Stewart and Chuck Missler, *The Coming Temple: Center Stage For the Final Countdown*, Orange, California, Dart Press, 1991.

CHAPTER 2

MT. SINAI: GOD'S COVENANT AND THE TEN COMMANDMENTS

To understand the story of the Ark of the Covenant, we must go back in history some four thousand years to God's dealings with a man named Abram (Abraham). God singled out this one man from the rest of humanity and made specific promises to him and his descendants. The story of the Bible revolves around these promises:

Now the Lord said to Abram: "Get out of your country, from your kindred and from your father's house, to a land I will show you. I will make you a great nation; I will bless you and make your name great; and you shall be a blessing. I will bless those who bless you, and I will curse him who curses you; and in you all the families of the earth shall be blessed" (Genesis 12:1-3).

According to God's promise, Abraham's descendants, Israel, would inherit a land where they would live as His special people and be a witness of Him to the world. There was, however, a warning. God warned Abraham that before this happened, his descendants would have to live as slaves in a foreign land for 400 years.

Then He said to Abram: 'Know certainly that your descendants will be strangers in a land that is not theirs, and will serve them, and they will afflict them four hundred years.

And also the nation whom they serve I will judge; afterward they shall come out with great possessions (Genesis 15:13,14).

All of this was literally fulfilled. After 400 years of living as slaves in the land of Egypt, the time of their deliverance was at hand.

The Delivery

During the time of their oppression, the people cried out for a deliverer. God answered their prayers and gave them both a deliverer and a prophet, a man named Moses. Moses demanded of the Pharaoh of Egypt that he let God's people go. Pharaoh refused. This refusal led to a series of ten plagues which were inflicted upon the Egyptians and the land of Egypt.

After the last plague, "the death of the firstborn," the reluctant Pharaoh allowed the children of Israel to leave Egypt for the Promised Land.

As the children of Israel departed Egypt they took spoils with them from the Egyptians. This included much gold and silver.

Now the children of Israel had done according to the word of Moses, and they has asked from the Egyptians articles of silver, articles of gold and clothing. And the Lord had given the people favor in sight of the Egyptians, so that they granted them what they requested. Thus they plundered the Egyptians (Exodus 12:36).

This literally fulfilled what God had told Abraham. The people did not leave the land empty-handed but rather departed with much wealth.

Red Sea

On the way to the Promised Land the children of Israel camped by the Red Sea.[1] The name "Red Sea" (*Yam Suf* in Hebrew), literally means "Sea of Reeds."

While camped at the Red Sea, the children of Israel were pursued by the Egyptian army. The Israelites, trapped without any avenue of escape, cried out to God for deliverance. At that point one of the greatest miracles recorded in the Old Testament occurred—the parting of the Red Sea.[2]

The Bible says Moses stretched out His hand over the Red Sea and the Lord caused the waters to go back. The sea bed became as dry ground and the children of Israel went across.

The Egyptian army attempted to follow, but were not so fortunate. You see, as they began their ascent, God then then instructed Moses to stretch his hand over the sea again. As the Egyptians pursued the children of Israel, the Red Sea returned to full depth and drowned the entire Egyptian army.

With the Egyptian threat now gone, the children of Israel continued toward the land God had promised Abraham and his descendants. They were supernaturally lead by God along the way being guided by a pillar of cloud during the day and a pillar of fire given to them to light the night.

Mount Sinai

In the third month after their departure from Egypt, the children of Israel arrived at Mt. Sinai. The Bible alludes to Mt. Sinai by various names—among them "the mountain," the "mountain of God," and "Mount Horeb." Yet the exact location of Mount Sinai site remains a mystery.[3]

God had warned the people that anyone coming too close to the mountain would be instantly killed. Barricades were set up at the base of the mountain to keep the people away.

A Kingdom of Priests

At Mt. Sinai God revealed Himself to the people with great signs. The mountain smoked, lightning came from the sky and the thunder roared.

At the sacred mountain, the nation entered into a special relationship with God as she bound herself to His covenant. The Lord said:

> If you will indeed obey My voice and keep My covenant, then you shall be a special treasure to Me above all people; for all the earth is Mine. And you shall be to Me a kingdom of priests and a holy nation.' These are the words that you shall speak to the children of Israel' (Exodus 19:3-6).

This event is crucial in understanding the history of the nation Israel. The Lord entered into an agreement with them where they would become a kingdom of priests to God on behalf of the nations. Israel would be God's unique representative to the nations on the earth. This would begin to fulfill part of the promise God made to Abraham.

> In your seed all the nations of the earth shall be blessed (Genesis 12:3).

The nation Israel, and its descendants would be a blessing to the entire world. This, like all of God's other promises, has been literally fulfilled.[4]

A Covenant Made

An altar was built at the foot of Mt. Sinai and sacrifices were offered. The people agreed with the terms of the covenant.

> And they said, 'All that the Lord has said we will do, and be obedient' And Moses took the blood and sprinkled it on the people, and said, 'Behold, the blood of the covenant which the Lord has made with you according to all these words' (Exodus 24:4,7,8).

This covenant would signal a unique relationship between God and the nation Israel:

> And He said: 'Behold, I make a covenant. Before all your people I will do marvels such as have not been done in all the earth, nor in any nation; and all the people among whom you are shall see the work of the Lord. For it is an awesome thing that I will do with you . . . Then the Lord said to Moses, 'Write these words, for according to the tenor of these words I have made a covenant with you and with Israel' (Exodus 34:10).

The Ten Commandments

While on Mt. Sinai, God gave Moses the Ten Commandments[5] written on tablets of stone.[6] These words which had already been spoken were now to be put in permanent form. God, with His own hand, wrote the Ten Commandments to testify to their importance.

Moses breaking the original set of the Ten Commandments

Then the Lord said to Moses, 'Come up to Me on the
mountain and be there; and I will give you tablets of stone,
and the law and commandments which I have written,
that you may teach them (Exodus 24:12).

The written form of the Ten Commandments was
God's pledge to His people. This required the people's
response in belief and obedience. The significance of the
Ten Commandments can scarcely be exaggerated, for they
have served as the basis of morality for a great part of the
world.

While Moses was on Mt. Sinai for forty days receiving
the Ten Commandments, he was miraculously supported
by the Lord. For the entire forty days Moses did not eat
bread nor drink water.

When he descended from the mountain with the Ten
Commandments, he found the people in rebellion against
God. They had fashioned a golden calf and were praising it
for their deliverance from Egypt. The original Ten
Commandments were then destroyed when Moses threw
them down in anger after seeing the Israelites sinning
against the Lord.[7]

Two More Tablets

God then instructed Moses to hew two more tablets of
stone like the first where He [the Lord] would again write
the Ten Commandments.

And the Lord said to Moses, 'Cut two tablets of stone
like the first ones, and I will write on these tablets the
words that were on the first tablets which you broke'
(Exodus 34:1).

Moses obeyed and a second set of tablets were made.
The agreement between God and His people had now been
memorialized in stone.

A Symbolic Presence to be Given

The children of Israel had gone from slavery to
freedom, from certain death at the Red Sea to miraculous
deliverance. They were now on their way to the land of
Promise. The covenant that God had made with Abraham
was being fulfilled. Four hundred years were spent in a
foreign land but the people left with considerable wealth

while their taskmasters, the Egyptians, were judged by God.

At Mt. Sinai, another covenant was made with the Israel. They were to be a special people. The Lord would uniquely meet and speak with only them as they testified to the existence of the One True God.

To confirm this, the Ten Commandments were supernaturally given to the people on two tablets of stone. After the first set was destroyed by Moses, a second set was built.

With the gold, silver and the other articles that they had taken from the Egyptians, the materials were at hand to construct certain holy objects as God would command them.

It was now time to construct a sacred object which God had chosen to symbolize Himself and which would house the Ten Commandments —the Ark of the Covenant.

Endnotes for Chapter 2

1. As for the origin of the name "Red Sea," a number of suggestions have been given. These include the color of its reeds, the corals in the water, the color of the mountains bordering the coasts, or the glow in the sky reflected on it. It is also said to have derived its name from the ancient nation of Erythria, so named because their inhabitants painted their faces red. It is possible that the name may also be associated with Edom, which means red. It is also said that it is called the Red Sea because it lies to the south, and the south is called the "red zone."

2. There is no consensus of opinion where the children of Israel crossed the Red Sea. In ancient times, the term Red Sea referred to what is now the Red Sea as well as its two arms, the Gulf of Suez and the Gulf of Aqaba. It also included waters to the south of Asia Minor, such as the Persian Gulf and the Indian Ocean.

   The route of the Exodus is an also an area of controversy. Tied up with this problem is the identification of the Red Sea.

3. The traditional site of Mt. Sinai is Jebel Musa in the Sinai Peninsula where St. Catherine' Monastery, a fourth century structure, today marks the spot. Dozens of different mountains, both in the Sinai desert and in Arabia have been suggested as the site. The Arabian sites are thought to have been volcanic in the past. Since there is controversy as to the exact route of the Exodus there remains no consensus as to the location of Mt. Sinai.

4. For further documentation see Don Stewart, *10 Reasons to Trust the Bible*, Orange, California, Dart Press, 1991.

5. The Ten Commandments are numbered according to two different traditions. The Roman Catholic and Lutheran churches combine the commandment forbidding the worship of other gods with that of the prohibiting of making images. They treat the coveting of the neighbor's wife and his possessions as two separate commandments. The Talmud, Eastern Orthodox, and Reformed Church treat the commandment against coveting as one commandment. They separate the worship of other gods from the making of images.

   The Ten Commandments differed from other stone monuments of antiquity in that they were portable and designed to be kept as a sacred treasure. Stone monuments usually stood upright and were kept in the open air.

   Moses placed these commandments from God in the "Book of the Covenant." There is no agreement as to the identity of the Book of the Covenant. Some authorities believe that this includes all of the Book of Genesis and Exodus up to the giving of the Ten Commandments. Other scholars believe that it was all the laws discussed up until this point, particularly Exodus 21:1-23:19. Still others say it was merely the Ten Commandments. Because the Bible does not specifically say, we cannot be certain as to what is contained in the Book of the Covenant.

6. We are not told as to the type of stone the commandments were written upon. These may have been made of the sapphire brick that the Israelites had previously seen (Exodus 24:10). This, however, is only a conjecture.

7. The question arises as to what did Moses hope to achieve by breaking the tablets. Since it is forbidden to break even the smallest vessel, how much more an object so precious and sacred as this? The action of breaking the tablets appears to be prompted by sheer anger though other explanations have been offered.

CHAPTER 3

BUILD ME AN ARK

As God had previously told Noah to build an Ark of wood to save the world from the Great Flood, He also told Moses to build an Ark—whose ultimate meaning would later be revealed.

During his stay on Mt. Sinai, God gave Moses the plans for the Ark of the Covenant. The command to build the Ark is recorded in the Book of Exodus:

> And they shall make an Ark of acacia wood; two and a half cubits shall be its length, a cubit and a half its width, and a cubit and a half its height. And you shall overlay it with pure gold, inside and out you shall overlay it, and shall make on it a molding of gold all around. You shall cast four rings of gold for it, and put them in its four corners; two shall be on one side, and two rings on the other side. And you shall make poles of acacia wood, and overlay them with gold. You shall put poles into the rings on the sides of the Ark, that the Ark may be carried by them. The poles shall be into the rings of the Ark; they shall not be taken from it. And you shall put into the Ark the Testimony which I will give you (Exodus 25:10-16).

What was the Ark?

The Ark of the Covenant, was a rectangular container or chest made out of acacia wood and lined inside and outside[1] with pure gold, the appropriate metal for God's presence.

The Hebrew word translated "Ark" means "box" or "chest." The word is used elsewhere in the Old Testament of a chest.[2]

> Then Jehoida the priest took a chest, bored a hole in its lid, and set it beside the altar . . . So it was, whenever they saw that there was much money in the chest (2 Kings 12:9,10).

This suggests that the primary function of the Ark was to be a container.

Size of the Ark

The exact size of the Ark is difficult to determine. The standard of measurement at that time was the cubit. The cubit was measured from the elbow to the tip of the middle finger. There is no agreement as to the exact length of the cubit.[3] Various estimates range from fourteen to twenty-four inches. Using an eighteen inch cubit, the Ark would have been three and three quarters feet long, two and one quarter feet wide, and two and one quarter feet high.

The thickness of the walls of the Ark is not stated. Estimates range from three quarters of an inch to three inches thick. The Bible simply does not say. The exact size of the Ark, therefore, cannot be determined with precision.

Acacia Wood

The Ark was made out of acacia wood (*shittim* in the Authorized Version). The acacia is a tall tree with a thick trunk. It is one of the few trees that will grow in a hot dry desert climate. Acacia trees are common in the Sinai Peninsula and are good for construction purposes. Acacia wood is strong and durable and resists insects and rot. The Septuagint, the Greek translation of the Hebrew Old Testament, renders this word as "incorruptible" wood or "decay proof" wood. The wood is very light and hard and it does not absorb moisture. The Talmud[4], (Jewish Commentaries on the Old Testament) states that it is a member of the cedar family.

Covered with Gold

The Ark was lined inside and outside with gold, so that nothing but gold was visible. Jewish commentator Umberto Cassuto explains the possible methods used:

From archaeological finds in Egypt we learn that wooden furniture was covered with gold in one of two ways: either hammered plates of gold were attached to the wood by means of small nails, or thin leaves of gold were glued to a fine layer of plaster spread over the wood. Here, apparently the first method is intended, since if the second method were used, the overlay would not hold very long, especially inside the ark, where two tables of stone were to be kept.[5]

Around the top of the Ark was a "molding" or "border" made of gold. The exact look and purpose is debated.[6]

The Ark also had four "corners" or "feet." Their appearance and purpose is likewise debated.[7]

Rings and Poles

The Ark had four golden rings,[8] two on each side. Two poles, made of acacia wood and then covered with gold were permanently inserted into the rings for the Ark's transporting. The poles would always remain in the rings whether the Ark was stationary or moving. This made the carrying of the Ark more practical.

Some authorities believe that the carrying poles actually went through the walls of the Ark, and these rings were like reinforcements.[9]

It is uncertain on the exact placement of the poles that were used to carry the Ark. Some authorities believe they ran lengthwise alongside the Ark, while others believe the poles were parallel to the shorter ends of it.[10]

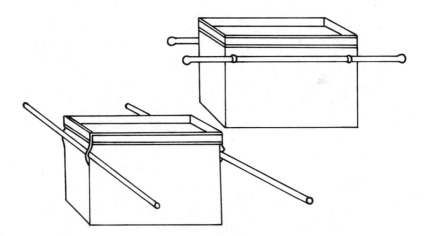

The Mercy Seat

All around the top of the Ark was a gold rectangular plate known as the Mercy Seat. The Mercy Seat was to be placed on top of the Ark having the exact same dimensions.

> You shall make a Mercy Seat of pure gold; two and a half cubits shall be its length and a cubit an a half its width . . . You shall put the Mercy Seat on top of the Ark (Exodus 25:17,21).

The translation "Mercy Seat"[11] can lead to misconceptions. The basic meaning of the Hebrew word *kapporeth* is "to cover." The Mercy Seat was the cover of the Ark. However the Mercy Seat was more than a simple covering,[12] it was an "atonement covering"—the place where sins were covered up.

God promised that He would speak to His people from above the Mercy Seat.

> And there I will meet with you, and I will speak with you from above the Mercy Seat, from between the two cherubim which are on the Ark of the Testimony, of things which I will give you in commandment to the children of Israel (Exodus 25:22).

An Independent Object?

Some Bible scholars have assumed that the Mercy Seat was a separate object, independent of the Ark.[13] It is more likely, however, that they are two components of the same thing. Each of them is incomplete without the other. Without the Mercy Seat the Ark would be open at the top and the contents in the Ark would be uncovered. There is nothing in Scripture that states that the Ark had a cover on its top, hence the need for the Mercy Seat.

Likewise, without the Ark, the Mercy Seat would not have a base to rest upon. Therefore, both the Ark and the Mercy Seat needed each other. This is why Scripture uses the term "Ark" while referring to both the Ark and the Mercy Seat.

Cherubim

Facing each other at opposite ends of the Mercy Seat stood two cherubim[14] made out of hammered gold.

Cherubim are winged creatures that represent heavenly beings in God's service. The cherubim covered the Mercy Seat with their spread out wings.

And you shall make two cherubim of gold; of hammered work you shall make them at the two ends of the Mercy Seat. Make one cherub at one end, and the other cherub at the other end; you shall make the cherubim at the two ends of it of one piece with the Mercy Seat. And the cherubim shall stretch out their wings above, covering the Mercy Seat with their wings, and they shall face one another; and the faces of the cherubim shall be toward the Mercy Seat (Exodus 25:18-20).

Unknown Appearance

Neither the size nor the form of the cherubim are described. The Bible, in other passages, gives various descriptions of cherubim. The two cherubim in the Tabernacle and Solomon's Temple seem to have two wings each (Exodus 25:20; 1 Kings 6:24,27) and one face (Exodus 25:20).

In the vision of Ezekiel, the cherubim have four wings and four faces. Most likely positioned in front was the face of a man, with a lion on the right side, an ox on the left side, and an eagle behind. In describing cherubim the prophet Ezekiel wrote:

Also from within it came the likeness of four living creatures. And this was their appearance: they had the likeness of man (Ezekiel 1:5).

Some authorities assume the cherubim on the Ark also had four faces. Samuel Ridout wrote:

They were composite creatures with four faces—of a lion, of an ox, of a man, and of an eagle (Ezek I: 4-14; Rev 4:6,7).[15]

Some have thought they resemble Egyptian models such as the Sphinx. Jewish writer Abba Eban states.

There in the shadows the sacred Ark was placed, and the presence of YHWH[16] resided enthroned upon two huge, human-headed, lion-bodied, winged creatures called cherubim. In other cultures of the time, where those figures were also found, they were called by different names. We know them too as sphinxes.[17]

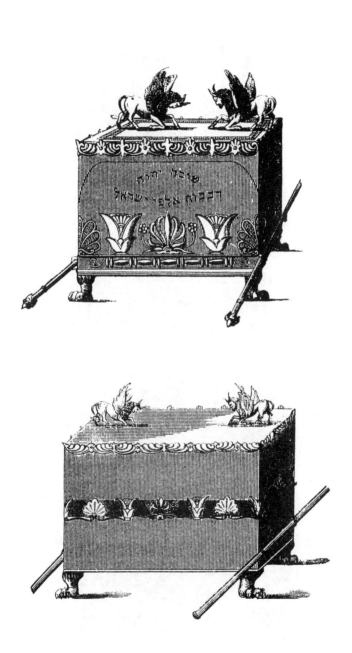

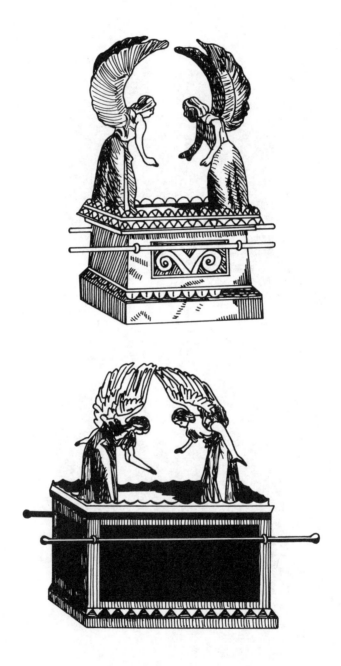

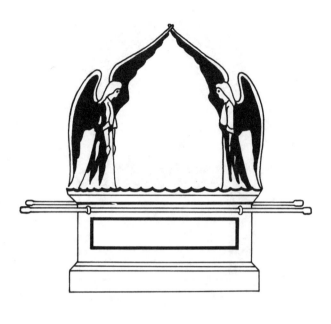

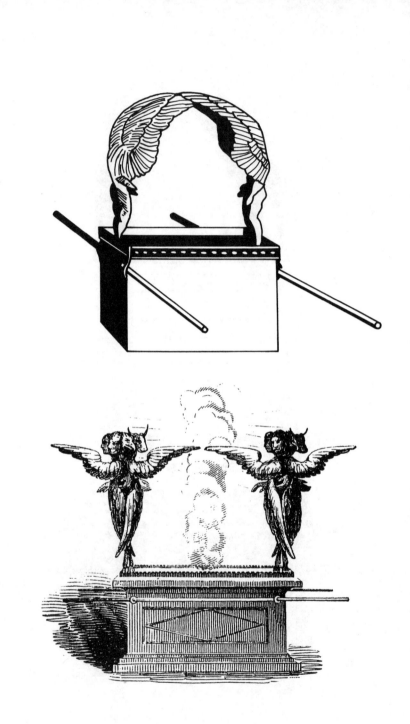

First century writer Flavius Josephus[18] declared that the cherubim resemble figures that were once known to men but that in his day their form was utterly lost. As to their appearance there has been much conjecture.[19]

What Did They Represent?

Though no one can be certain of the exact appearance of the cherubim, they represented the presence of the Lord. God is called "He who dwells between the cherubim."

> Give ear, O Shepherd of Israel, You who lead Joseph like a flock; You who dwell between the cherubim, shine forth! (Psalm 80:1).

The Book of Genesis describes the cherubim as the ones guarding the Garden of Eden. God had stationed them at the entrance to the garden to guard the way to the tree of life:

> So He drove out the man; and He placed cherubim at the east of the garden of Eden, and a flaming sword which turned every way, to guard the way to the tree of life. (Genesis 3:24).

One Solid Piece of Gold?

It is also said that the cherubim were fashioned from the same piece of gold as the Mercy Seat.

> Make one cherub at one end, and the other cherub at the other end; you shall make the cherubim at the two ends of it of one piece with the Mercy Seat (Exodus 25:18).

Although it is possible they were formed from one piece of gold, this is not necessarily the case. The text may convey that, when *finished*, the cherubim should be seen connected to the Mercy Seat. It does not necessarily mean that they were fabricated out of the same mass of gold.

Contents of the Ark

The Lord gave specific orders as to what the Ark would contain. The Ten Commandments, written by the hand of God, were placed inside the Ark. Later in Israel's history, Moses recounted the story:

Then I turned and came down from the mountain, and put the tablets in the ark which I had made; and there they are, just as the Lord commanded me (Deuteronomy 10:2-5).

The depositing of the Ten Commandments inside the Ark was not an unusual practice. In the ancient Near East, it was common practice to place the treaties of alliance in a temple. This served as a testimony for the future. Similarly, the tablets which contained the essential requirements of the Covenant were also called 'Testimonies' and were kept in the Ark of the Covenant, the only visible sign of the invisible presence of God.

Two Tablets

Two tablets of the Law were placed inside the Ark. First century writer Flavius Josephus says that each of the tablets contained five precepts. Jewish and Christian tradition have held that one tablet contained four commandments, and the other tablet six. The Scripture does not state it as such. It is possible, however, that each tablet contained all Ten Commandments.

The Ten Commandments were written on two stone tablets. This probably means two copies. The reason for having two copies of the Ten Commandments has only recently been understood. When a written covenant was made in the world of the Bible, each party making the covenant had a copy of its contents. If the covenant was between two nations, for instance the Hittites and the Egyptians, the two copies would be kept far apart, in the temple of the god of each land. In Israel, though the covenant was between God and his people. Both copies of the Ten Commandments were kept in the Covenant Box (Ark). This was the centre of Israel and it was also the place of God's presence. So God's copy and Israel's copy could be kept together. The Ten Commandments, then, were the terms of the covenant that God had made with his people. At Sinai, in response to all that God had done for them, the people of Israel accepted these terms.[20]

Other Contents

Aaron's rod that budded was also later placed inside the Ark:[21]

And the Lord said to Moses, 'Bring Aaron's rod back before the Testimony, to be kept as a sign against the rebels, that you may put their murmurings away from Me, lest they die' (Numbers 17:10).

Upon Moses' orders, Aaron put two quarts of manna[22] in a jar and placed it before the Lord:

> And Moses said to Aaron, 'Take a pot and put an omer of manna in it, and lay it up before the Lord, to be kept for your generations. As the Lord commanded Moses, so Aaron laid it up before the Testimony, to be kept (Exodus 16:33,34).

That the pot of manna and Aaron's rod were to be placed inside the Ark is not stated in these passages, but it is assumed that it took place from the words "before the Lord." Both the golden jar and Aaron's rod came later to rest inside the Ark. The writer to the Hebrews says:

> The Ark of the covenant overlaid on all sides with gold, in which were the golden pot that had manna, Aaron's rod that budded, and the tablets of the covenant (Hebrews 9:5).

Later Moses put the complete book of the law by the side of the Ark of the Covenant.

> Take this Book of the Law, and put it beside the Ark of the Covenant of the Lord your God, that it may be there as a witness for you (Deuteronomy 31:26).

Church father John Chrysostom said that the contents of the Ark were significant memorials of Israel's rebellion; the tables of the covenant, for the first were broken on account of their sin; the manna reminding them of their murmuring; and the rod that budded of their jealousy of Aaron.

Work Finished

The Ark was built by Bezalel and Oholiab[23] upon Moses' order. To complete their task, they were given special wisdom from the Lord. God said to Moses:

> I have put wisdom in the hearts of all who are gifted artisans, that they may make all that I have commanded

you: the tabernacle of meeting, the Ark of the Testimony and the Mercy Seat that is on it (Exodus 31:6,7).

The Bible records that the work was finished as ordered. It was at the beginning of the second year of the Exodus that the components of the Ark of the Covenant were brought to Moses.

And the children of Israel did according to all that the Lord had commanded Moses; so they did. And they brought . . . the Ark of the Testimony with its poles, and the Mercy Seat (Exodus 39:33,35).

The Ten Commandments were then placed in the Ark of the Covenant and the Mercy Seat secured on top.

He took the Testimony and put it into the ark, inserted the poles through the rings of the ark, and put the Mercy Seat on top of the ark (Exodus 40:29).

The Ark of the Covenant was now completed.

Sacred Object

The completed Ark was a sacred object as can be seen from the different titles the Old Testament uses to identify it. Over twenty different terms are used to describe this holy artifact.

Ark of God

Thirty-four times the title "Ark of God" was used in describing this object.

And before the lamp of God went out in the tabernacle of the Lord where the Ark of God was (1 Samuel 3:3).

Ark of Your Strength

It was also called the "Ark of Your strength."

Arise O Lord, to Your resting place, You and the Ark of Your strength (Psalm 132:8).

This reference is to the power of the Ark. The Ark was sometimes spoken of as representing God's power and glory.

So that He forsook the tabernacle in Shiloh, the tent which He had placed among me, and delivered His strength into captivity, and His glory into the enemy's hand (Psalm 78:60,61).

The references here to His "strength" and "glory" are to the Ark when it was taken captive by the Philistines.

Ark of God the Lord

Later in Israel's history, it was called, the Ark of God the Lord.

And David and all Israel went up to Baalah, to Kirjath Jearim, which belonged to Judah, to bring up from there the ark of God the Lord, who dwells between the cherubim, where His name is proclaimed (1 Chronicles 13:6).

Ark of the Testimony

One of the earliest titles used is Ark of the Testimony.[24]

And there I will meet with you, and I will speak with you from above the Mercy Seat, from between the two cherubim which are on the Ark of the Testimony, of things which I will give you in commandment to the children of Israel (Exodus 25:22).

Ark of the Covenant

The most significant title is the "Ark of the Covenant." A covenant is an "agreement" or "testament". This title is used because the Ark contained the two tablets on which were written the Ten Commandments, the covenant between Israel and the Lord. Old Testament authority Marten Woudstra writes:

The phrase "ark of the covenant" no doubt refers to the fact that the ark was to contain and did contain the tables of the covenant. These tables were called the "testimony."[25]

Ark of the Covenant of the Lord

Because the Ark revealed the presence of the Lord, the sacred object was called the "Ark of the Covenant of the

Lord." This term is used some thirty-one times in Scripture.

> At that time the Lord separated the tribe of Levi to bear
> the ark of the covenant of the Lord, to stand before the
> Lord to minister to Him and to bless His name to this day
> (Deuteronomy 10:8).

God's Presence

The now completed Ark of the Covenant was the most holy object Israel possessed, for it symbolized God's presence among them in a special way. In the future, God would speak to His people from the Ark. King David later recognized that God dwelt in a unique way between the cherubim.

> And David and all Israel went up to Baalah, to Kirjath
> Jearim, which belonged to Judah, to bring up from there
> the Ark of God the Lord, who dwells between the
> cherubim, where His name is proclaimed (1 Chronicles
> 13:6).

King Hezekiah also realized that the Ark was symbolic of God's presence:

> Then Hezekiah prayed before the Lord and said: "O
> Lord God of Israel, the One who dwells between the
> cherubim, You are God, You alone, of all the kingdoms of
> the earth. You have made heaven and earth (2 Kings
> 19:15).

As God appeared upon Mt. Sinai, He promised that His visible presence would remain with His people. The glory cloud in which God had brought deliverance at the Exodus would regularly appear between the wings of the cherubim over the Mercy Seat of the Ark.

Summary

This sacred object is described for us in basic terms in Scripture. It was a small chest lined inside and outside with gold. Though the acacia wood formed the dimensions of the Ark, its appearance was all gold—no wood could be seen. There are, however, many points which we cannot express with certainty including: the Ark's size, its "feet" or "molding," and the look of the cherubim. Hence any artists conception can only be viewed as an approximation of what it looked like.

What is known for certain is that the Ark of the Covenant was the most sacred object God has ever ordered humanity to construct. Not only did it contain the tablets of the Law, the Ten Commandments, written with the finger of God, it symbolized the Covenant, the promises that God has made with His people and continues to keep.

Endnotes for Chapter 3

1. Biblical authority R.C.H. Lenski noted:

> The ark is described as "having been overlaid with gold." Exodus 25:11 says "within and without," it also has "a crown of gold round about." That is why the word which is used here is not gold as material, but the diminutive, wrought gold, gold work in designs (R. C. H. Lenski, *The Interpretation of Hebrews*, Minneapolis, Augsburg Publishing House, 1966, p. 278).

2. In Genesis 50:26 the word *aron* אֲרוֹן is translated "coffin." *Aron* is probably related to the Akkadian *aranu* meaning box.

Allen Cole writes:

> 'Chest' (rather like a small seaman's chest, or a Chinese camphorwood box) given the meaning of *aron* is better than the older translation 'ark.' A different word is used for the 'ark' of Noah and Moses (R. Alan Cole, *Exodus*, Downers Grove, Illinois, Inter-Varsity Press, 1973, p. 190).

3. James G. Murphy notes that the:

> Babylonian cubit, which consisted of seven palms seems to have been sometimes employed (2 Chron iii. 3, Ezek. xi. 5), but only after the captivity (James G. Murphy, *The Book of Exodus*, Boston, W. H. Halliday and Company, 1868).

4. The Word *Talmud* comes from the Hebrew word "to study." It was a written compendium of oral law, completed by about the fifth century A.D. It is comprised of the Misnah and Gemara, a commentary on the Misnah. The Talmud exists in two versions: the Jerusalem and the Babylonian.

5. Umberto Cassuto, *Commentary on Exodus*, Jerusalem, The Magnes Press, 1967, p. 329.

On the covering with gold Murphy says:

> This was not a mere gilding but covering of the surface with thin plates of gold as we infer from 1 Kings vi. 16 and 2 Chron. iii. 3. The Talmud goes so far as to conclude that three chests were made, an outer one of gold, a middle one of shittah, and an inner one of gold plate (Murphy, ibid. p. 168).

Jewish commentator Rashi said:

Bezalel made three arks, two of gold and one of wood, each having four walls (sides) and a bottom, being however open at the top. He put the wooden ark into the larger golden one and the smaller golden one into that of wood and covered its upper rim (that of the wooden ark) with gold; consequently it can be said that the wooden ark was overlaid with gold within and without (*Pentateuch with Rashi's Commentaries*, London, Shapiro, Valentine and Co., 1945, p. 133).

6.   Concerning the molding or crown W.H. Gispen writes:

The molding ran probably around the top of the ark on all four sides; it is possible that the lid rested on this molding. However it is also possible that the molding encased the atonement cover, so that the cover could not slide, e.g., when the ark was lifted up or put down (W.H. Gispen, *Exodus*, Grand Rapids, Michigan, Zondervan, 1982, p, 246,247).

Cassuto wrote concerning the molding of gold:

an adornment in the form of a garland of flowers or leaves running right round the four sides of the ark on the outside, bisecting its height, and resembling in its form a similar adornment that was to be made for the table and its frame and the altar of incense; all the sacred appurtenances were to be fashioned in the same style. (Cassuto, ibid. p. 329).

This was a border or cornice of pure gold round the upper edge of the ark, adorning, and and the same time strengthening it for support of the Mercy Seat (Murphy. ibid. p. 168).

7.   Some scholars think the Ark was a simple box without legs while others believed that it had legs or a lower rim. The "legs" would have had to have been small but of adequate size to raise the Ark above ground level. Old Testament authority Walter Kaiser, writes:

The meaning of feet is uncertain but "its . . . artificial feet" probably is the closest to its basic meaning . . . Whatever it was, four rings were attached to it. The King James Version reads "four corners" which is to be rejected. Whatever it was, the four gold rings were attached there (Walter Kaiser, Exodus, in *The Expositors*

Bible Commentary, General Editor Frank C. Gaebelein, Volume 2, Grand Rapids, Zondervan, 1990, p. 454,455).

8. We are not told where the rings were placed on the Ark. Some authorities maintain they were at the very top of the Ark while others contend they were about 7 inches (two and one third handbreadths) from the top. Still others state the rings were at the very bottom of the Ark.

9. Josephus, *Antiquities of the Jews*, 3:6:5.

10. For example, commentator Henry Soltau believed the poles (staves) were to be placed sideways:

> It will be seen that the Staves are . . . placed sideways, and not lengthways in the Ark. This seems to be their right position, because it is not probable that the Ark would be turned about, when it was taken up to be carried in the journeys, but would be borne straightforward. Also from 1 Kings viii. 8, it would appear, that, when drawn out of the rings, the Staves reached forwards toward the holy place; and the high priest, when taking in the incense and blood on the great day of atonement, would (if this were the position of the Staves) go in between them up to the Mercy Seat, instead of going up as it were against one of them (Henry Soltau, *The Holy Vessels and Furniture of the Tabernacle*, Grand Rapids, Michigan, Kregel Publications, 1971, p. 43).   See or diagrams on page 33.

11. William Tyndale was the first to translate this word as "Mercy Seat." This was followed in 1534 by Martin Luther's translation. Modern translations have rendered the term variously such as "Place of Reconciliation" (Translators New Testament).

12. The verb that lies behind the noun "atonement" in the expression "atonement cover" means "to ransom or deliver by means of a substitute."

Concerning the weight of the Mercy Seat, Aryeh Kaplan notes:

> The Talmud states that the ark cover was one handbreadth (3 inches) thick (Sukkah 5a). It can easily be calculated that if it were solid gold, it would weigh, without the cherubs, some 2500 pounds, or 17 talents . . . Some sources state that the ark cover was considerably thinner (Tur), since we find the ark had to be light enough to be carried easily . . . One source states that the ark-cover weighed one talent (1500 pounds) just like the menorah

. . . The ark cover would therefore have been around 3/16 inch thick. It may have been made like an inverted open box, so that its sides were one handbreadth thick on the outside (Rabbi Aryeh Kaplan, *The Living Torah*, Brooklyn, New York, Moznaim Publishing Company, 1981, pp. 384, 385).

13. Some see the Ark and Mercy Seat as separate object. Frank White writes:

Notwithstanding the Ark and Mercy-Seat were inseparable, the latter frequently spoken of in Scripture as something distinct from the former, and a separate place is assigned it in the various descriptions given of the Tabernacle furniture . . . The fact goes to show that the Mercy Seat had a special purpose of its own, and was by no means to be regarded simply as the lid of the Ark. This implies that the Mercy-Seat was to be looked upon as the most prominent and important object contained in that part of the House of God, even beyond that of the Ark itself (Frank H. White, *Christ in the Tabernacle*, S.W. Partridge and Co., London, 1910, pp. 153,154).

14. On the position of the cherubim facing one another Kaplan writes:

Directly. Others say that they faced toward the east, toward the opening of the Holy of Holies, with their heads inclined toward each other (Bava Bathra 99a). Others say that their bodies faced toward the east, but their heads faced each other . . . They faced each other so that they would not appear to be gods (Moreh Nevukhim 3:45). (Kaplan, ibid. p. 384).

15. Samuel Ridout, *Lectures on the Tabernacle*, New York, Loizeaux Publishers, 1914, p. 44.

16. The Hebrew name Yahweh (the Lord) means "I am" (cf. Exodus 3:14).

17. Abba Eban, *Heritage: Civilization and the Jews:* New York, Summit Books, 1984, p. 38.

18. Flavius Josephus, *Antiquities of the Jews.* 3:6:5.

19. For example, see our diagrams as to the various artists conceptions of the cherubim (pp. 36-41).

20. *Eerdmans' Family Encyclopedia of the Bible,* First American Edition, Grand Rapids, Michigan, Wm. B. Eerdmans Publishing Company, 1978, p. 132).

21. The story of Aaron's rod is dealt with in chapter 6

22. Concerning the pot of manna, Kaplan notes:

> urn. A large clay jar . . . According to others, the word *tzintzeneth* denotes a glass jar, so that the manna could be seen . . . It might also have been a gold vessel (one possible translation of the Septuagint). In Egyptian, *tzenat* is a vase, and *snu* a jar, while *serbet* is a vessel of silver-gold alloy. *Sen* is a kind of precious stone (Kaplan, ibid. p. 338,341).

23. The name Bezaleel means "in the shadow of God's protection." He was a descendant of Caleb (1 Chronicles 2:19). His ability to work in the arts and his skills as a craftsman were gifts of the Holy Spirit. Oholiab, Bezaleel's assistant, was from the tribe of Dan. His name means "tent of my father." These two skilled craftsmen were responsible for the construction of all that pertained in the Tabernacle and its service, though they themselves possibly only supervised in the construction of various items.

24. This phrase is used 14 times in Scripture. Testimony is the Hebrew word meaning "sign" or "reminder." It speaks of the two stone tablets within the Ark. Concerning the "testimony" Walter Kaiser writes:

> vs. 16 *edut* means testimony or laws of the Ten Commandments that were placed inside the Ark. In Egypt, Babylonia, and the Hittite Empire, important documents were deposited in the sanctuary at the feet of the deity (Walter Kaiser, ibid. p. 455).

25. Marten H. Woudstra, *The Ark of the Covenant From Conquest to Kingship,* Philadelphia, Presbyterian and Reformed, 1965, p. 79.

CHAPTER 4

A TEMPORARY HOME
FOR THE ARK
IS CONSTRUCTED:
THE TABERNACLE

At Mt. Sinai, the holy Ark of the Covenant was the first and most important object that God commanded to be built. In the same manner that the Lord gave Moses instructions to build the Ark, He also gave him the plans for its resting place. This structure would be the earthly counterpart to one that is in heaven. The most common designation for this sanctuary was the "Tabernacle"[1] or "tent of meeting."

The Tabernacle was a "tent of testimony" to remind Israel that God does dwell with His people and reveals Himself to them.

During their years of wandering in the wilderness, this structure was portable. It was built in such a way that it could be easily taken apart and carried when the people journeyed toward the Promised Land.

According to Pattern

Several articles of furniture were to be built and kept inside the Tabernacle. All the furnishings of the Tabernacle were to be made according to the pattern God showed Moses.

> According to all that I show you, that is, the pattern of
> the Tabernacle and the pattern of its furnishings, just so
> you shall make it (Exodus 25:9).

Since the Tabernacle and its furniture were to be
constructed according to a divinely-given blueprint, strict
attention had to be paid to the smallest of details.[2] Moses,
not only received detailed instructions, God may have also
supernaturally shown him a pattern or model of the
Tabernacle.

After Moses was given the pattern, the materials were
brought to him, supplied by the free will offerings of the
children of Israel.[3] The building materials included three
different metals (gold, silver, bronze), the skins of animals,
wood, oil and precious stones.

Holy Place

The Tabernacle itself was a rectangular structure that
consisted of two rooms: the first, called the "Holy Place,"
comprised two thirds of the area. The smaller inner room
was known as the "Holy of Holies."

The Holy Place contained several articles of furniture:
the Golden Altar for burning incense, a Golden
Lampstand (Menorah) that held seven lamps to give light,
and a Table of Showbread, where twelve loaves of bread
were placed. The bread was renewed every Sabbath. The two
rooms of the Tabernacle were separated by a veil. The veil,
made of fine linen, was colored blue, purple, and scarlet.
Embroidered upon it were the figures of the cherubim. The
veil that divided the two chambers of the Tabernacle had
the function of sealing off the way into the inner room.

The outer room was used on a regular basis. This,
however, was not true of the inner room of the Tabernacle.

Holy of Holies

The Holy of Holies was the most sacred place in the
Tabernacle. Only one article of furniture was to stand
inside the Holy of Holies—the Ark of the Covenant.

> And you shall hang the veil from the clasps. Then you
> shall bring the Ark of the Testimony in there, behind the
> veil. The veil shall be a divider for you between the holy
> place and the Most Holy (Exodus 26:33).

The Holy of Holies could be entered only by the High Priest, and he could only come in one day a year—the Great Day of Atonement. On that special day, the High Priest presented an offering for the sins of the people as he sprinkled blood on the Mercy Seat above the Ark.

No Natural Light

Daylight was not allowed to penetrate either the Holy Place or the Holy of Holies. The Holy Place was illumined only by the Golden Lampstand. The Holy of Holies, however, was left in total darkness. This is symbolic of the invisible God whom no man has seen or can see. The Apostle Paul wrote of God's nature:

> Who alone has immortality, dwelling in unapproachable light, whom no man has seen or can see, to whom be honor and everlasting power (1 Timothy 6:16).

Ark is Outlined First

The Bible describes several articles of the Tabernacle's furniture before the Tabernacle itself. This shows that they were of greater importance. The building instructions began with the Holy of Holies and worked outward. The Ark was the first, and most important piece of furniture in the Tabernacle. Jewish Commentator Umberto Cassuto writes:

> After the general introduction regarding the contribution to the Tabernacle, the Divine communication deals separately with each of the holy articles that are to be placed within the Tabernacle and kept there. The articles are described here before the Tabernacle itself, because they are of primary importance, and their sanctity is greater than that of the Tabernacle. The Tabernacle serves to protect them; but they do not serve the Tabernacle.[4]

The Ark was the primary article of furniture in the Tabernacle. Thirteen verses are dedicated to its construction, more than any other article of furniture.

The Ark of the Covenant, in the Holy of Holies, was the spot from where the God of the Covenant communicated with His people.

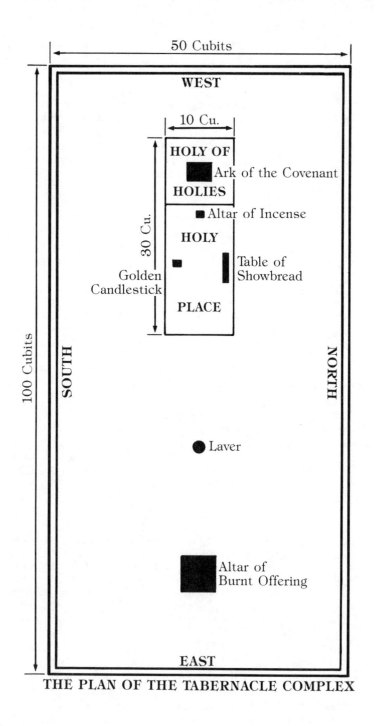

THE PLAN OF THE TABERNACLE COMPLEX

Now when Moses went into the Tabernacle of meeting to speak with Him, he heard the voice of One speaking to him from above the Mercy Seat that was on the Ark of the Testimony, from between the two cherubim; thus He spoke to him (Numbers 7:89).

Work Finished

The Bible records that the Tabernacle was constructed exactly to the pattern God had given Moses.

Thus all the work of the Tabernacle of the tent of meeting was finished. And the children of Israel did according to all that the Lord had commanded Moses; so they did. And they brought to the Tabernacle to Moses, the tent with all its furnishings . . . the Ark of the Testimony with its poles and the Mercy Seat (Exodus 39:32,33,35).

The furniture of the Tabernacle were copies of the same furniture in heaven. The writer to the Hebrews said:

For Christ has not entered the holy places made with hands, which are copies of the true, but into heaven itself, now to appear in the presence of God (Hebrews 9:24).

When the Tabernacle was dedicated to the Lord the two tablets containing the Ten Commandments were placed inside the Ark by Moses.[5] The Ark of the Covenant was then placed in the Tabernacle. This occurred on the first day of the first month of the second year after the children of Israel had departed from the land of Egypt.

Then the Lord spoke to Moses, saying: 'On the first day of the month you shall set up the Tabernacle of the tent of meeting. You shall put in the Ark of the Testimony, and partition off the Ark with the veil' . . . He took the Testimony and put it into the Ark, inserted the poles through the rings of the Ark, and put the Mercy Seat on top of the Ark (Exodus 40:1-3,29).

When the Ark was placed in the Tabernacle, the poles pressed up against the veil that separated the Holy of Holies from the Holy Place. By being pressed against the veil the priests could see that the Ark was in its proper place without entering.

When the Tabernacle was completed it was dedicated to the Lord. At the dedication of the Tabernacle the glory of the Lord came to rest over it.

> Then the cloud covered the Tabernacle of meeting, and the glory of the Lord filled the Tabernacle. And Moses was not able to enter the Tabernacle of meeting because the cloud rested above it, and the glory of the Lord filled the Tabernacle (Exodus 40:34-36).

The Ark of the Covenant now resided in its temporary home.

Importance of the Ark

As we conclude our brief summary of the Tabernacle, we observe that the Ark of the Covenant ranked the highest of all the vessels, standing alone in the Holy of Holies. In the Biblical order, before the Tabernacle was even described and commanded to be built, God gave orders to build this most important piece of furniture.[6]

All the rituals of the Tabernacle were conducted with reference to the Ark. Without the Ark of the Covenant, all the other vessels of the Tabernacle and all the service of the priests would have been useless.

The Ark of the Covenant, the most important object in the Tabernacle, was now ready to make its trek to the Promised Land and a permanent resting place.

Endnotes for Chapter 4

1. The name for the structure is tent. The English translators exalted it to the more high sounding "Tabernacle" following the Latin Vulgate *tabernaculum*. The name house and temple were also used for this structure but only when it was in a more settled condition.

It is called "the tent," which usually refers to its outer covering; the tent of meeting" where God met His people (27;21); the tent of witness" or testimony because it contained the Ark and the Ten Commandments (25:16); the dwelling and the dwelling of the Lord (Numbers 16:9) or the dwelling of the Testimony (Exodus 38:21) and the sanctuary or holy place (Exodus 25:8). The Tabernacle is mentioned 139 separate times in the Old Testament. It comes from the word "dwell" — *Mishkan*. It is the place God dwells with His people.

2. The Tabernacle with its furniture contains spiritual truths. Jewish sage Abravanel wrote:

> Does every detail of the Tabernacle and its furnishings have symbolic meaning or can we accept that God commanded them purely for ornamental and aesthetic reasons? It is difficult to imagine that the two cherubim in the form of babes crowning the Ark or the seven-branched candlestick with its elaborate carvings of almonds, cups and flowers have no specific symbolic significance. . . We have no alternative but to assume they have an allegorical meaning over and above their immediate literal sense. Our Sages, accordingly tried to provide us with insights into their symbolism.

It is important to realize that the study of the Ark and Tabernacle need to be done through the lens of Scripture. C.H. Mackintosh comments about correctly understanding the Tabernacle and its furniture:

> Nature can do nothing here Reason is blind—imagination utterly vain—the most gigantic intellect, instead of being able to interpret the sacred symbols, appears like a bat in the sunshine, blindly dashing itself against the objects which it is utterly unable to discern. We must compel reason and imagination to stand without, while with a chastened heart a single eye, and a spiritual mind, we enter the hallowed precincts and gaze upon the deeply significant furniture. God the Holy Ghost is the only One who can conduct us through the courts of the Lord's house,and expound to our souls the true meaning of all that there meets our view. To attempt the exposition, by the aid of intellect unsanctified powers,

would be infinitely more absurd than to set about the repairs of a watch with a blacksmith's tongs and hammer. "The pattern of things in heaven" cannot be interpreted by the natural mind, in its most cultivated form. They must all be read in the light of heaven. Earth has no light which could at all develop their beauties. The One who furnished the patterns can alone explain what the patterns mean. The One who furnished the beauteous symbols can alone interpret them (C. H. Mackintosh, *Notes on the Book of Exodus*, New York, Loizeaux Brothers, 1862, p. 275).

3.   R. Alan Cole remarks that there are three fundamental principles in Exodus 25:1-9 that are eternally valid.

The first (in verse 2) is that giving to God must be voluntary, not forced (2 Cor. 9:7). God's grace will prompt men to give: and man will then give his most costly treasures gladly to God. . . Secondly, it is God's aim and purpose to live in the midst of His people (verse 8): that is the whole reason for making the Tent. Thirdly, obedience in carrying out God's master-plan is essential (verse 9) (R. Alan Cole, *Exodus*, Downers Grove, Illinois, Inter-Varsity Press, 1973, p. 189).

4.   Umberto Cassuto, *Commentary on Exodus*, Jerusalem, The Magnes Press, 1967, p. 328.

5.   The tablets would not have been very large. Apparently they laid side by side inside the Ark and were wrapped in linen so when the Ark was carried the writing on them would not be rubbed away.
Cassuto remarks on the tablets being inside the Ark.

If the question be asked, why the tables, which comprise the principles of the Covenant and the basic precepts incumbent on the Israelites, were lying in an enclosed place, and were not exhibited before the people, it can easily be answered that there were undoubtedly copies of the Decalogue engraven on stone, or written on parchment or papyrus, available for the people to see, and that it was only the original testimony that was put in the Ark for safe keeping (Umberto Cassuto, *Commentary on Exodus*, Jerusalem, The Magnes Press, 1967, p. 331).

Note on the Golden Altar and the Book of the Law:

The Golden Altar of Incense was not in the Holy of Holies. It stood before the entrance to the inner sanctuary. The smoke of the incense was designed to penetrate the veil and permeate the Holy of Holies as it ascended before the Ark. There was an intimate relationship between the Altar of Incense and the Ark. In Israel's later history, the Altar of Incense became more closely associated with the Ark and the Holy of Holies.

Was the Book of the Law placed inside the Ark or in a chest next to it? The words, "by the side of it" seem to refer to next to it rather than inside. Prideaux believes it was on the outside for the following reasons:

> 1st. The same word, *Mitzzad*, is made use of, where it is said that the Philistines sent back the Ark with an offering of Jewels of Gold put in a coffer by the side of it. And there it is certain the word must be understood of the outside, not the inside. 2dly, The Ark was not of Capacity enough to hold the volume of the whole law of Moses with the other things placed therein. 3dly, The end of laying up the original volume of the Law in the Temple was, that it might be reserved there, as the Authentick Copy, by which all others were to be corrected, and set right, and therefore had to answer to this end it must have be placed so, as that access might be had thereto on all occasions acquiring it, which could not have be done, if it had been put within the Ark, and shut up there by the Cover of the Mercy Seat over it, which was not to be removed. 4thly, When Hilkiah the High Priest in the time of Josiah found the Copy of the Law in the Temple, there is nothing said of the Ark, neither is it there spoken of, as taken from thence, but as found elsewhere in the Temple. And therefore putting all this together it seems plain, that the volume of the Law was not laid within the Ark, but had a particular Coffer, or repository of its own, in which it was placed by the side of it (Humphrey Prideaux, *Old and New Testament Connected*, Part 1, Vol. 1, 10th edition, 1729, pp. 205,206).

6. *Smith's Bible Dictionary* notes:

> This [the Ark], taken together with the mercy-seat was the one piece of the tabernacle's furniture especially invested with sacredness and mystery, and it therefore the first for which precise directions were delivered ("Ark of the Covenant," *Dr. William Smith's Dictionary of the Bible*, Revised and edited by Ezra Abbot, Vol 1, 1872, p. 155).

CHAPTER 5

WHAT WAS THE PURPOSE OF THE ARK?

A box that contained God? An instrument of War? A container that held a meteorite and not the Ten Commandments?

These are just some of the theories that have been put forward regarding the meaning of Ark of the Covenant and its contents.

We have now arrived at one of the areas of controversy surrounding the Ark—its purpose? Did the Israelites believe God actually lived inside the Ark? Was it some superstitious relic? Was it a weapon that no army could withstand?

Theories abound concerning the meaning and purpose of the Ark.[1] Some of the most well-known are:

1. A container where the Lord, the God of Israel, dwelt.

2. An idea borrowed from other nations.

3. A "Talisman" or "Good Luck" charm.

4. A device that Moses constructed with advanced scientific knowledge.

5. An Ancient war machine.

6. A container for the Ten Commandments as well as a representation of God's presence.

We will consider each of these suggestions as to what the Ark may have represented.

1. Container For the Lord?

Some interpreters see the Ark as a container that housed God's presence. The Lord, they believe, was somehow confined to the Ark.

Why would God order the people to build an Ark where He would "dwell among them?" Does this not prove that they thought that God actually lived inside the Ark and was limited to a certain geographic space?

God Not in the Ark

The idea that the Lord was confined to the Ark does not fit the facts. The Bible makes its clear that God is not a material object and cannot be limited to one place.

> Thus says the Lord, "Heaven is My throne, and earth is My footstool. Where is the house you will build for Me? And where is the place of My rest? (Isaiah 66:1).

When the Ark was placed in Solomon's Temple, Solomon's prayer showed that the people did not believe God was limited to one particular area.

> But will God dwell on the earth? Behold, heaven and the heaven of heavens cannot contain You. How much less this temple which I built! (1 Kings 8:27).

The Lord existed before the Ark was built. He is spoken of as the Creator of all things.

> Who has made man's mouth? Or who makes the mute, the deaf, the seeing, or the blind? Have not I, the Lord? (Exodus 4:11).

Not only was the Lord the one who commanded the Ark to be built, the Bible says He existed apart from it.

In addition, the Lord also was in open opposition to the Ark when it was wrongly used (1 Samuel 4:3-11). Its value ceased when God did not bless it.

Finally, the Lord continued to exist *after* the Ark disappeared.

The Scripture makes it clear that the God of Israel was not confined to the Ark. The Ark symbolized the presence of God without any attempted physical resemblance.

2 Borrowed Idea

A common theory about the Ark is that its design and purpose were borrowed from similar structures that were current in the ancient Near East. The Ark of the Covenant, it is contended, looked similar to other "sacred objects" that were in use at that time. Ancient analogies to the Ark have been sought in model temples, tent-shrines chariots for gods, squared thrones and even coffins for the gods. Therefore, it is argued there is nothing unique or supernatural about the Ark since it was one of many such objects.

For example, the tomb of King Tutankhamun (King Tut), who lived about the same time as Moses, contained a portable chest similar to the Ark of the Covenant. This container was probably made to house the heavy royal robes.

King Tut's wooden box had four poles for carrying, two at each end. When the chest was stationary, the poles were slid into rings underneath it.

Similar "arks" were supposedly common in Israel's time.

Three Problems With This View

There are three basic problems with the view that Israel's Ark was one of many such "arks" in the ancient world.

First, the references to the ark-like objects in other cultures have only a superficial resemblance. They are not the same structure or pattern as the Biblical Ark. A similarity in design does not prove one necessarily "borrowed from the other."

Second, many of the similar structures were built after the Ark of the Covenant. If any borrowing was done, it was probably from the Ark of the Covenant, not the reverse.

Egyptian chest or box from Thebes

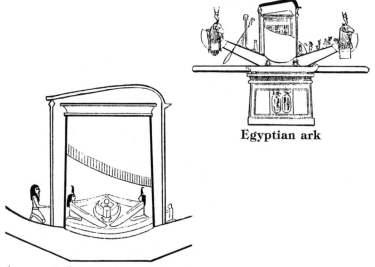

Egyptian ark

A sacred Egyptian boat or ark
with two figures perhaps
representing cherubim

Assyrian Sphinx

Old Testament authority George Bush observes:

> It is to be remarked that similar arks or chests, containing the mysteries of their religions, were common among nearly all the ancient heathen nations, the hint of which was probably taken from the Jews. The Egyptians, for instance, carried in solemn procession a sacred chest, containing the secret things and mysteries of their religion.[2]

Finally, and by far the most important, the history of the Ark shows that it was not some ancient pagan box devoid of power. Supernatural events took place around the Ark. The idea that the Ark was somehow ordinary or commonplace does not fit with or follow the facts.

3. Magical Object (Talisman)

The Ark has been viewed as a magical object or talisman, like a "rabbits foot," or a "good luck" charm. Though the people may have treated the Ark as a good luck charm, they learned that it did not guarantee victory. When Israel attempted to use the Ark as a "rabbits foot," in a battle with the Philistines, they lost both the battle and the Ark:

> So the Philistines fought, and Israel was defeated, and every man fled to his tent. There was a very great slaughter, and there fell of Israel thirty thousand foot soldiers. Also the ark of God was captured; and the two sons of Eli, Hophni and Phineas died (1 Samuel 4:10,11).

Ark and Islam

Islam holds a superstitious view of the Ark. John Lawson and John M. Wilson note:

> The Mohammedans pretend that the Ark was given to Adam ready made, and that it was handed down from patriarch to patriarch until the time of Moses; and the portraits of the patriarchs and prophets were engraven upon it; that in times of war a mighty rushing wind came forth from it which discomfited the enemies of Israel, and hence they carried it about with them as a protection in the wanderings from place to place. The followers of the Arabian prophet allege that in addition to the tables of stone, the ark of the covenant contained the shoes which Moses put off at the burning bush on Horeb, the pontifical

head-dress which Aaron wore, and a piece of wood with which Moses sweetened the waters of Marah.[3]

The idea that the Ark had some magical qualities is not taught in Scripture.

4. Mosaic Deception?

One theory has the Ark as a man-made device constructed by Moses with the skills he learned in Egypt. British author Graham Hancock wondered:

> As a magician skilled in Egyptian 'sacred science', might not Moses have had at his disposal far more in the way of knowledge and technology than had hitherto been recognized by the archaeologists? And might he not have applied that knowledge and technology to the construction of the Ark of the Covenant?[4]

Moses, with his knowledge of Egyptian science, supposedly built this terrible warlike object. Hancock concludes:

> I find myself drawn to the strange passages in the Old Testament books of Exodus and Deuteronomy which described the encounters between God and Moses on Mt. Sinai. Amidst thunder and fire, electrical storms and clouds of smoke, Yahweh supposedly disclosed the blueprint of the Ark of the Covenant to the Hebrew magus and presented him with the stone Tablets of the Law inscribed on the Ten Commandments. Then the Ark itself was built by the artificer Bezaleel who slavishly followed the 'divine' plan, almost as though he knew that he was forging some monstrous instrument.
> And this, I suspect, is what the Ark really was: a monstrous instrument capable of releasing fearful energies in an uncontrolled and catastrophic manner if it was mishandled or misused in any way—an instrument that was not conceived in the mind of God, as the Bible teaches, but rather in the mind of Moses.[5]

According to Hancock and others, Moses was not a prophet of God but rather a simple con artist. This view assumes that the God of the Old Testament does not exist, but was rather a creation of the desert-dwelling Hebrews. This is contradicted by the evidence that God not only exists, but that He has revealed Himself to us in both the Old and New Testament.

5. Instrument of War

The idea that the Ark was some type of war instrument is well-known but the evidence is non-existent. Apart from the use of the Ark at Jericho, the Ark does not receive mention at any of the other battles in the Book of Joshua. Other Old Testament references to the Ark used in battle are few.

In addition, no military purpose can be found in the Ark's construction: neither in its form nor its contents. It was not shaped like a weapon, it was *never* used as a weapon. The Bible gives no report of lightning, electricity, or any other force emanating from the Ark as it was taken to battle. The importance of the Ark in fighting wars was not because of its design or purpose, rather it was due to its symbolizing the invisible God of Israel. God was the One fighting for Israel, not the Ark. The Ark symbolized His presence.

6. Biblical View

Though there have been many different attempts to discern the purpose of the Ark, the only one that fits the facts is the Biblical explanation.

The Ark was a container for the Ten Commandments, the Covenant between God and His people. More than that, it was symbolic of the presence and character of God. He did not exist only there, but He revealed Himself from that sacred object. The Ark represented God's presence in the midst of His people.

The Lord told Moses:

> And there I will meet with you, and I will speak with you from above the Mercy Seat, from between the two cherubim which are on the Ark of the Testimony, of things which I will give you in commandment to the children of Israel (Exodus 25:22).

The Power of the Ark

The Bible does say that there was great power connected to the Ark of the Covenant. When the Ark was brought to the Jordan River, at flood stage, the waters immediately stopped flowing and rolled back to the city of Adam allowing the children of Israel to pass safely into the promised land (Joshua 3).

Shortly thereafter, the Ark was carried by priests around the city of Jericho once each day for six straight days and then seven times around on the seventh day. After the seventh time around; the wall collapsed and the victory belonged to Israel (Joshua 6:6-20).

When the Ark was later captured by the Philistines all sorts of terrible evils befell them. A plague caused them to send the Ark back to the children of Israel (1 Samuel 5-6). A number of men perished at Beth-Shemesh when the Israelites did not treat the Ark with proper respect.

God's Presence Symbolized

The power of the Ark lay not in its fallacy of being some magic box. Its power was in the fact that it symbolized God's Divine presence.

The Israelites went to battle with the Philistines without the Ark leading them. They were soundly defeated. Thinking that their defeat came about because of the absence of the Ark, they obtained it and went to do battle with the Philistines a second time. Again they were routed and the Ark was captured. God was making the point that that it was not the mere presence of the Ark that would win the battle, it was His presence that was needed to win and His presence did not necessarily come with the Ark. Therefore, the idea that the Ark had some magic power, making any army that possessed it invincible, does not square with the facts. God had promised His presence in the Ark as long as the people obeyed Him. When they disobeyed, the glory departed.

> The glory of God had departed from Israel, for the Ark of God has been captured (1 Samuel 4:22).

When news came that the Ark had been captured the high priest Eli fell backward and broke his neck. His daughter-in-law, dying in childbirth, named the son Ichabod, "no glory,"

Thus, the power of the Ark went hand in hand with obedience to God.

Law not Image

The Ark of the Covenant was unique in that it housed the *law* of God, not some image of Him. The Ten Commandments forbade any image of God to be made.

You shall not make for yourself any carved image, or any likeness of anything that is in heaven above, or that is in the earth beneath, or that is in the water under the earth (Exodus 20:4).

This commandment extended to Temple vessels and replicas of the sacred furniture.

The Ark of the Covenant was not to be worshiped. Rather worship was to be extended to the invisible God which it symbolized.

God-Given

We close this section with the emphasis on the supernatural construction of the Ark. The Ark cannot be compared to any pagan object that has ever been made, because its origin came from Almighty God Himself. Samuel Ridout writes:

We are told that the Israelites represented a stage in the natural development of the human race in their upward progress. But who taught them to cast away idols? How could they, or Moses, have conceived the thought that God was infinitely great and almighty, but not corporeal? There is but one answer—God was pleased to make Himself known. And how constantly, patiently, and carefully, did He reiterate that lesson. . .

The ark, then, and the Mercy Seat, with the attendant cherubim, were not idols, but they emphasized the spirituality of that all-glorious Being who fills heaven and earth, and yet had come to dwell among His people and manifest Himself to them.[6]

To those who consider the Ark merely some man-made superstitious object and who reject the God of Israel and His sacred artifact, we offer them the comments of the psalmist. . .

Why do the nations rage, and the people of the earth plot a vain thing? The kings of the earth set themselves, and the rulers of the earth take counsel together, against the Lord and against His anointed saying, "Let us break Their bonds in pieces and cast away their cords from us." HE WHO SITS IN THE HEAVENS SHALL LAUGH; THE LORD SHALL HOLD THEM IN DERISION (Psalm 2:1-4).

Endnotes for Chapter 5

1. Marten Woudstra writes:

> There is hardly a single type of Old Testament interpretation which has not in some way drawn the ark within its own particular orbit. Thus the ark has been the subject of sane spiritualization and extreme allegorizing . . . The solemn words of David, spoken at the entry of the ark into the sanctuary, "Arise O Yahweh, into thy restingplace, thou and the ark of thy strength" (Ps. 132:8) cannot be applied to the many studies devoted to the ark in the course of time. The ark has not enjoyed a restingplace but has constantly moved about from one theory to the next (Marten H. Woudstra, *The Ark of the Covenant From Conquest to Kingship*, Philadelphia, Presbyterian and Reformed, 1965, p. 10).

2. George Bush, *Notes on the Book of Exodus*, Volume, 1, Boston, Henry A. Young & Co., 1841, p. 92. Bush also wrote:

> The Trojans also had their sacred chest; and the palladium of the Greeks and Romans was something not very unlike. It is remarkable too, that as the Hebrew Tabernacle and Temple had a holy of holies, in which the ark was deposited, so had the heathen, in the inmost part of their temples . . . which none but the priests might enter. . .
> Something very similar may be traced among barbarous and savage nations. Thus Tacitus speaking of the nations of Northern Germany, of whom our Saxon ancestors were a branch, says that they generally worshiped Hertham, or Mother Earth (Terram matrem); believing her to interpose in the affairs of men, and to visit nations; and that to her, within a grove in a certain island, was consecrated a vehicle covered with a vestment, and which none but the priests were allowed to touch. The same thing has been frequently noticed in the connection with religious systems of other heathen nations, and among the inhabitants of Mexico and the South Sea Islands, very curious analogies with the Mosaic ark have been discovered (ibid. p. 93).

J. Barton Payne notes:

> His presence came and dwelt over the ark (25:22) though He remained free to reject those who should prove faithless (19:5). For contrary to Canaanitish theology, the testament did not put God "in a box." Israel in the consolidation period may indeed have succumbed to a

belief in the magical efficacy of the ark. (It is mentioned four times in the three verses, 1 Samuel 4:3-5). But to treat it as a "container" of God became in itself nothing short of a violation of the testament concept; and how God reacted to this externalization, they learned to their sorrow. "Man looketh on the outward appearance, but Yahweh looketh upon the heart" (I Samuel 16:7).

Old Testament authority Umberto Cassuto writes:

The conception of the ark as the Lord's footstool enables us to understand why the tablets of the covenant were placed within it, and to realize that the conjectures . . . that inside the ark were not the tables but sacred stones (kinds of fetishes, or idols, and the like), are without foundation. It was the custom in the ancient East to deposit the deeds of a covenant made between human kings in the sanctuaries of the gods, in the footstool of the idols that symbolized the deity, so that the godhead should be a witness to the covenant and see that it was observed. . . This custom makes it clear why the testimony to the covenant made between the Lord and Israel were enshrined in the ark. Among the Israelites there was no image to symbolize the God of Israel, but there was His footstool, and therein the testimony of the covenant was placed and preserved (Cassuto, ibid. p. 331).

The *International Standard Bible Encyclopedia* notes:

The statement of Moses "Arise O Lord, and let thy enemies be scattered" (Nu. 10:35), is not the command addressed to those who carry the ark to lift it up and thereby elevate Yahweh for the journey, but is a demand made upon Yahweh, in accordance with His promise, to go ahead of Israel as the ark does. According to 1 S. 4:3 the Israelites did not say, "We want to go and get the Lord," but "We want to go and get the ark of the Lord, that He may come among us." They wanted to induce Him to come by getting the ark. This, too, the priests and the soothsayers of the Philistines say: "Do not send away the ark of the God of Israel empty [i.e. without a gift]" (1 S. 6:3), but they do not speak as though they thought Yahweh was Himself confined therein. . .
Ancient Israel was therefore evidently of the conviction that the ark was closely connected with Yahweh, and that something of His power was inherent in the ark; consequently the feeling prevailed that when near the ark they were in a special way in the presence of the Lord. But this is something different from the opinion that the ark was, in the very literal sense, a seat or dwelling place of Yahweh. Ancient man was not conscious to the extent we

are of the difference between the symbolic presence and the literal reality, but that this difference was felt is not a matter of doubt (W. Lotz, M.G. Kyle, C.E. Armerding in *International Standard Bible Encyclopedia*, Volume 1, Revised Edition, Grand Rapids, Michigan, Wm. B. Eerdmans Publishing Company, 1979, p. 293).

They conclude:

In all the discussion it is foolish to press the aspect of physical presence to great lengths. That Yahweh was present with His people is clear from the texts. But that Yahweh was confined to the ark runs counter to both Hebrew notions about the nonspatial nature of God, and to the explicit statements of Scripture which, dating from the same times, mention God dwelling in many places both within and outside of Canaan (ibid. p. 294).

3. John Lawson and John M. Wilson, *A Cyclopaedia of Biblical Geography, Biography, Natural History, and General Knowledge*, Vol 1, Aaron to Egypt, Edinburgh, A Fullarton & Co., 1867, p. 184.

According to the Catholic Encyclopedia, the Ark of the Covenant is a title given to the Virgin Mary to signify her divine motherhood (*The Catholic Encyclopedia*, Robert C. Broderick, Nashville, Thomas Nelson Publishers, 1976, p. 52).

It has been alleged that the Ark was a specially built transmitter to talk to God. Science fiction writer Erik von Daaniken wrote:

Without actually consulting Exodus, I seem to remember that the Ark was often surrounded by flashing sparks and that Moses made use of this "transmitter" whenever he needed help and advice (Erik von Daaniken, *Chariots of the gods*, pp. 58,59).

He should have consulted Exodus. There are no references in that book or any other in the Old Testament where the Ark is said to have been surrounded by flashing light. Furthermore, the Book of Exodus records a number of occasions where God spoke to Moses before the Ark was constructed.

The Bible says the Ark contained the tablets of the Ten Commandments. Others have assumed something else was inside the Ark such as sacred stones or a piece of a meteor! There is nothing in Scripture that even remotely suggests that the tablets of Ten Commandments had any secret power or that they had fallen down from outer space. Imagination runs wild when attempting to give a natural explanation for supernatural phenomena. J. Barton Payne writes:

> The Mosaic traditions concerning the contents of the ark have been discounted by many. It has been supposed that the ark originally contained a fetish or other sacred stones. But these theories have been refuted by others, cf. R. Kittel, A History of the Hebrews, I, London, 1895, p. 238, "There is not a trace of its having resembled the heathen arks in containing an image or Yahweh or a holy stone" (J. Barton Payne, in *Zondervan Pictorial Encyclopedia of the Bible*, Volume 1, Merrill C. Tenney General Editor, Grand Rapids, Zondervan, 1975, p. 306).

4.   Graham Hancock, *The Sign and the Seal: The Quest for the Lost Ark of the Covenant*, New York, Crown Publishers, Inc,1992, p. 339,340.

5.   Hancock, ibid. p. 304

6.   Samuel Ridout, *Lectures on the Tabernacle*, New York, Loizeaux Publishers, 1914, p. 268, 269.

James Murphy notes:

> The contents of this cabinet distinguished it from all heathen chests of a similar kind in which were deposited certain symbols of the powers of nature which man regarded with superstitious veneration. Here are placed the two tables, on which are traced in plain and literal characters, the great principles of eternal rectitude, not as an object of worship, but as the basis of all moral dealing in the intercourse between God and man (James G. Murphy, *The Book of Exodus*, Boston, W. H. Halliday and Company, 1868, p. 291).

After Mt. Sinai, where did the Ark go? What was its history? We will now follow the travels of the Ark to the Promised Land, from its miraculous entry, to the time of its mysterious disappearance.

SECTION TWO

THE HISTORY OF
THE ARK OF THE COVENANT

CHAPTER 6

LEADING THE WAY TO THE PROMISED LAND

The command had been given, the materials gathered, and the sacred Ark had been built. The Ark of the Covenant was now ready to make its mark in history, the final chapter of which is still unwritten.

The history of the Ark of the Covenant parallels the history of the children of Israel. The Ark was the sacred object that the Lord used to lead the way to the Promised Land.[1]

Seven weeks after the Tabernacle had been inaugurated, the children of Israel left Mt. Sinai as "the people of God." While the other components of the Tabernacle occupied the central part of the column of march, the Ark of the Covenant went before the line of march "to seek out a resting place for them."

So they departed from the mountain of the Lord on a journey of three days; and the ark of the covenant of the Lord went before them for the three days' journey, to search out a resting place for them. And the cloud of the Lord was above them by day when they went out from the camp. So it was, whenever the ark set out, that Moses said, 'Rise up, O Lord! Let Your enemies be scattered, and let those who hate You flee before You.' And when it rested he said: Return O Lord, to the many thousands of Israel (Numbers 10:33-36).

During the wanderings of the children of Israel in the desert, the Ark was carried on the shoulders of the priests. The poles were never removed from the Ark.

The Bible gives us no explanation as to why the poles were to remain with the Ark and never to be removed. The poles that were used to carry the altar of sacrifice and the altar of incense were allowed to be removed, but the poles carrying the Ark were never removed.

It is possible that this order was given to make it unnecessary for the Ark itself to be touched, when set down or taken up, by those who bore it on the march.[2]

Unseen by the People

The Ark was transported in such a way that the people could not see it. It was covered by the veil from the dismantled Tabernacle. Then a curtain of badger skins covered that, and finally a blue cloth[3] covered the two. This made it near to impossible for anyone to see the Ark except the priests.

> When the camp prepares to journey, Aaron and his sons shall come, and they shall take down the covering veil and cover the Ark of the Testimony with it. Then they shall put on it a covering of badger skins, and spread over that a cloth entirely of blue (Numbers 4:5,6).

Levites

The Levites were responsible for putting up and taking down the Tabernacle, and carrying the coverings and furniture when the people wandered in the wilderness.

> At that time the Lord separated the tribe of Levi to bear the ark of the covenant of the Lord, to stand before the Lord to minister to Him and to bless His name, to this day (Deuteronomy 10:7).

One of the families of the Levites, the Kohathites, were responsible for the Ark.

> And the leader of the fathers' house of the families of the Kohathites was Elizaphan the son of Uzziel. Their duty included the Ark (Numbers 3:30,31).

The Kohathites were given the task of lowering the veil and placing it over the Ark along with the hides and cloths. They could not touch the Ark upon pain of death.[4]

The Ark and
Mercy Seat
Partly Covered

This covering was to keep the Ark from being seen by the people as well as to protect it from the elements. The coverings could be touched, but not the things covered.

No Permanent Rest

During the time of wandering in the wilderness, the Ark of the Covenant never found a permanent resting place. C.H. Mackintosh writes:

> The ark of the covenant was to accompany the people in all their wanderings. It never rested while they were travelling . . . It moved from place to place in the wilderness. It went before them in the midst of Jordan; it was their grand rallying point in all the wars of Canaan; it was the sure and certain earnest of power wherever it went. No power of the enemy could stand before that which was the well-known expression of the divine presence and power. The ark was to be Israel's companion in travel, in the desert; and "the staves" and "the rings" were the apt expression of its traveling character.[5]

Centerpoint of Camp

When the Israelites would make camp, the Ark and the Tabernacle would be placed in the center of the multitude (Numbers 10:14-27). It was truly central to the worship of the people. Everything in the camp pointed to the Ark. The purpose of entering the court of the Tabernacle was to enter the presence of God Himself.

God was not only present with His people in the Ark of the Covenant, He was also a God who speaks and acts. Before the Ark was constructed He promised to speak to His people through this sacred object. The first example of this is recorded in the Book of Leviticus:

> Now the Lord called to Moses, and spoke to him from the Tabernacle of meeting (Leviticus 1:1).

God continued to speak to Moses in an audible voice on other occasions:[6]

> Now when Moses went into the Tabernacle of meeting to speak with Him, he heard the voice of One speaking to him from above the Mercy Seat that was on the ark of the Testimony, from between the two cherubim; thus He spoke to him (Numbers 7:89).

Day of Atonement

During their wilderness wanderings and beyond, the children of Israel celebrated one sacred day when their sins would be atoned for. This event centered around the Ark of the Covenant.

As we have mentioned, the High Priest could not march into the Holy of Holies anytime he wanted.

> And the Lord said to Moses: Tell Aaron your brother not to come at simply any time into the Holy Place inside the veil, before the Mercy Seat which is on the ark, lest he die; for I will appear in the cloud above the Mercy Seat (Leviticus 16:2).

Only once a year, on the Great Day of Atonement, was the High Priest allowed to enter the holiest of all. This was the day the Ark achieved its highest sacrificial significance. Before the priest could enter, he had to observe the sacrificial rites and ceremonies outlined in Leviticus 16. Blood had to shed for his sins as well as for the sins of the people.

On that day the High Priest entered the Holy of Holies three times, first with incense, then with the blood of a bull which atoned for his own sins and those of his house, and finally, he entered with the blood of a goat that atoned for the sins of the people.

The Mercy Seat, on top of the Ark, was the most sacred place in the Sanctuary, being the visible throne of the invisible presence of God. The Mercy Seat was so named because on the Great Day of Atonement the High Priest sprinkled it with the blood of the victims of the substitutionary sacrifice.

> Then he shall kill the goat of the sin offering, which is for the people, bring its blood inside the veil, do with that blood as he did with the blood of the bull, and sprinkle it on the Mercy Seat and before the Mercy Seat (Leviticus 16:15).

The Great Day of Atonement spoke of a future time when the sins of the people would not merely be covered up but actually taken away.[7]

God's Provision—Manna

While the children of Israel wandered in the wilderness they were supernaturally fed by manna from heaven.

> And when the layer of dew lifted, there, on the surface of the wilderness, was a small round substance, as fine as frost on the ground. So when the children of Israel saw it they said to one another, "What is it?" For they did not know what it was. And Moses said to them, "This is the bread which the Lord has given you to eat" (Exodus 16:14)

The people were allowed to gather enough for one day. Any that was left over would spoil. On the day before the Sabbath, they were able to gather a double portion to keep them from working on the day of rest.

To remind the people of God's provision, a golden pot of manna was placed inside the Ark of the Covenant.

Aaron's Rod

After God had sent a plague on some of the rebellious people, there were still those who were murmuring against the leadership of Moses and Aaron. God then performed a miracle to show the people that it was Aaron whom he had chosen to be the priest.

God commanded Moses to collect twelve staffs, one from each of the tribes of Israel. Each owner was to write his name on the staff. Aaron's name was written on the rod of Levi. The staffs were to be placed in the Tabernacle before the Ark of the Covenant. God then told Moses:

And it shall be that the rod of the man whom I choose
will blossom; thus I will rid myself of the murmuring of
the children of Israel, which they murmer against you
(Numbers 17:5).

The next morning they found that Aaron's rod[8] had
budded and produced almonds.

Now it came to pass on the next day that Moses went
into the Tabernacle of witness, and behold the rod of
Aaron, of the house of Levi, had sprouted and put forth
buds, had produced blossoms and yielded ripe almonds
(Numbers 17:8).

God's response to the test left no doubt as to its
meaning.

And the Lord said to Moses, "Bring Aaron's rod back
before the Testimony, to be kept as a sign against the
rebels, that you may put their murmurings away from
Me, lest they die." Thus did Moses; just as the Lord had
commanded him, so did he (Numbers 18:10,11).

The writer to the Hebrews states at some point the rod
of Aaron was placed inside the Ark of the Covenant.

The ark of the covenant overlaid on all sides with gold,
in which were the golden pot that had the manna,
Aaron's rod that budded, and the tablets of the covenant
(Hebrews 9:4).

Ronald B. Allen makes an appropriate observation:

Aaron's rod was not returned to him. It was to be a
perpetual reminder of the wonder of the night and the
choice of God in his priest. Hence it was to remain in the
Tabernacle in perpetuity . . .
The interesting thing is that these memorials were put
in a place where no one would ordinarily see them. They
would be told of them in later generations, but they would
not be on public display. None, save the High Priest, would
enter the Holy Place, excepting Moses on rare occasions
such as this chapter presents. While the text focuses on
the role these symbols have in the memory of the people,
the placement of these symbols in the seclusion of the
shrine indicates that the one who will ever be reminded is
the Lord! These holy symbols were ever before him as
memorials of his special works with his people. Should
anyone of a later age dare to question the unique and holy

place of the Aaronic priests in the service of the Lord, this memorial of God's symbolic choice of Aaron would stand poignantly in opposition to his audacity.[9]

God's Providence

During their wilderness wanderings, the Lord providentially acted through the Ark even without their inquiring.

Now it came to pass on the twentieth day of the second month, in the second year, that the cloud was taken up from above the Tabernacle of the Testimony (Numbers 10:11).

When the cloud was lifted up, this was the signal for the people to advance. The Ark went before them to "seek out a resting place" (Numbers 10:33).

Fighting Without the Ark

On one occasion, the people attempted to fight a battle without the consent of the Lord and His Ark. The Ark remained behind and the people were defeated.

But they presumed to go up to the mountaintop; nevertheless, neither the ark of the covenant of the Lord nor Moses departed from the camp. Then the Amalekites and the Canaanites who dwelt in that mountain came down and attacked them, and drove them back as far as Hormah (Numbers 14:44,45).

When the Israelites attempted to enter the land without the guidance from the Lord, they were slaughtered at the border. The battle was lost because the children of Israel did not consult the Lord, not because they neglected to take along the Ark.

Moses' Speech

After forty years[10] of wandering in the wilderness, the people were positioned to enter the Promised Land. Moses then gave a speech to the multitude reminding them of their history. He indicated that God had showed them mercy in allowing a second set of tablets to be formed.[11] Moses prayer on behalf of the people, had kept them from experiencing the wrath of God.

At that time the Lord said to me, 'Hew for yourself two tablets of stone like the first and come to Me on the mountain and make yourself an ark of wood. And I will write on the tablets the words that were on the first tablets, which you broke; and you shall put them in the ark. So I[12] made an ark of acacia wood, hewed two tablets of stone like the first and went up the mountain, having two tablets in my hand. And He wrote on the tablets according to the first writing, the Ten Commandments, which the Lord had spoken to you in the mountain from the midst of the fire in the day of the assembly; and the Lord gave them to me. Then I turned and came down from the mountain, and put the tablets in the ark which I had made; and there they are, just as the Lord commanded me (Deuteronomy 10:1-5).[13]

Moses testified that the tablets were still in the Ark at the time of his speech to the people.

Moses' Death

Moses, the man God used to deliver his people from Egyptian bondage and to make the Ark of the Covenant, was not allowed to enter the Promised Land.[14]

So Moses the servant of the Lord died in the land of Moab, according to the word of the Lord. And he buried him in a valley in the land of Moab, opposite Beth Peor; but no one knows his grave to this day (Deuteronomy 34:5,6).

Though the exact burial place of Moses is still unknown, this location has figured into modern-day searches for the Ark of the Covenant.[15]

Time to Enter

The children of Israel had wandered for forty years in the wilderness. They were now perched on the border, about to enter the Promised Land. There was, however, a seemingly impossible obstacle in their way and a great miracle from God would be needed to allow them to enter their land.

Endnotes for Chapter 6

1. Marten Woudstra writes:

   To speak about the ark inevitably means to speak about the God whose intimate association with the ark is frequently stated. This lends to the ark-stories a peculiar significance. . . at some time during the history of the Old Testament the notion prevailed that Yahweh (the Lord) had set aside one solemn object for the purpose of being the supreme manifestation of his presence with Israel (Marten H. Woudstra, *The Ark of the Covenant From Conquest to Kingship*, Philadelphia, Presbyterian and Reformed, 1965, p. 13.)

   One Jewish legend says:

   The Ark gave the signal for breaking camp by soaring high and then swiftly moving before the camp at a distance of three days' march (Louis Ginzberg, *Legends of the Jews*, Philadelphia, Jewish Publication Society of America, 1911, Vol 3. p. 243).

2. One Jewish writer stated why he thought this was so:

   The ark is the dwelling place of the Torah, our foundation and glory, and we have to show it the greatest reverence and respect. We are bidden not to remove it poles, since we might be called upon to go forth with the ark in haste, and in the hurry of the moment forget to examine whether the poles are properly secured and, God forbid, the ark might slip from our hold. If the poles are always secured in their place such a thing could never happen, since the ark would always be ready for transportation (Sefer Ha-hinukh).

   Umberto Cassuto writes

   Whereas the poles of the other sacred vessels were not fitted into them permanently, but only when they were moved from one place to another in the course of the Israelites' journeys. The reason for this distinction is, apparently, the fact that the ark was due to be carried not only when the camp as a whole was on the move, but also in connection with solemn processions, like those described in Joshua iii. 3 f.; vi 4 ff.; and consequently, it was fitting that whatever was necessary to its transportation should always be ready. The poles, were, so to speak, an inseparable part of the ark, which was always intended to be carried. (Umberto Cassuto,

Commentary on Exodus, Jerusalem, The Magnes Press, 1967, pp. 321, 322).

Keil writes that there were four poles:

> It has four carrying poles so that bearers could support it on their shoulders. Each pole slides through two bronze rings attached to the base of the box (C.F. Keil, *Biblical Commentary on the Old Testament,* Volume II, The Pentateuch, C.F. Keil and F. Delitzsch, Grand Rapids, Eerdmans, reprinted 1971, p. 167).

3. The blue covering on the Ark stood in contrast to the other articles of furniture which were covered first by a blue, purple, or scarlet cloth and afterward badgers' skins.

4. The Bible is clear on this matter.

> When the camp prepares to journey, Aaron and his sons shall come, and they shall take down the covering veil and cover the ark of the Testimony with it . . . And when Aaron and his sons have finished covering the sanctuary and all the furnishings of the sanctuary, when the camp is set to go, then the sons of Kohath shall come to carry them; but they shall not touch any holy thing, lest they die (Numbers 4:5,15).

5. C. H. Mackintosh, *Notes on the Book of Exodus,* New York, Loizeaux Brothers, 1862, pp. 278,279.

The great Jewish commentator Maimonides wrote the following concerning the transporting of the Ark.

> When the ark is moved from place to place it is not moved on a beast or wagon but must be carried on the shoulder. Because David forgot and had it moved on a wagon, the breach was broken against Uzzah. This duty of carrying it on the shoulder is distinctly stated: "for the service of the holy things belonged to them: they bore it upon their shoulders" (Num 7:9). The porters carried it facing each other, their backs to the outside, their faces inwards, taking care that the poles should not slip out of the rings, since he who removes one of the poles from the rings is liable to the penalty of lashes, as it is stated: "the poles shall remain in the rings of the ark, they shall not be removed therefrom." (Rambam in his code Klei Ha-Mikdash, 2, 12-13).

6. William Brown notes:

> It is not necessary to suppose that Moses or the High Priest, when consulting Jehovah, entered the Holy of Holies. The probability is, that Moses or the priest inquired of the Lord in the Holy Place, standing, while so engaged, before the golden altar, and there would hear the voice of the Lord coming from between the cherubim (William Brown, *The Tabernacle*, Edinburgh, William Oliphant and Company, Third Edition,1874, pp. 153, 154).

Nadab and Abihu are said to have offered strange fire before the Lord which cost them their life (Leviticus 10). Some feel their sin was going into the Holy of Holies before the Ark.

7. This is developed in Chapter 29.

8. On Aaron's rod that budded George Bush writes:

> The original word for "rod" (*matteh*) is for the most part used to denote a staff, stick, walking stick, or wand, rather than a green rod, branch or bough. It would seem, from Num 21:18, that the princes of the tribes carried staves in their hands, as a kind of baton, that should serve as a badge of authority. The rods or staves were doubtless official ensigns of the authority with which the heads of the tribes were invested. Hence the Scripture frequently uses the word rod as equivalent to sceptre;' and indeed the more modern use of sceptres is derived from this ancient custom. These staves were of course dry, and had probably been for years in use; and that such should blossom and bear fruit again is a moral impossibility (George Bush, *Notes Critical and Practical on the Book of Numbers*, Boston, Henry A. Young & Co, 1858, p. 251).

9. Ronald B. Allen, *The Expositors Bible Commentary*, Volume 2, Frank C. Gaebelein, General Editor, Grand Rapids, Zondervan, 1990, p. 848.

10. The reason it took the people forty years to enter the Promised Land was because of their unbelief. Initially God led them to the border at Kadesh Barnea. Twelve men were sent to spy out the land. Ten of them came back with reports of giants in the land and no tangible evidence that it was a wonderful land. Two of the spies, Joshua and Caleb brought back a positive report along with tangible evidence: grapes, pomegranates and figs. The people believed the ten and complained to Moses that they had been brought to a place of

death. As a judgment for their unbelief, God turned them southward, their backs to the Promise Land where they wandered for forty years. Every person twenty years and older died in the wilderness, with the exception of Joshua and Caleb. When God initially said to them, "Go into the land," the people refused. Later God told them *not* to go up against the Amalekites. On this occasion they did go up and were soundly defeated.

11. There has been some question whether Moses put the broken set of the Ten Commandments into the Ark of the Covenant. The first set of tablets were most likely destroyed when Moses threw them down. No other mention is ever made of them. John Lawson and John M. Wilson write:

> The rabbis allege that the two tables of the law were deposited in the ark, not only those which were entire, but those also which were broken. This opinion they found upon a mistranslation of Deut. x. 2, which they render thus: "And I will write on the tables the words that were on the first table, which thou breakest and hast put in the ark." The last clause is more correctly translated in our version, "thou shalt put" (John Lawson and John M. Wilson, *A Cyclopaedia of Biblical Geography, Biography, Natural History, and General Knowledge*, Vol 1, Aaron to Egypt, Edinburgh, A Fullarton & Co., 1867, p. 184).

C.H. Mackintosh writes:

> When, therefore, we read of the "ark of the covenant," we are led to believe that it was designed of God to preserve his covenant unbroken, in the midst of an erring people. In it, as we know, the second set of tablets were deposited. As to the first set they were broken in pieces, beneath the mount . . . The ark could not contain within its hallowed inclosure, broken tablets. Man might fail to fulfill his self-chosen vow; but God's law must be preserved in its divine integrity and perfectness. If God was to set up his throne in the midst of his people, he could only do it in a way worthy of himself. His standard of judgment and government must be perfect (C.H. Mackintosh, ibid. p. 288).

12. "I made" probably refers to the instructions Moses gave to Bezaleel, the artist employed for the work. He probably gave the orders before he ascended Mt. Sinai in order that the Ark would be finished upon his descent. Thus he could deposit the Ten Commandments.

13. Were there two Arks? When Israel was on the march, the Ark "went before" them seeking places to camp. However, the impression left by Scripture is that the Kohathites, who had charge of the Ark and the Tabernacle, were somewhere in the middle of the marching column. When the nation was camped, the Ark was placed at its center. This had led some to believe there were actually two Arks.

The difficulty which this passage offers has prompted Jewish interpreters to speak of two different Arks. The first, housing the broken tables of the law, preceded the people through the wilderness. The other, the depository of the second set of the law tablets, marched with the group.

The probable explanation is that rest of the Tabernacle and its furniture were carried at the center, but the Ark was an exception. The object that represented God's presence would lead the way.

Others find a second Ark in Deuteronomy 10:1. It is, however, not necessary to argue for two Arks for Deuteronomy 10:1 summarizes the making of one Ark. It does not to suggest a second Ark was constructed after the golden calf incident.

14. Moses was not allowed to enter because he disobeyed a commandment of God. God had told him to speak to a rock and water would come forth. Instead Moses struck the rock. This act of disobedience kept him from the Promised Land.

15. See Chapter 23 Has the Ark Been Found on Mt. Nebo?

CHAPTER 7

THE WATERS OF JORDAN MIRACULOUSLY PART

At last, the Promised Land! After wandering for forty years in the wilderness, the children of Israel were about to enter the land God had promised to Abraham and his descendants. A major obstacle, however, stood in the way. Between them and their dream was the swift current of the river Jordan. As God had previously parted the Red Sea, He would now work another outstanding miracle to bring His people to the land of promise. This miracle would center around the Ark of the Covenant.

Holy War

Because the land would have to be taken by conquest the people began to prepare for a Holy War. God reminded them that the battle they were fighting was holy by drawing their attention to the Ark of the Covenant. The Ark was not only the outward symbol for the presence of God, it also contained the covenant that God had made with His people. Part of the covenant included ownership of the Promised Land. The Ark represented to all the people that God was going before Israel to lead them to victory.

The Ark would precede the people into the Promised Land:

When you see the ark of the covenant of the Lord your God, and the priests, the Levites bearing it, then you shall set out from your place and go after it . . . (Joshua 3:3,6).

The Mighty Jordan

The Jordan River has an important place in Biblical history. Growing wider with each mile, the Jordan begins its sixty mile course near the slopes of Mount Hermon and flows south to the Dead Sea, some 1286 feet below sea level. The slopes on each side of the Jordan are steep and sometimes form huge precipices. At best, it is not an easy river to cross.

The children of Israel arrived during the month of Nisan (March-April), the first month of their year. Ordinarily the river around Jericho is about fifty to sixty yards across, but this was the time of the barley harvest when the river would be twice as wide as normal. The river at flood stage must have presented an ominous sight for the people. As they were waiting at its bank for three days, they probably wondered how they were going to be able to cross this wide river: who would make a way?

New Leader

This was the appropriate occasion for God to raise up Joshua in the sight of the people. It was now his time to be confirmed by God as Israel's new leader.

And the Lord said to Joshua, 'This day I will begin to magnify you in the sight of all Israel, that they may know that, as I was with Moses, so I will be with you. You shall command the priests who bear the ark of the covenant, saying 'When you have come to the edge of the water of Jordan, you shall stand in the Jordan' (Joshua 3:7,8).

Joshua had been in the shadow of Moses since the time of the deliverance from Egypt. He would now participate in a similar miracle as the parting of the Red Sea. The Ark would accomplish the same thing as Moses' rod at the Red Sea, miraculously parting the water. Joshua's involvement was more indirect than Moses. Moses lifted up the rod and the Red Sea parted while Joshua merely gave the orders. Though the Ark had not been built when the Israelites crossed the Red Sea, it was now leading the way symbolizing God's power over His enemies.

God With Them

The purpose for this miracle was to show that God was with them. He had kept His promise to bring them to this land and now He would drive out their enemies:

> So Joshua said to the children of Israel, 'Come here, and hear the words of the Lord your God.' And Joshua said, 'By this you will know that the living God is among you, and that He will without fail drive out from before you the Canaanites and the Hittites and the Hivites and the Perizzites and the Girgashites and the Amorites and the Jebusites: Behold the ark of the covenant of the Lord of all the earth is crossing over before you into the Jordan (Joshua 3:10,11).

The method that God prescribed would show the people that a miracle was occurring. Joshua commanded:

> And it shall come to pass, as soon as the soles of the feet of the priests who bear the ark of the Lord, the Lord of all the earth, shall rest in the waters of the Jordan, that the waters of Jordan shall be cut off, the waters that come down from upstream, and they shall stand as a heap (Joshua 3:12,13).

The priests were to step into the river by faith and then God would part the waters. Here the Ark would lead and be carried by the priests. This same procedure happened on other important occasions.[1]

Kept at a Distance

The people were commanded to keep a distance of 2,000 cubits (3,500 feet) behind the Ark at the command of God.[2] This command probably served two purposes. The first was to emphasize the necessity of being separate from a holy God.

The second was of a practical nature. By being some distance from the Ark, the people could visibly witness the miracle of the waters of Jordan parting. This would clearly testify that God was leading them.

The priests were ordered to cross over with the Ark. The people were not told how they were going to be able to get across the Jordan and its overflowing banks. Obviously this was going to be a journey of faith.

> And they commanded the people, saying, 'When you see the ark of the covenant of the Lord your God, and the priests, the Levites, bearing it, then you shall set out from your place and go after it. Yet there shall be a space between you and it, about two thousand cubits by measure. Do not come near it, that you may know the way by which you must go, for you have not passed this way before (Joshua 3:3,4).

This would allow the entire multitude to see the great event that was about to happen. Marten Woudstra notes:

> The distance of 2000 cubits was approximately that of the outer bank of the Jordan to the inner bed . . . Thus the people would still be on the outer bank while the feet of the priests touched the water's edge.[3]

The Miracle Occurs

As God promised, the waters parted.

> So it was, when the people set out from their camp to cross over the Jordan, with the priests, bearing the ark of the covenant before the people, and as those who bore the ark came to the Jordan, and the feet of the priests dipped in the edge of the water (for the Jordan overflows all its banks during the whole time of harvest), that the waters which came down from upstream stood still, and rose in a heap very far away at Adam, the city that is beside Zaretan. So the waters that went down into the Sea of the Arabah, the Salt Sea failed, and were cut off; and the people crossed over opposite Jericho. Then the priests who bore the ark of the covenant of the Lord stood firm on dry ground in the midst of the Jordan; and all Israel crossed over on dry ground until all the people had crossed completely over the Jordan (Joshua 3:14-17).

Thus, the Lord, of Whom the Ark symbolized, was the One who actually entered the Promised Land first, ahead of Joshua and the people. Donald Madvig writes:

> The ark of the covenant is the most prominent feature in these two chapters. The presence of the ark indicates that the crossing of the Jordan was much more than a military maneuver: It was a religious procession. . . When

the ark was carried across the Jordan, the Lord was marching to claim his land.[4]

The Water was Rolled Back

As soon as the priests put their feet into the Jordan the waters were rolled back. This miracle reminded the people of their deliverance from Egypt when the Red Sea parted.

The people crossed the river on dry ground. However, this does not necessarily mean the ground was not moist. Marten H. Woudstra comments:

> The Hebrew term for "dry ground" (*harabah*) does not require that the riverbed be powdery dry but simply means it was no longer covered with water. This indicates *terra firma* as contrasted with the flooding river (cf. 4:18, where the term "dry ground" is used to distinguish the bank from the riverbed.[5]

The water drained off below and the river bottom was dry as the people walked across. Not only did the water stop flowing, it went all the way back to a town called Adam, some fifteen miles to the north! Adam is identified with ed Damieh about twenty miles from the Dead Sea. Since Israel crossed the Jordan opposite Jericho (Joshua 3:16) about five miles from the Dead Sea, they were about fifteen miles from Adam.

How Did God Do It?

At Adam, the Jordan flows through clay banks forty feet high. In the past, rock slides have occurred near Adam temporarily stopping the Jordan. The suggestion is often made that God used a landslide to stop the river from flowing. Although this is possible, the account suggests that the waters separated immediately in front of the priests.

The parting of the waters of the Jordan was a miracle. It happened at the precise time the Ark was placed in the river and the river bed continued to be dry until the entire procession made its way into the Promised Land. Some have tried to give a natural explanation by citing an earthquake that happened on December 8, 1267. That earthquake caused the banks of the Jordan to collapse and the river was damned up for ten hours. A similar event

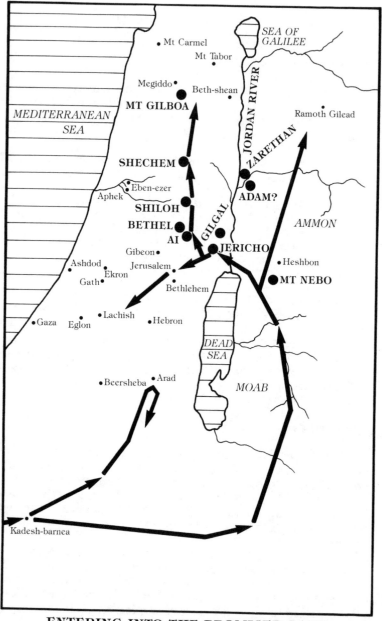

ENTERING INTO THE PROMISED LAND

occurred on July 11, 1927 which stopped the river for twenty-one hours. Neither of these stoppages occurred during flood season.

A close examination of the text will reveal that this crossing was a supernatural event due to the following circumstances:

1. Predicted

First, the event occurred as predicted. God had promised Joshua that this event would show His power to their enemies.

2. Timing

The timing of the event was exact. As soon as the priests stepped into the water the Jordan parted.

3. Flood Stage

To add to the miraculous character of the event, it occurred when the river was at flood stage.

4. Dry

The bottom of the river was dry enough for all the people to walk across.

5. Long Duration

The wall of water lasted the entire time it took the children of Israel to cross the dry river.

6. Water Returns

Immediately after the people entered the Promised Land and the priests came out of the river, the water returned. Again the timing was perfect. Donald Madvig comments on the miraculous nature of the event:

> If an earthquake was responsible for stopping the Jordan River, it was still a miracle. The discovery of secondary causes only serves to explain how God did what he did, and only God's intervention can account for the miraculous timing. This must have been a remarkable example of what H.L. Ellison (Joshua—2 Samuel [Grand

Rapids: Eerdmans, 1966], p. 7) calls "the supernatural use of the natural.[6]

The result of this miracle, led by the Ark of the Covenant, was that God was glorified among all the people.[7] In addition, Joshua was lifted up as their new leader. The nation Israel was encouraged to possess the land of promise, and the inhabitants of the land of Canaan became fearful at the power of the Lord.

Memorial

After the crossing of the Jordan, two piles of stones were erected as memorials. One was where the Ark stood on the east edge of the river the other on the west side of Gilgal. This was to be a witness for generations to come of this miracle.

> When your children ask in time to come, 'What do these stones mean to you?' Then you shall answer them that the waters of Jordan were cut off before the ark of the covenant of the Lord; when it crossed over the Jordan, the waters of Jordan were cut off. And these stones shall be a memorial to the children of Israel forever (Joshua 4:4-8).

Battle of the Gods

This episode was a continuation of the battle of the Gods, begun in Egypt. The god of the Canaanites was named Baal. Supposedly Baal was the god of nature. The fact that God lead Israel into the Promised Land by superseding the laws of nature demonstrated that He was the true and living God. Baal was powerless in the presence of the Lord. The Bible makes it clear that the God of Israel is the true God of nature.

Joshua assured the people that the living God would prove His presence among them and drive out the Canaanites. The God of Israel, whom the Ark of the Covenant symbolized, is spoken of as "the Lord of all the earth."[8]

> Behold the ark of the Covenant of the Lord of all the earth is crossing before you into Jordan (Joshua 3:11).

Once this mighty miracle occurred the Passover was celebrated (Joshua 4:19-5:10). The next day the manna ceased:

Now the manna ceased on the day after they had eaten the produce of the land; the children of Israel no longer had manna, but they ate the food of Canaan that year (Joshua 5:12).

Fulfilled Prophecy

The crossing of the Jordan into Canaan was the beginning of the fulfillment of promises that God had made to Abraham. Thus it was appropriate that the Ark,[9] the symbol of the covenant, led the way:

Then He brought him outside and said, "Look now toward heaven, and count the stars if you are able to number them." And He said to him, "So shall your descendants be . . . On the same day God made a covenant with Abram saying: "To your descendants I have given this land, from the river of Egypt to the great river Euphrates (Genesis 15:5,18).

As God had promised Abraham, his descendants would mightily increase. Moses had earlier reminded them:

Your fathers went down to Egypt with seventy persons, and now the Lord your God has made you as the stars of heaven in multitude (Deuteronomy 10:22).

The Conquest Begins

Israel was now committed to fight against the inhabitants of Canaan. This included overcoming well-protected cities and armies with chariots. There was no going back. The first city to be conquered was the fortified city of Jericho. The Ark of the Covenant would again figure prominently in this battle.

Endnotes for Chapter 7

1.   J. Barton Payne notes;

> On important occasions, such as the entrance into Canaan, the Ark might be carried by the priests (Josh 3:3; 4:10; cf. Deut 31:9; 1 Kings 8:3) or as a joint undertaking by priests and Levites (2 Sam 15:24; 1 Chron. 15:11,12) J. Barton Payne, *The Zondervan Pictorial Encyclopedia of the Bible,* Merill Tenney General Editor, Volume 1, 1975, p. 308.

2.   Donald Madvig notes the emphasis given on staying away from the Ark.

> In Hebrew the warning to stay far away from the ark comes first and gives greater emphasis to the sacredness of the ark. The same order in English would be confusing. It would seem to say that they would know the way to go by keeping away from the ark rather than by following it (Donald Madvig, *The Expositors Bible Commentary,* Frank C. Gaebelein General Editor, Volume 3, Grand Rapids, Zondervan, 1992, p. 267, note 4).

3.   Marten H. Woudstra, *The Book of Joshua,* Grand Rapids, Eerdmans, 1981, p. 81.

> The distance of 2000 cubits (about five eights of a mile) was later used to mark off an allowable Sabbath day's journey (cf. Acts 1:12). This was fixed by Jewish rabbis on the basis of Exodus 16:29 and Numbers 35:5.

4.   Donald H. Madvig, ibid. p. 265.

5.   Woudstra, ibid. p. 81.

6.   Madvig, ibid. p. 272

7.   Marten Woudstra writes:

> Until the very end of the account, due stress is given to ark and priests (vv. 3,8,13). The ark, the supreme symbol of God's indwelling, is view as directing silently the whole proceeding as the priests *stood firm on dry ground.* The narrators chief concern with this chapter has been to focus attention upon the stupendous miracle, wrought under the watchful eye of the Lord, whose ark led the way into the waters and then stood in the river bed while *the whole nation had finished crossing over the Jordan.* (Woudstra, ibid.,p. 88).

8. Zechariah speaks of a future time when Israel is established in her kingdom after all of their enemies had been judged. In referring to the Lord, he uses the same title we find here in Joshua "Lord of all the earth."

So he said, 'These are the two anointed ones, who stand beside the Lord of the whole earth . . . And the angel answered and said to me, 'These are the four spirits of heaven, who go out from their station before the Lord of all the earth (Zechariah 4:14; 6:5) .

9. Marten Woudstra makes an appropriate comment on the entire episode.

The ark's prominence should be noted, though this ought not to be considered in terms of magic. There is a certain way in which it is not the ark but the faith of those who carry and follow it that will bring about the miracle. The stories in 1 Samuel 4ff. show clearly that a superstitious belief in the ark's potency does not bring about the desired end (Woudstra, ibid. p. 86).

CHAPTER 8

CONQUERING A CITY
GOD'S WAY: JERICHO

The God who reveals Himself in Scripture does things His own way. His ideas and thoughts are not the same as we human beings. The prophet Isaiah records the Lord as saying:

'For My thoughts are not your thoughts, nor are your ways My ways,' says the Lord. 'For as the heavens are higher than the earth, so are My ways higher than your ways, and My thoughts than your thoughts' (Isaiah 55:8,9).

This statement was never more true than when Joshua received the battle plan from the Lord to take the city of Jericho.

Once the children of Israel entered the land God had promised, they practiced the neglected rite of circumcision. Then they were ready to fulfil the promises of God and conquer the land. The first battle would be the city of Jericho.

Jericho

Jericho is one of the oldest cities in the world, situated about seventeen miles northeast of Jerusalem. In Joshua's day, Jericho was by no means the largest city of Canaan, but it was located in a strategic area. It lay a few miles west of the Jordan River, where most nomads and travelers crossed to enter Canaan.

Jericho was a fortified city: a city with walls constructed to repel enemy attack. Excavations have uncovered ruins that prove it was already an ancient city at the time Joshua arrived. Many fortified cities had walls up to twenty feet thick and over twenty-five feet high. If standing atop them, one could see for miles. The inhabitants of Jericho were constantly on guard, watching for the enemy.

Jericho was a strong city, able to defend itself against a large army. However, strength of stone or brick was not strong enough to stop the army of the Lord.

The Battle Plan

The battle fought against Jericho employed one of the oddest strategies ever used to fight a battle. Joshua told the men of war:

> You shall march around the city, all you men of war; you shall go all around the city once. This you shall do for six days (Joshua 6:3).

The seventh day the strategy would be different.

> And seven priests shall bear seven trumpets of rams' horns before the ark. But the seventh day you shall march around the city seven times, and the priests shall blow the trumpets. Then it shall come to pass, when they make a long blast with the ram's horn, and when you hear the sound of the trumpet, that all the people shall shout with a great shout; then the wall of the city will fall down flat. And the people shall go up every man straight before him (Joshua 6:4,5).

The battle plan, therefore, consisted of the people, led by the Ark of the Covenant, marching once around the city for six straight days. On the seventh day they were to march around seven times and then give a shout after hearing the sound of the trumpet. The walls, then, were going to fall down.

Since the people had just experienced the miracle of the parting of the Jordan, it was probably easier for them to accept this odd way of conquering a fortified city.

We are not given any specific details as to the line of march. Nothing is told of the number of people marching or the length of the column. Donald Madvig writes:

No details are given as to how the march was conducted (i.e., how many marched abreast or how long the column was). Jericho occupied only about five or six acres of land. Even though the Israelites must have maintained sufficient distance from the city to be safely beyond the range of bow and arrow, it is possible that the head of the column had arrived back at the camp before the last of the rear guard left.[1]

The children of Israel marched around the city of Jericho a total of thirteen times with the Ark leading the way. At the head of the procession were priests with trumpets, followed by the Ark, and then the Israelite men of war.

Throughout each one of these marches the men were not allowed to utter one word. One can only imagine the confusion this caused for the inhabitants of Jericho as they watched this silent procession march around their city.

And The Walls Come Tumbling Down

On the seventh day they marched around the city seven times, blew a trumpet and, as predicted, the walls of the city fell down.

So the people shouted when the priests blew the trumpets. And it happened when the people heard the sound of the trumpet, and the people shouted with a great shout, that the wall fell down flat. Then the people went up into the city, every man straight before him, and they took the city (Joshua 6:20).

The city of Jericho had been conquered by the unusual battle tactics of the God of Israel.

Why Did the Walls Fall Down?

Critics of the Bible have raised objections to the Biblical account as recorded in Joshua. Rejecting the supernatural explanation found in Scripture, these individuals have attempted to give alternative explanations as to what the Bible says occurred. There have been a variety of non-supernatural explanations offered as to why the wall fell down at the precise moment that the priests blew the trumpets and the people shouted.

One popular suggestion is that an earthquake occurred at that precise moment. Others have alleged that

The walls of Jericho falling down

the marchers served to distract the citizens of Jericho from other Israelites who were digging under the city walls.

It has also been alleged that vibrations from the people caused the walls to collapse. All the marching around supposedly caused the walls to weaken and fall down.

Whatever the explanation, it is clear that the fall of Jericho was a miracle. That it was supernatural is attested to by the fact that the entire wall fell down, except for one portion—the house of Rahab, a woman who hid Israel's spies.

The New Testament commented on the event in this manner:

> By faith the walls of Jericho fell, after the people had marched around them for seven days (Hebrews 11:30).

The blast from the trumpets and the shout of the people is not what brought the walls down, it was the miraculous power of God.

The Evidence Says Yes

Recent archaeological evidence has substantiated the Biblical account of the destruction of the city of Jericho by Joshua. After evaluating all the facts, scholar Bryant Wood writes:

> Was there a destruction at the hands of the Israelites? The correlation between the archaeological evidence and the Biblical narrative is substantial.
> The city was strongly fortified (Joshua 2:5,7,15,6:5,20).
> The attack occurred just after harvest time in the spring (Joshua 2:6, 3:15, 5:10).
> The inhabitants had no opportunity to flee with their foodstuffs (Joshua 6:1).
> The siege was short (Joshua 6:15).
> The walls were leveled, possibly by an earthquake (Joshua 6:20).
> The city was not plundered (Joshua 6:17,18).
> The city was burned (Joshua 6:24).[2]

Joshua's Prophecy

After the destruction of Jericho, Joshua pronounced a curse upon the city.

Then Joshua charged them at that time saying,
'Cursed be the man before the Lord who rises up and
builds this city Jericho; he shall lay its foundation with
his firstborn, and with his youngest he shall set up its
gates (Joshua 6:26).

Though the site of the city was later occupied for brief
periods the prohibition against building the city was not
violated until the time of Ahab, 500 years later.

Hiel the Bethelite attempted to rebuild the city's wall.
This act cost the lives of his two sons Abiram and Segub.[3]
The exact site where the ancient city stood has not been
rebuilt to this day.

God's Power

Jericho, the fortified city of Canaan, was conquered by
the miraculous power of God. Led by the Ark of the
Covenant, the city was taken with a battle plan that clearly
showed the superiority of the God of Israel. The conquest
of the Promised Land had begun.

Endnotes for Chapter 8

1. Donald Madvig, *The Expositors Bible Commentary,* Volume 3, Frank C. Gaebelein General Editor, Grand Rapids, Zondervan, 1992, p. 280.

John Rea observes:

> On that day they compassed the city seven times. One can easily walk around the nine-acre mound in fifteen or twenty minutes. John Rea, Joshua, *The Wycliffe Bible Commentary,* Edited by Charles F. Pfeiffer and Everett F. Harrison, Chicago, Moody Press, 1962, p. 213.

2. Bryant G. Wood, Did the Israelites Conquer Jericho? *Biblical Archaeology Review,* March/April, 1990, p. 57.

3. The verse reads:

> In his days, Hiel of Bethel built Jericho. He laid its foundation with Abiram his firstborn, and with his youngest son Segub he set up the gates according to the word of the Lord, which He had spoken through Joshua the son of Nun (1 Kings 16:34).

CHAPTER 9

BATTLING FOR THE PROMISED LAND

We recall that God had promised
Abraham that the entire land of Canaan would belong to
his descendants. Jericho was the first city of the Promised
Land to be conquered. After Jericho was destroyed,
Joshua set his sights on the smaller city of Ai. With the
success at Jericho, it seemed that victory at Ai would be a
simple matter. This, however, would not be the case.

Fighting Without the Lord

If Joshua thought that having the Ark would be an
automatic guarantee for victory in battle, he would soon
learn differently.

> Now Joshua sent men from Jericho to Ai, which is
> beside Beth Aven, on the east side of Bethel, and spoke to
> them, saying. 'Go up and spy out the country.' So the
> men went up and spied out Ai. And they returned to
> Joshua and said to him. 'Do not let all the people go up,
> but let about two or three thousand men go up and attack
> Ai. Do not weary all the people there, for the people of Ai
> are few (Joshua 7:2,3).

The victory at Jericho was not won because of the
superior fighting ability of Israel but because of the power

of the Lord. Unfortunately, the overconfident people went to fight the battle with Ai without consulting Him.

> So about three thousand men went up there from the people, but they fled before the men of Ai (Joshua 7:4).

The army was defeated at Ai. The main reason for the defeat was that one of the Israelites, a man named Achan, took some of the booty from the destroyed city of Jericho. God had commanded that Jericho be utterly destroyed with no spoils taken. The Israelites had to be judged for their disobedience. After the loss at Ai, Joshua fell before the Ark:

> Then Joshua tore his clothes, and fell to the earth on his face before the ark of the Lord until evening, both he and the elders of Israel; and they put dust on their heads (Joshua 7:6).

Ai was eventually conquered, but a valuable lesson was learned: mere possession of the Ark did not guarantee victory.

Nowhere is it recorded that the Ark of the Covenant was involved in either battle with Ai. Marten Woudstra observes:

> The God who gives the victory at Jericho permits defeat at Ai. It is not the absence or presence of the ark which causes the defeat. . . . It is obvious therefore, that the narrator had no intention to suggest that the ark's role had been somewhat magical in character at the time of Jordan's crossing and the conquest of Jericho. . . Any doubt as to the true nature of the ark is quickly dispelled.[1]

Altar Built

After the victory at Ai, the children of Israel built an altar to the Lord at Mt. Ebal in the area of Shechem. Shechem is in the heart of the promised land. The purpose of the altar was to commemorate the victories of Jericho and Ai. In addition, the covenant[2] was renewed between God and His people. The Ark of the Covenant was the central focus at this assembly.

> Now Joshua built an altar to the Lord God of Israel in Mt. Ebal, as Moses the servant of the Lord had commanded the children of Israel, as it is written in the Book of the Law of Moses: "an altar of whole stones over

which no man has wielded any iron tool." And they offered on it burnt offerings to the Lord, and sacrificed peace offerings. And there, in the presence of the children of Israel, he wrote on stones a copy of the law of Moses which he had written. Then all of Israel, with their elders and officers and judges, stood on either side of the ark before the priests, the Levites, who bore the ark of the covenant of the Lord, the stranger as well as he who was born among them. Half of them were in front of Mt. Gerizim and half of them in front of Mt. Ebal, as Moses the servant of the Lord had commanded, that they should bless the people of Israel. And afterward he read all the words of the law, the blessings and the cursings, according to all that is written in the Book of the Law. There was not a word of all that Moses had commanded which Joshua did not read before all of the congregation of Israel, with the women, the little ones, and the strangers who were living among them (Joshua 8:30-35).

There is no indication that the Ark was ever permanently at this location. It seems that it was brought there only for the renewing of the covenant.

Ark as War Machine?

We have seen that the Ark is often viewed as some type of war object. The Book of Joshua, however, speaks against this view as Marten Woudstra notes:

The evidence for this alleged use of the ark in the book of Joshua is virtually non-existent. Barring the extensive use of the ark at the fall of Jericho, a most exceptional and miraculous occasion, the ark does not receive mention at any of the other battles in Joshua. It is doubtful whether it was carried along to Ai. One must infer from the relevant passages that the initial battle did not cause Joshua to go along with the armed band. This would be an indication that the ark also stayed in the camp. It was before the ark, which had remained in the camp, that Joshua prostrated himself.[3]

As long as Canaan remained unconquered, and the people were still an army, the Tabernacle was moved from place to place wherever the people of Israel at the time were camped. It rested finally in the place where the Lord had chosen.

Shiloh

Once the people settled into the land the Ark went to Shiloh,[4] approximately twenty miles from Jerusalem. First, an altar was built.

And that day Joshua made them woodcutters and water carriers for the congregation and for the altar of the Lord, in the place which He would choose, even to this day (Joshua 9:27).

Then the Tabernacle was set up:

Then the whole congregation of the children of Israel assembled together at Shiloh, and set up the Tabernacle of meeting there. And the land was subdued before them (Joshua 18:1)

There it stayed for nearly four hundred years. The Tabernacle at Shiloh must have been like the one constructed by Moses at Mount Sinai. However, some permanent features developed. This special sanctuary was known as the "House" or "Temple" of the Lord.

So Hannah arose after they had finished eating and drinking in Shiloh. Now Eli the priest was sitting by the doorpost of the tabernacle of the Lord (1 Samuel 1:9).

The word translated "Tabernacle" in this verse is the Hebrew word *hekal,* meaning "palace" or "temple."

The Ark was now placed in this permanent house of the Lord (1 Samuel 1:7,9). Shiloh had the only recognized altar in Israel where the people would go for the yearly feasts:

Then they said, "In fact, there is a yearly feast of the Lord in Shiloh, which is north of Bethel, on the east side of the highway that goes up from Bethel to Shechem, and south of Lebonah (Judges 21:19).

The reason why Shiloh was chosen is not stated. Part of the reason may be because of the central location that it had, as well as the fact that it belonged to the powerful tribe of Ephraim, the tribe Joshua was a part of. Shiloh was a focal point for the children of Israel during the entire period of the Judges.[5]

Days of the Judges

For a three hundred year period after the time of Joshua, the references to the Ark are rare. The *International Standard Bible Encyclopedia* notes:

Just where the ark was during the period of the judges is still a matter of some uncertainty. . . [6]

The period of the Judges was a dark time in Israel's history. The last verse of the book of Judges comments on that time.

In those days there was no king in Israel; everyone did what was right in his own eyes (Judges 21:25).

As we have noted, the Ark was not carried into every battle that the children of Israel fought. At a later period, the Ark was temporarily moved south from Shiloh to Bethel on the Benjamite border during the war with Gibeah. We have the record of the High Priest Phineas receiving counsel from God concerning the civil war with Benjamin.[7]

So the children of Israel inquired of the Lord (the ark of the covenant of God was there in those days, and Phineas the son of Eleazar, the son of Aaron, stood before it in those days), saying, "Shall I yet again go out to battle against the children of my brother Benjamin or shall I cease? And the Lord said, "Go up, for tomorrow I will deliver them into your hand" (Judges 20:27,28).

Apart from this one event, the Bible is silent about the Ark during the time of the Judges.

Conclusion

For several hundred years after the battle of Jericho, references to the Ark are few. It is assumed the Ark traveled with the Tabernacle and came to rest in Shiloh, where it stood for a period of four hundred years.

We now come to an incident where the Ark is again brought out to battle, and this time with disastrous results.

Endnotes for Chapter 9

1. Marten H. Woudstra, *The Ark of the Covenant From Conquest to Kingship*, Philadelphia, Presbyterian and Reformed, 1965, p. 56. He also observes:

> It is not clear from the narrative whether the ark remained behind in the camp, or whether taken along to the battle. In Josh. 7:6 Joshua is seen prostrating himself in front of the ark, but there is no indication whether the ark had accompanied the warriors. It seems plausible to assume that did had not. (p. 56, note 1).

2. The act of copying the law obeyed an earlier command of Moses (Deuteronomy 27:2-8). We are not told specifically what the law that was copied on stones was. It may have been the Ten Commandments and other laws. It may have been the book of Deuteronomy. The custom of inscribing law codes on stone is ancient practiced by the Sumerians and the Babylonians. The code of Hammurabi in 1700 B.C. is such an example.

3. Woudstra, ibid. p. 119

4. Jeremiah 7:12 records God's presence had been in Shiloh.

> But go now to My place which was in Shiloh, where I set My name at the first, and see what I did to it because of the wickedness of the people Israel.

5. The word often used to describe is these religious shrines is amphictyony. It comes from the Greek word meaning "those that dwell around" or neighbors. In ancient Greece, amphictyony referred to a confederation of states that were established around a religious center, such as Delphi. In the ancient world it was a common religious practice to have a focal point or shrine. These include the oracle at Delphi; the Etruscan shrine in Italy; the temple of the moon-god Sin at Haran.

6. W. Lotz, M.G. Kyle, C.E. Armerding in the *International Standard Bible Encyclopedia*, Volume 1, Revised Edition, Grand Rapids, Wm. B. Eerdmans Publishing Company, 1979, p. 292.

7. The *International Standard Bible Encyclopedia* notes

> A brief reference in Jgs. 2:1 to a movement of the "angel of the Lord" from Gilgal to Bochim (LXX adds "unto Bethel") has given rise to the idea that . . . [the ark was] in

Bethel during the entire period. This, so the argument goes is confirmed by the ark's appearance in Bethel at the close of the period of the Judges (Jgs. 20:18, 26-28), and the lack of mention of Shiloh in Jgs. 20. Such arguments are not entirely convincing when it is noted that Judges does, like Joshua, place the religious center . . . in Shiloh (18:31). . . the ark could well have been resident in Shiloh but simply moved to Bethel for convenience at the battle, although 20:27 seems to indicate a period of the general residence of the ark in that place. In view of the otherwise unbroken testimony to the ark's presence in Shiloh (excepting only the LXX of Jgs. 2:1) it seems best to explain the Bethel reference by some means as suggested above(*International Standard Bible Encyclopedia*, ibid. p. 292).

Marten Woudstra writes:

With regard to the ark's sojourn at Bethel we note the following. Although the ark was for this occasion removed from its customary place, it did not accompany the Israelites into battle. This is clear from the fact that the camp was in Mizpah, whereas the ark was at Bethel. This is another argument against the theory of the ark's habitual use as a palladium of battle (Woudstra, ibid. p. 128).

CHAPTER 10

THE ARK IS LOST TO THE PHILISTINES

Human beings are a superstitious lot. We put our trust in good luck charms such as "rabbits feet," "crosses," or "lucky numbers," thinking it will give us some advantage over others. Many people believe physical objects have some untapped power lying within them. The children of Israel were no different. They attempted to use the Ark of the Covenant as their "rabbit's foot," to gain victory in a battle. The Lord, however, would not allow them to achieve success.

The time of this battle was at the end of the days of the Judges. The High Priest at that time was a man named Eli. He had two worthless sons who were performing the priestly duties. Judgment was about to begin in the house of the Lord.

The Ark was still housed in the Tabernacle at Shiloh.

Now there was a certain man . . . and his name was Elkanah . . . This man went up from his city yearly to worship and sacrifice to the Lord of hosts in Shiloh. Also the two sons of Eli, Hophni and Phineas, the priests of the Lord, were there . . . where the Ark of God was (1 Samuel 1:1,3;3:1).

Though it was a time of spiritual darkness, one light did shine forth—a man named Samuel.

Samuel

The Bible records that a woman named Hannah prayed constantly to have a child. She told the Lord that if He would give her a child, she promised to dedicate the child to Him. That prayer was answered in the birth of Samuel.

Samuel's life was dedicated to God's service. When he was a young man he often would sleep in the Tabernacle at Shiloh where the Ark was located. The Bible records an episode where the Lord spoke to Samuel while he was sleeping in the Tabernacle:

> And it came to pass at that time, while Eli was lying down in his place, and when his eyes had begun to grow dim that he could not see, and before the lamp of God went out in the Tabernacle of the Lord where the ark of God was, and while Samuel was lying down to sleep, that the Lord called Samuel. And he answered "Here I am!" (1 Samuel 3:2-4).

Assuming that it was Eli who had called him, Samuel came to the old priest to find out what he wanted. Eli told Samuel that he had not called him. The episode was repeated again with the same results. The third time Samuel heard the voice and approached Eli, the priest realized it was the Lord speaking to Samuel. Eli then told the young man:

> 'Go, lie down; and it shall be, if He calls you, that you must say, "Speak Lord for Your servant hears"' (1 Samuel 3:9).

This account illustrates that the people did not think that God lived inside of the Ark. When Eli realized that God was speaking to Samuel, he did not tell the young man to address the Ark, he told him merely to answer the Lord. Though they were sleeping in the same building as the Ark nowhere in this account do they identify the Ark with the voice speaking to Samuel.

When the Lord called Samuel a third time, the young man responded. Samuel was then told by the Lord that a mighty event was going to occur that would shake up all of Israel.

> Then the Lord said to Samuel: "Behold, I will do something in Israel at which both ears of everyone who hears it will tingle" (1 Samuel 3:11).

The incident would be something the people would not have thought of in their worst nightmare—the loss of the Ark of the Covenant.

False Trust in the Ark

In the days of Samuel, the event in question occurred. Israel mistakenly put their trust in the Ark, rather than the Lord of Whom the Ark symbolized. They learned a lesson that the Ark itself was no guarantee of victory. The result was the physical death of the High Priest Eli and his two sons, as well as the loss of the Ark. In addition, the glory of the Lord departed from Israel. These events happened in a war with the Philistines.

The Philistines had been Israel's major enemy during the last period of the Judges. They were the "Sea people" coming originally from Crete, or some other part of the Aegean Sea.

They lived in five major towns on the southern coast of Palestine. Technologically advanced, they were pioneers in the use of iron.

Israel Attacks

In this first battle, Israel attacked the Philistines and were defeated.

> Now Israel went out to battle against the Philistines, and encamped beside Ebenezer; and the Philistines encamped in Aphek. Then the Philistines put themselves in battle array against Israel. And when they joined battle, Israel was defeated by the Philistines, who killed about four thousand men of the army in the field (1 Samuel 4:2,3).

After this loss in battle, the people decided to take the Ark with them for the next encounter.

> And when the people had come into the camp, the elders of Israel said, 'Why has the Lord defeated us today before the Philistines? Let us bring the ark of the covenant of the Lord from Shiloh to us, that when it comes among us it may save us from the hand of our enemies (1 Samuel 4:3).

Though the Ark did symbolize God's presence, it was victorious only when the people were led by Him. Ronald Youngblood comments:

The elders doubtless remembered the account of Joshua's victory over Jericho, in which the ark was a highly visible symbol of divine help and strength (Josh 6:2-20; cf. also Num. 10:35). It would accompany Israel's army on at least one other occasion in the future as well (2 Samuel 11:11). What the elders failed to understand, however, was that the ark was neither an infallible talisman nor a military palladium that would insure victory. If God willed defeat for his people, a thousand arks would not bring success. . . The elders understood clearly that if God was not "with" them, defeat was inevitable (Num. 14:42; Deut 1:42). They mistakenly assumed, however, that wherever the ark was, the Lord was.[1]

The people went to get the Ark for the next skirmish:

So the people sent to Shiloh, that they might bring from there the ark of the covenant of the Lord of hosts, who dwells between the cherubim. And the two sons of Eli, Hophni and Phineas were there with the ark of the covenant of God (1 Samuel 4:4).

Arrival of Ark

When the Ark arrived at the camp there was much fanfare.

And when the ark of the covenant of the Lord came into the camp, all Israel shouted so loudly that the earth shook (1 Samuel 4:5).

The noise that was made attracted the attention of the Philistines.

So when the Philistines heard the noise of the shout, they said, 'What does the sound of this great shout in the camp of the Hebrews mean?' Then they understood that the ark of the Lord had come into the camp (1 Samuel 4:6).

Once the Philistines realized the source of all the commotion they became afraid:

So the Philistines were afraid, for they said, 'God has come into the camp!' And they said, 'Woe to us! For such a thing has never happened before. Woe to us! Who will deliver us from the hand of these mighty gods? These are the gods who struck the Egyptians with all the plagues in the wilderness. Be strong and conduct yourselves like men, you Philistines, that you do not become servants of the Hebrews, as they have been to you. Conduct yourselves like men and fight! (1 Samuel 4:9).

The Philistines also had the pagan idea of equating God with the Ark. They too assumed that the Ark was going to guarantee victory for Israel for they were well aware of what happened 300 years earlier when God had brought His people out of Egypt.

Yet on this day, the Ark would not save the children of Israel. The battle was won by the Philistines and the Ark captured.

So the Philistines fought, and Israel was defeated, and every man fled to his tent. There was a very great slaughter, and there fell of Israel thirty thousand foot soldiers. Also the ark of God was captured; and the two sons of Eli, Hophni and Phineas died (1 Samuel 4:10,11).

This episode would put to rest any idea that God was confined to the Ark. J. Barton Payne writes:

The pagan theory of having God "in a box," as if the presence would automatically guarantee salvation (1 Sam 4:3,7), was dispelled once and for all when the Philistines captured the Ark at the . . . battle of Ebenezer.[2]

The Ark is Lost

A messenger was sent back to the camp to deliver the bad news about the battle and the Ark:

Then a man of Benjamin ran from the battle line the same day, and came to Shiloh with his clothes torn and dirt on his head. Now when he came, there was Eli, sitting on a seat by the wayside watching, for his heart trembled for the ark of God. And when the man came into the city and told it, all the city cried out (1 Samuel 4:12,13).

The message reached the High Priest Eli that the Ark had been lost:

When Eli heard the noise of the outcry, he said, 'What does the sound of the tumult mean?' And the man came hastily and told Eli. . . 'Israel had fled before the Philistines, and there has been a great slaughter among the people. Also your two sons, Hophni and Phineas, are dead; and the ark of God has been captured.' Then it happened, when he made mention of the Ark of God, that Eli fell off the seat backward by the side of the gate; and his neck was broken and he died (1 Samuel 4:14,17,18).

More than the loss of the battle or the death of his sons, when Eli heard the news of the Ark's capture, he fell back and died.

Glory Departed

The combination of bad news, the Ark's capture, and the death of the High Priest Eli and his sons, sent the pregnant wife of Phineas into labor.

Now his daughter-in-law, Phineas' wife, was with child, due to be delivered; and when she heard the news that the ark of God was captured, and that her father-in-law and her husband were dead, she bowed herself and gave birth, for her labor pains came upon her. And about the time of her death the women who stood by her said to her, 'Do not fear for you have borne a son.' But she did not answer, nor did she regard it (1 Samuel 4:19,20).

The child was then given a befitting name:

Then she named the child Ichabod, saying, 'The glory has departed from Israel!' because the ark of God had been captured and because of her father-in-law and her husband (1 Samuel 4:21).

When the Ark of the Covenant was taken, the Tabernacle lost its glory, never again to receive it.[3] The children of Israel were left without the Ark, without priests, and without a successor to the priesthood. Their foolish gesture in taking the Ark to battle cost them a terrible price.

The Philistines now had the Ark. Yet, they too would discover that the mere possession of this sacred object was no formula for success. They were about to personally experience the power of the Lord, the God of Israel.

Endnotes for Chapter 10

1. Ronald Youngblood, *The Expositors Bible Commentary*, Volume 3, Frank C. Gaebelein General Editor, Zondervan, Grand Rapids, 1992, p. 595.

2. J. Barton Payne, in The *Zondervan Pictorial Encyclopedia of the Bible*, Volume 1, Merill Tenney General Editor, 1975, p. 309.

Marten Woudstra notes

> There is no indication of the exact reason which, in the opinion of the elders, may have brought on defeat. What should be noted, however, is that the defeat is attributed to Yahweh, even though the emblem of his presence had not yet been carried into the field. This fact may certainly be cited as proof that the narrative knows nothing of a mere identification of Yahweh with the cultic emblem. Quite apart from the presence or absence of the ark, the elders are led to think of Yahweh as the ultimate cause of the discomfiture (Marten H. Woudstra, *The Ark of the Covenant From Conquest to Kingship*, Philadelphia, Presbyterian and Reformed, 1965, p. 42).

3. When this sanctuary was destroyed as a result of the first battle of Ebenezer the sacrifices ceased at Shiloh. The prophet Samuel treated Shiloh as an abandoned shrine and sacrificed instead at Mizpeh(1 Samuel 7:9) at Ramah (1 Samuel 9:12;10:3) and at Gilgal (1 Samuel 10:8;11:15).
    This gives the impression that the Tabernacle again became a movable sanctuary. The psalmist wrote:

> So that He forsook the Tabernacle of Shiloh, the tent which He had placed among men (Pslam 78:60).

CHAPTER 11

THE ARK BECOMES A PROBLEM FOR THE PHILISTINES

Victory at last! The Lord, the God of Israel, had been defeated by the Philistines and their god Dagon. Possession of the holy Ark symbolized their superiority over Israel and its God. At least, this is what the Philistines thought. They would soon learn otherwise.

The Philistines did not destroy the Ark because they understood its importance. To them, it was an objective symbol of their victory over Israel and its God, and was to be displayed for their people to see. The Ark, however, remained in the Philistine country for only a short time:

Now the ark of the Lord was in the country of the Philistines seven months (1 Samuel 6:1).

The stay was not a happy one for the people of Philistia. They found that Israel's holy object was not going to be a prized possession for them.

Ashdod and Dagon

When the Philistines conquered the earlier inhabitants of the land of Canaan, they also acquired several of their deities. One such god was a corn deity named Dagon.[1]

Dagon was ranked very high among the gods as the father of Baal. As a god of the Philistines, Dagon was a rival to the Lord.

Dagon, however, proved not very powerful against the God of Israel. At Gaza, Samson pulled the temple of Dagon to the ground, killing himself and 3,000 Philistines (Judges 16:23-30).

With this dismal history against Israel, the Philistines rejoiced in capturing the Ark. The Ark then was placed before Dagon in his temple.

> Then the Philistines took the Ark of God and brought it from Ebenezer to Ashdod. When the Philistines took the ark of God, they brought it into the temple of Dagon and set it by Dagon (1 Samuel 5:1,2).

The Philistines treated the Ark like it was a trophy of *their* great victory. They brought it to Ashdod, some fifty miles southwest of Shiloh laying it at the feet of Dagon. This act indicated that the God of Israel was subject to Dagon. Though this was a house of worship to the Philistines, it was an abomination to the Lord.

The Philistines did not realize that it was not Dagon who defeated Israel or captured the Ark, this was the Lord's doing. Though the presence of the Lord was not confined to the Ark, He did not abandon it when it was in the hands of the Philistines.

> And when the people of Ashdod arose early in the morning, there was Dagon fallen on its face before the ark of the Lord. So they took Dagon and set it in its place again (1 Samuel 5:3).

Dagon had fallen on its face before the Lord. The Philistines assumed some accident had occurred and placed their god back on its pedestal.

> And when they arose early the next morning, there was Dagon, fallen on its face to the ground before the Ark of the Lord. The head of Dagon and both the palms of its hands were broken off on the threshold; only the torso of Dagon was left of it (1 Samuel 5:4).

Now Dagon was prostrate before the Ark with its head and hands broken. Only the torso was left. The Philistines realized that this was more than an accident. Without a head Dagon could not think for them, see them, or hear their prayers. Having no hands it could not work for them.

Severed heads and hands were considered battlefield trophies in the ancient world. Naturally, the Philistines were very upset by these circumstances.

> Therefore neither the priests of Dagon nor any who come into Dagon's temple tread on the threshold of Dagon in Ashdod to this day (1 Samuel 5:5).

The Philistines would not enter their temple because of fear. They realized their god had no power over the Ark of the Lord.

Problems Suffered

The destruction of Dagon was not the only problem the Philistines suffered because of the Ark:

> But the hand of the Lord was heavy on the people of Ashdod, and He ravaged them and struck them with tumors, both Ashdod and its territory. And when the men of Ashdod saw how it was, they said, 'The ark of the God of Israel must not remain with us, for His hand is harsh toward us and Dagon our God' (1 Samuel 5:6,7).

The nature of this plague is uncertain. It seems to have consisted of growths, particularly in the rectal area. It could have been a hemorrhoid-like condition. The mention of mice have caused some commentators to speculate it was the bubonic plague, an epidemic which is spread by rodents. One of the characteristics of this disease is swollen lymph glands in the groin area.

The Philistines were now at a loss to know what to do with the Ark.

> Therefore they sent and gathered to themselves all the lords of the Philistines, and said, 'What shall we do with the ark of the God of Israel?' And they answered, 'Let the ark of the God of Israel be carried away to Gath.' So they carried the ark of Israel away (1 Samuel 5:8).

Gath

When the Philistines sent the Ark to Gath, twelve miles to the southeast, a similar disaster happened.

> And so it was, after they had carried it away, that the hand of the Lord was against the city with a very great

destruction; and He struck the men of the city, both small and great, and tumors broke out on them (1 Samuel 5:9).

The Ark then moved to Ekron with its reputation preceding it.

Therefore they sent the ark of God to Ekron. So it was, as the ark of God came to Ekron, that the Ekronites cried out saying, 'They have brought the ark of God of Israel to us, to kill us and our people!' (1 Samuel 5:10).

The people of Ekron wanted nothing to do with the Ark.

So they sent and gathered together all the lords of the Philistines and said, 'Send away the ark of the God of Israel, and let it go back to its own place, so that it does not kill us and our people.' For there was a deadly destruction throughout all the city; the hand of God was very heavy there. And the men who did not die were stricken with tumors, and the cry of the city went up to heaven (1 Samuel 5:11,12).

The plague from the Ark caused a deadly destruction. The Philistines victory trophy had caused them nothing but trouble. They decided the Ark must go back to Israel.

Having no God-ordained priesthood to return the Ark, the Philistines placed it upon a cart.

A Fleece

Knowing that they had received divine judgment, the Philistines decided to send the Ark back to Israel with symbolic gifts. The gifts were a representation of what they sought deliverance from. Therefore, they fashioned five golden mice (or rats) and five golden images of their tumors. The rodents were probably chosen because they were destroying their fields. The Philistines also sent a chest containing articles of gold.

The Philistines put "the Ark" to a final test. Two milk cows, which were mothers with young, were chosen to transport the Ark back to Israel. If the cows turned their back on their young, then the people would know that it was the Lord who afflicted them. If the animals did the natural thing and returned to their young, then it would signify that the Lord was not involved in their suffering. The Bible records that the cows went straight toward Israel without turning to the left or right. There was no doubt that the Lord had judged the idolatrous Philistines.

Ronald Youngblood aptly summarizes the lessons these chapters teach us:

> The lesson of chapters 4 and 5 is clear: Neither Israelites nor Philistines—not even Dagon himself—can control or resist the will of the sovereign Lord, who Presence, though enthroned between the cherubim surmounting the ark of the covenant, is not limited by that location and therefore cannot be manipulated by the whim of whoever happens to be in possession of it at any particular time.[2]

The Ark of the Covenant had been nothing short of a catastrophe in a land where it did not belong.[3] The Philistines learned, to their great pain, that the Lord, the God of Israel, was superior over all the so-called gods of the nations. After sending the Ark from city to city they wanted nothing more to do with it. It was time for the Ark to come back home.

Endnotes for Chapter 11

1. The older etymology of דָּגוֹן (dagon) from דָּג (dag, "fish")—assuming that Dagon was a fish-god or that he was the god of a maritime people—has now been almost universally abandoned in favor of a derivation from דָּגָן (dagan "grain"). Ugaritic epic literature claims that Dagon was the father of Baal, the storm-god of fertility, a paternity compatible with his role as a grain god. From early times he was worshiped by the Semitic peoples of the Levant. Numerous towns are named after him including Beth Dagon in Judah (Josh 15:41) and Beth Dagon in Asher (Josh 19:27), neither of which has been located (Ronald Youngblood, *The Expositors Bible Commentary*, Volume 3, General Editor Frank Gaebelein, Grand Rapids, Zondervan, pp. 601,602 note 2).

2. Youngblood, ibid, p. 601.

3. Marten H. Woudstra comments about the different qualities of the Ark.

In the book of Joshua, so the argument goes, the ark was a rather solemn object, carried about in great silence. Buy in its heyday the ark seems to have been of a different kind. It was the representation of the warrior god. It was mortally dangerous, Not only that, it also had certain unpredictable features and behaved rather impishly. . .

In response it should be noted that some of these supposed differences may be due to a difference in the circumstances under which the ark functioned. . . The story of the ark's sojourn among the Philistines . . . does indeed possess certain humorous features. But is this out of keeping with the true nature of the ark? Is not the ark the emblem of Him who sitteth in the heavens and who shall laugh at his adversaries (Marten H. Woudstra, *The Ark of the Covenant From Conquest to Kingship*, Philadelphia, Presbyterian and Reformed, 1965, p. 117).

CHAPTER 12

BACK COMES THE
ARK TO ISRAEL

Homeward bound. It was time for the Ark of the Covenant to come back to the land and the people to which it belonged. After a short stint with the Philistines, with disastrous results, the holy object was sent back to Israel to the city of Beth Shemesh, about fifteen miles west of Jerusalem.

It arrived during the time of the wheat harvest (June). The excited people decided to chop up the wood of the cart that carried the Ark and sacrifice the cows as a burnt offering to the Lord. A large rock in the field of a man named Joshua of Beth Shemesh became the temporary resting place of the Ark.

Then the cart came into the field of Joshua of Beth Shemesh, and stood there; a large stone was there. So they split the wood of the cart and offered the cows as a burnt offering to the Lord. The Levites took down the ark of the Lord and that chest that was with it, in which were the articles of gold, and put them on the large stone. Then the men of Beth Shemesh offered burnt offerings and made sacrifices the same day to the Lord (1 Samuel 6:14,15)

The celebration over the Ark's return soon turned to tragedy. Many people were killed at Beth Shemesh for trifling with the Ark.[1]

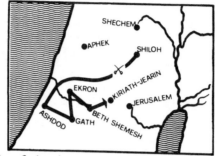

The travels of the Ark of the Covenant after its capture
by the Philistines

Return of the Ark to Beth Shemesh

Then He struck the men of Beth Shemesh, because they had looked into the ark of the Lord. He struck fifty thousand and seventy men of the people (1 Samuel 6:19).

The people were killed for desecrating the Ark. By opening it up and looking inside, they broke the commandment of God. Only the priests were allowed to handle the Ark and even they were not allowed to open it and gaze at its contents. As we have seen, God gave strict orders on the disposition of the Ark.

When the camp prepares to journey, Aaron and his sons shall come, and they shall take down the covering veil and cover the ark of the Testimony with it . . . And when Aaron and his sons have finished covering the sanctuary and all the furnishings of the sanctuary, when the camp is set to go, then the sons of Kohath shall come to carry them; but they shall not touch any holy thing, lest they die (Numbers 4:5,15).

The people were not even allowed to watch the holy items being covered:

But they shall not go in to watch while the holy things are being covered, lest they die (Numbers 4:20).

We are not told the reason why the people of Beth Shemesh looked into the Ark. Whether it was mere curiosity or a desire for its safety we do not know. Israel had morally declined during this period and this episode with the Ark is a further example of their lack of spirituality. The Ark of the Covenant was holy, it was not to be trifled with.[2]

Moreover, the Ark had been returned to Israel without any effort of the people to retrieve it. God's presence with the Ark had again been demonstrated. He compelled the cows that were hitched to its new wagon to abandon their own calves in order to drag it to Beth Shemesh. He then put to death those who looked into it. For those who may think God was unfair for this harsh judgment, Marten Woudstra puts the matter into perspective:

In our evaluation of this story the fact should not be overlooked that the ark in this particular context has just manifested its extreme power and holiness in the country of the Philistines. The latter had been confronted with the majesty of the God whose ark this was. Although grudgingly, they had learned to treat the ark with

circumspection and awe, witness also the gifts that were
sent along with its return. In vivid contrast to this show
of reverential fear on the part of the Philistines stand the
conduct of the Beth-shemites. Whether these were fully
aware of what had transpired in the Philistine cities of
the plain, we cannot tell. Beth-shemesh was situated in
the proximity of Philistia. Some reliable information of
the terrifying events that took place there may have been
transmitted onto them.[3]

We should keep these things in mind when we consider
the sudden death of the people of Beth Shemesh. They
were without excuse.

The Ark of the Covenant would now remain in Israel
until the time of its disappearance.

Kirjath Jearim

After the death of the men of Beth Shemesh, the Ark
of the Covenant was moved to the house of Aminadab in
the city of Kirjath Jearim.[4] Kirjath Jearim lay some nine
miles northeast of Beth Shemesh, in the direction of
Shiloh. The fact that Shiloh was in ruins explains why the
Ark did not return there. At Kirjath Jearim, Aminadab's
son cared for the Ark while it remained at the house:

Then the men of Kirjath Jearim came and took the ark
of the Lord and brought it into the house of Aminadab on
the hill, and consecrated Eleazar his son to keep the ark
of the Lord. So it was the ark remained in Kirjath Jearim
a long time; it was there twenty years. And all the house of
Israel lamented after the Lord (1 Samuel 7:2).

There was no attempt to restore the Tabernacle during
this period.[5]

Confirming Evidence Found?

This Biblical account of the Ark's capture by the
Philistines and return to Israel may have some present-
day confirmation. There is the possibility that the oldest
reference to the Ark of the Covenant, outside of the Old
Testament, has just recently been discovered. Ronald
Youngblood relates how an ostracon (pottery or bone
fragment) was deciphered.

In the late 1970's an ostracon containing a five-line
inscription was recovered from an Early Iron Age grain

silo in the ruins of Izbeth Sarteh. The fifth line was soon identified as an alphabet, but the first four lines remained undeciphered until recently. According to William H. Shea, they read as follows: "Unto the field we came, (unto) Aphek from Shiloh. The Kittim took (it [the ark of the covenant] and) came to Azor, (to) Dagon lord of Ashdod, (and to) Gath. (It returned to) Kirath Jearim. The companion of the foot soldiers, Hophni, came to tell the elders, "A horse has come (and) upon (it was my) brother for us to bury.' " (The 'Izbeth Sartah Ostracon," Andrews University Seminary Studies 28, 1 [1990]: 62). Shea (p. 81) observes that eleven of the key words of the inscription appear in the parallel account in the capture of the ark in chapters 4-6: "Aphek" 4:1), "field" (4:2), "elders" (4:3), "Shiloh" (4:3-4), "Hophni" (4:4, 11,17), "foot soldiers" (4:10), "take/capture (4:11ff.), "tell" (4:13), "Ashdod" (5:1-7), "Gath" (5:8), "Kiriath Jearim (written Jearin Kiriah"; (6:21). If Shea's reading holds up under further analysis, the Izbeth Sarteh ostracon contains the earliest known extrabiblical reference to an OT event (the capture of the ark by the Philistines) and an OT person (Hophni) (cf. William H. Shea, Ancient Ostracon Records Ark's Wanderings," *Ministry* [1991]: 14).[6]

If this discovery holds it would indeed be exciting. The oldest confirmation of an Old Testament account would be that of the Ark's capture and return.

Neglected by Saul

After Samuel, came the reign of Saul, the first King of Israel. It seems that during his rule the Ark was generally neglected.

And let us bring the ark of our God back to us, for we have not inquired at it since the days of Saul (1 Chronicles 13:3).

Saul seems to have brought the Ark with him prior to one of his campaigns, the battle of Michmash:[7]

And Saul said . . . "Bring the ark of God here" (1 Samuel 14:18).

This is the only reference we have to the Ark during Saul's reign. From the time the Ark was taken by the Philistines, through the time of Saul, no lasting place was found for the holy object.[8]

The Ark was now about to make a journey to a permanent resting place, the city of Jerusalem. Unfortunately, another tragic episode was about to occur.

Endnotes for Chapter 12

1. The number of men who died at Beth Shemesh is listed as 50,070. Yet this figure does not seem to be possible. Ronald Youngblood writes:

> The . . . reading 50,070 is attested in all the major ancient versions and is therefore textually secure. The number is far too large, however, to have constituted only "some" of the men at Beth Shemesh; at the same time the death of "seventy would hardly be a heavy blow," especially in light of 4:10 (where "thirty thousand" men died in a "slaughter" that was very great . . . A suggested solution is to change . .. "He struck down among the people seventy men [and] fifty thousand men" to read . . . He struck down the people for seven days, men for five days, a thousand men . . . The number slain at Beth Shemesh becomes a "thousand" rather than "seventy" of "50,070" (Ronald Youngblood, *The Expositors Bible Commentary*, Volume 3, General Editor Frank Gaebelein, Grand Rapids, Zondervan, p. 606, note 19).

2. The Jerusalem Bible as well as the New English Bible imply that the men were killed because they had not rejoiced when the saw the Ark:

> But the sons of Jeconiah did not rejoice with the rest of the men of Beth-Shemesh when they welcomed the Ark of the Lord, and he struck down seventy of them. The people mourned because the Lord struck them so heavy a blow (1 Samuel 6:19, New English Bible).

This translation, however, is not to be preferred.

3. Marten H. Woudstra, *The Ark of the Covenant From Conquest to Kingship*, Philadelphia, Presbyterian and Reformed, 1965, p. 51.

4. Kirjath Jearim was built over a large hill. Jerusalem, eight miles away, can be seen in the distance. Today, the church of the Ark of the Covenant stands over the traditional site of the house of Aminadab.

5. At some point after this event, the Tabernacle was moved to Gibeon where it is mentioned in connection with Zadok's high priestly ministry.

> And Zadok the priest and his brethren the priests, before the tabernacle of the Lord at the high place that was at Gibeon, to offer burnt offerings to the Lord on the

altar of burnt offering regularly morning and evening, and to do according to all that is written in the Law of the Lord which He commanded Israel (1 Chronicles 16:39,40).

6. Ronald Youngblood, ibid. p. 596,597.

7. The Septuagint reads "ephod" in place of "Ark" in 1 Samuel 14:18.

8. *Smith's Dictionary of the Bible* notes:

It sojourned among several probably Levitical families (1 Samuel vii. 1; 2 Sam vi. 3,11; 1 Chr. xiii. 13, xv. 24,25) in the border villages of Eastern Judah (*Dr. William Smith's Dictionary of the Bible*, Revised and edited by Ezra Abbot, Vol 1, 1872, p. 156).

CHAPTER 13

THE ULTIMATE
DESTINATION:
JERUSALEM

The first King of Israel, Saul, neglected the Ark of the Covenant while he ruled. The next King of Israel, however, was a man after God's own heart. Arguably, he would become Israel's most famous King, his name was David.

After a seven-year reign over his own tribe of Judah, David became king over a united Israel. Soon after this event he captured the city of Jerusalem from the Jebusites. David then proceeded to make Jerusalem his political capital (2 Samuel 5:6-10).

Shortly thereafter, he brought within its walls the Ark of the Covenant, thereby making Jerusalem the religious center of his realm as well. Until David's time, Jerusalem did not belong to any of the tribes of Israel.

Brought to Jerusalem

David brought the Ark to Jerusalem around 1000 B.C. A tragic instance involving a man named Uzzah occurred along the way.

And when they came to Nachon's threshingfloor, Uzzah put his hand on the ark of God and took hold of it, for the oxen stumbled. Then the anger of the Lord was aroused against Uzzah, and God struck him there for his error: and he died there by the ark of God (2 Samuel 6:6,7).

This event further illustrated that the Ark was sacred, not to be treated lightly. The Bible is very clear concerning the manner in which the Ark was to be transported.

No one may carry the ark of God but the Levites, for the Lord has chosen them to carry the ark of God and to minister before Him forever (1 Chronicles 15:2).

The fault was David's. He had attempted to transport the Ark in the same manner as the Philistines had, and not according to the manner that God had prescribed. The Philistines were seemingly excused for their ignorance on transporting the Ark, the same did not hold true for those who knew better.

God had clearly instructed that poles should be placed in the rings attached to the Ark and that they were never to be removed. This would allow it to be carried by the priests on their shoulders. The Philistines had to put the Ark on a new cart because this was their only means of transporting it. Had the children of Israel carried the Ark in the way in which God had prescribed, then it never would have tottered.

In addition, Uzzah was a descendant of Aminadab, who previously had had custody of the Ark. He obviously knew better than to touch it. Though well-intentioned, it cost him his life.

The Uzzah incident interrupted the happy procession into Jerusalem. His impulsive gesture to save the Ark was a direct violation of the law. He did not die because of some pagan taboo connected with the Ark, as some commentators have claimed. J. Barton Payne writes:

Those who seek to explain Scripture on the basis of comparative religion have attributed much of the . . . material found in the Old Testament to the primitive concept of taboo. It is asserted that "holy" objects were once thought to contain "other, separate" spirits in themselves and were therefore to be left alone. Such superstition is unworthy of Scripture. It is true that certain holy objects were required to be kept separate and that contact with them could mean death, as when Uzzah touched the ark. But Uzzah died because God struck him, not because of an intrinsic taboo.[1]

Obed Edom

The Ark, stopped short of Jerusalem, resting at the house of a Levite named Obed-Edom for three months. Obed-Edom and his house received blessing while the Ark remained there.

> The ark of the Lord remained in the house of Obed-Edom the Gittite three months. And the Lord blessed Obed-Edom and all his household (2 Samuel 6:11,12).

King David then brought the Ark to Jerusalem in the way in which God had prescribed, on the shoulders of the priests. It was then placed in a "tent" or "booth" that had been built on Mt. Zion.[2]

> So they brought the ark of God, and set it in the midst of the tabernacle that David had erected for it. Then they offered burnt offerings and peace offerings before God (1 Chronicles 16:1).

This was the first time in history that the Ark of the Covenant had come to Jerusalem.

Ark Brought Out

Once the Ark had been brought to Jerusalem, the Bible states that it was removed on only one occasion. This was during the rebellion of Absalom, David's son. Without David's consent, the Ark had been taken out of Jerusalem by his well-meaning supporters.

> There was Zadok also, and all the Levites with him, bearing the ark of the covenant of God. And they set down the ark of God, and Abiathar went up until all the people had finished crossing over from the city. Then the King said to Zadok, "Carry the ark of God back into the city. If I find favor in the eyes of the Lord, He will bring me back and show me both it and his habitation. But if he says thus, 'I have no delight in you,' here I am, let Him do to me as seems good to Him.' . . . Therefore Zadok and Abiathar carried the ark of God back to Jerusalem and they remained there (2 Samuel 15:24-29).

David refused to treat the Ark as a "good luck charm" or a "war machine." He would not bring it with him to battle. His trust would be in God alone.

A House for the Lord

Throughout its entire existence, the Ark dwelt in a portable sanctuary. King David recognized the need of a permanent house for the Ark.

> Now it came to pass when the king was dwelling in his house, and the Lord had given him rest from all his enemies all around, that the king said to Nathan the prophet, 'See now, I dwell in a house of cedar, but the ark dwells inside tent curtains (2 Samuel 7:1,2).

God honored David for his desire to build a more lasting structure to house the Ark. But David was told by the Lord that he could not build it because he was a man of war. David then gathered the materials and made the preparations, but the actual building would have to be left to another.[3]

He told the people what was in his heart.

> Then King David rose to his feet and said, "Hear me, my brethren and my people: I had it in my heart to build a house of rest for the ark of the Lord, and for the footstool of our God and had made preparations to build it. But God said to me, 'You shall not build a house for My name, because you have been a man of war and have shed blood (1 Chronicles 28:2,3).

The building of a permanent house for the Ark was never carried out during David's lifetime. This honor would fall to his son Solomon.[4] To house the Ark, he constructed one of the most magnificent structures in the ancient world—the Temple of Jerusalem.

Author at Capernaum where fourth century synagogue ark is depicted.

Close-up of synagogue ark in Capernaum.

Synagogue at Beth Alpha where Ark is depicted
in floor mosaic.

Author at the site of Jericho, one of the places a
miracle occurred with the Ark of the Covenant.

Ancient tower at Jericho, one of the oldest cities in the world.

Top area of the Temple Mount looking toward the Mount of Olives. Some feel the Ark is buried somewhere underneath these stones.

El Kas fountain on the Temple Mount. Possible site of the Holy of Holies, and location of the Ark.

Dome of the Rock Shrine, another viable site of
the Holy of Holies and the Ark.

Dome of the Tablets where it is also proposed the
Holy of Holies stood. Ark may be buried
somewhere near this spot.

In the background, the caves of Qumran where
the Dead Sea Scrolls were found and Ark hunting
is taking place.

In the background is Gordon's Calvary, one
possible site of Christ's crucifixion as well as a
potential resting place for the Ark.

The caves of Ein Gedi where Ark exploration has taken place.

Author with Lambert Dolphin at First Annual
Temple Conference in Jerusalem.

Author speaking to First Annual Temple
Conference about the Ark of the Covenant.

Chief archaeologist of Jerusalem, Dan Bahat
addressing the Temple Conference. He does not
believe any of the Temple vessels are still buried
underneath the Temple Mount.

Rabbi Chaim Richman of the Temple Institute tells the audience of the Ark's discovery underneath the Temple Mount.

Depiction of the Arch ot Titus in the Temple Institute in Jerusalem.

Newly constructed model of Second Temple,
displayed in the Rabbinical Tunnel underneath
the Western Wall.

Model of the Third Temple, housed in the Old City
of Jerusalem.

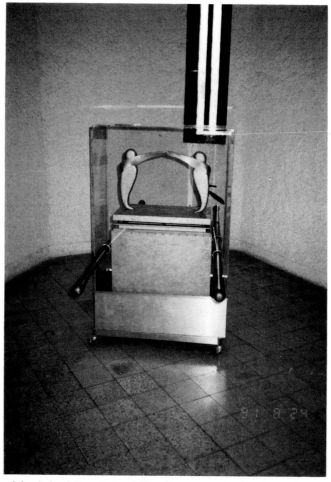

Model of the Ark of the Covenant, displayed in the Old City of Jerusalem.

Replica of the sacred Menorah, hoped to be
reconstructed for the Third Temple.

ארון הברית עולי

نقل تابوت الرب الى اورشليم

The Ark of the Lord to Jerusalem

"So David and all the house of Israel brought up the ark of the Lord with shouting, and with the sound of the trumpet"

Depiction of the Ark of the Lord being brought to Jerusalem by King David. Displayed in newly renovated David's Tower in Jerusalem.

Endnotes for Chapter 13

1.   J. Barton Payne, *The Theology of the Older Testament*, Grand Rapids, Zondervan, 1962, p. 123.

J. Barton Payne also notes:

Certain great Psalms seem to have been composed for the occasion and for its subsequent celebration (Pss. 24:7-10; 132:8). No hint, however, exists of any annual Babylonian style "enthronement festival" for Yahweh: sentiments such as God has gone up with a shout (Ps 47:5) express rather His reign over all the earth. J. Barton Payne, *The Zondervan Pictorial Encyclopedia of the Bible*, Volume 1, Merill Tenney General Editor, 1975, p. 310.

2.   Once the Ark was brought to Jerusalem the Tabernacle began to lose its significance. It retained only the old altar of burnt offerings.

For the tabernacle of the Lord and the altar of the burnt offering, which Moses had made in the wilderness, were at that time at the high place in Gibeon (1 Chronicles 21:29).

For a while the double service went on as Zadok the High Priest officiated at Gibeon.

And Zadok the priest and his brethren the priests, before the tabernacle of the Lord at the high place that was at Gibeon (1 Chronicles 16:39).

The divided worship continued all the days of David. When Solomon ascended to the throne he recognized the sanctity of both places:

The Solomon awoke; and it indeed had been a dream. And he came to Jerusalem and stood before the ark of the covenant of the Lord, offered up burnt offerings, offered peace offerings, and made a feast for all his servants. (1 Kings 3:15).

Yet Solomon went down to Gibeon to worship at the Tabernacle.

Then Solomon, and all the congregation with him went to the high place that was at Gibeon; for the tabernacle of meeting with God was there, which Moses the servant of the Lord had made in the wilderness. But David had brought up the ark of God from Kirjath Jearim to the place David had prepared for it, for he had pitched a tent in Jerusalem (2 Chronicles 1:3,4).

Because the Tabernacle may have caused a division among the people Solomon moved it all with all its holy vessels to Jerusalem.

And they brought up the ark of the Lord, the tabernacle of meeting, and all the holy furnishings that were in the tabernacle. The priests and the Levites brought them up (1 Kings 8:4).

3.   King David left behind a great legacy in the history of Israel as Jewish author Max Dimont notes.

Though David was a warrior king, his claim to fame among Jews rests on three achievements totally unconnected with war. He made Jerusalem a symbol, an ideal, and a holy place: first, by making Jerusalem the political capital of Palestine; second, by earmarking the Temple for that city; and third, by enshrining the Ark in Jerusalem (Max Dimont, *Jews, God, and History*, New York, Signet Books, 1962, p. 49).

4.   Solomon, like his father, realized the holiness of the Ark. He moved his pagan wife, daughter of Pharaoh, away from the area of the Ark.

Now Solomon brought the daughter of Pharoah up from the City of David to the house he had built for her, for he said, 'My wife shall not dwell in the house of David, king of Israel, because the places to which the ark of the Lord has come are holy' (2 Chronicles 8:11).

On one occasion, Solomon worshiped God in front of the Ark in its temporary shelter after he had been granted wisdom by God.

Then Solomon awoke; and indeed it had been a dream. And he came to Jerusalem and stood before the ark of the covenant of the Lord, offered up burnt offerings, and made a feast for all his servants (1 Kings 3:15).

CHAPTER 14

SOLOMONS TEMPLE: A PERMANENT HOME FOR THE ARK

One of the greatest building projects in ancient history was the golden Temple at Jerusalem. Once built, its fame spread to the ends of the earth. This building stood as a testimony to the true and living God.

The Bible records that Solomon built the Temple on Mt. Moriah.

Now Solomon began to build the house of the Lord at Jerusalem on Mount Moriah, where the Lord had appeared to his father David, at the place that David had prepared on the threshing floor of Ornan the Jebusite (2 Chronicles 3:1).

The dedication of the Temple was part of a great celebration attended by elders, tribal heads, leaders of clans, and all the assembly of Israel.

Now Solomon assembled the elders of Israel and all the heads of the tribes, the chief fathers and the children of Israel, in Jerusalem, that they may bring the ark of the covenant of the Lord up from the City of David, which is Zion (2 Chronicles 5:2).

The focal point of the dedication of the Temple was the placing of the Ark of the Covenant in its permanent home.

The Ark had remained in a tent David had built upon Mt.
Zion, located in the southeast portion of Jerusalem just
south of the Temple.

> David built houses for himself in the City of David; and
> he prepared a place for the ark of God, and pitched a tent
> for it (1 Chronicles 15:1).

The moment had arrived for the Ark to come to its
ultimate resting place in the Temple.

> Therefore all the men of Israel assembled together with
> the king at the feast, which was in the seventh month. So
> all the elders of Israel came, and the Levites took the ark.
> Then they brought up the ark, the tabernacle of meeting,
> and all the holy furnishings that were in the tabernacle.
> The priests and the Levites brought them up (2
> Chronicles 5:4,5).

King Solomon followed in the footsteps of his father
David by sacrificing a large number of animals in honor of
the Ark.

> Also King Solomon, and all the congregation of Israel
> who were assembled with him before the ark, were
> sacrificing sheep and oxen that could not be counted or
> numbered for multitude (2 Chronicles 5:6).

The time chosen for this event was the Feast of
Tabernacles (September-October). The year was
approximately 959 B.C.

> Then the priests brought in the ark of the covenant of
> the Lord to its place, into the inner sanctuary of the
> temple, to the Most Holy Place, under the wings of the
> cherubim. For the cherubim spread their wings over the
> place of the ark and the cherubim overshadowed the ark
> and its poles (2 Chronicles 5:7-9).

After forty years of traveling in the wilderness, and
hundreds of years in the Promised Land, the Ark finally
came to rest at the Temple in Jerusalem.[1]

A Cloud Appears

During the dedication ceremony, a cloud filled the
Temple.

Indeed it came to pass, when the trumpeters and singers were as one, to make one sound to be heard in praising and thanking the Lord, and when they lifted up their voice with the trumpets and cymbals of instruments of music, and praised God saying: 'For He is good, for His mercy endures forever,' That the house, the house of the Lord, was filled with a cloud, so that the priests could not continue ministering because of the cloud; for the glory of the Lord filled the house of God (2 Chronicles 5:13,14).

God had made His presence known to Moses in a similar way in the Tabernacle. His glory now filled the Temple.

Solomon's Prayer

It is important to note that Solomon realized that God was not confined either to the Temple or the Ark. During his prayer of dedication he said:

But will God indeed dwell with men on the earth? Behold, heaven and the heaven of heavens cannot contain You; how much less this temple which I have built! (2 Chronicles 6:18).

Solomon also repeated the wilderness prayer of Moses:

Now therefore, Arise O Lord God to Your resting place, You and the ark of Your strength. Let Your priests, O Lord God, be clothed with your salvation, and let your saints rejoice in goodness (2 Chronicles 6:41).

The Ark now rested in the Temple with only the poles visible:

And the poles extended so that the end of the poles of the ark could be seen from the holy place, in front of the inner sanctuary; but they could not be seen from the outside. And they are there to this day (2 Chronicles 5:9).

Only Tablets Remain

It seems that the contents of the Ark had changed. By the time of Samuel (1 Samuel 6:19), or at least by the time of Solomon, only the two tablets containing the Ten Commandments were in the Ark. Aaron's rod and the golden pot of manna were no longer there.

There was nothing in the Ark except for two tablets of stone which Moses put there at Horeb, when the Lord made a covenant with the children of Israel (1 Kings 8:9).

The writer to the Hebrews, in discussing the Tabernacle, says that the Ark had contained Aaron's rod and a jar of manna.

The Ark of the covenant overlaid on all sides with gold, in which were the golden pot that had manna, Aaron's rod that budded, and the tablets of the covenant (Hebrews 9:4).

The Old Testament, however, does not mention these items as being in the Ark. We are told these items were initially placed in front of the Ark, not inside of it.

And the Lord said to Moses, 'Bring Aaron's rod back before the Testimony, to be kept as a sign against the rebels, that you may put their murmurings away from Me, lest they die (Numbers 17:10).

There has been much speculation why this is so. Some people believe these other two objects may have been added later than the time of Solomon. It is also possible that they had been lost by Solomon's time. A removal of the articles may have occurred during the seven months when the Ark was in the land of the Philistines.

Whatever the case may be, they were not found inside the Ark at Solomon's dedication. All that was left in the Ark of the Covenant was the Ten Commandments.

Two Carved Cherubim

A new feature was added to the inside of the Holy of Holies: two giant cherubim[2] carved out of cedarwood and overlaid with gold. Their wings met in the middle of the Holy of Holies in a protecting arch. From tip to tip they measured about twenty feet. Underneath these wings dwelt the Ark as well as the Shekinah glory.

Then he set the cherubim inside the inner room; and they stretched out the wings of the cherubim so that the wing of the one touched one wall, and the wing of the other cherub touched the other wall. And their wings touched each other in the middle of the room (1 Kings 6:27).

Temple was Unique

The Temple of Jerusalem differed from other Temples in the ancient Middle East in that it had no idols. The Ark of the Covenant, in the Holy of Holies was its treasure. Jewish author Chaim Potok writes:

This we do know: the Solomonic temple was devoid of images. Israelites were called upon to offer sacrifices to their all-powerful and invisible God, who had covenanted with their ancestors in Canaan and at Sinai, and whose promise to the patriarchs had been clearly fulfilled—as evidenced by the empire of the united monarchy and the glittering splendor of Solomon's new Jerusalem. They were to offer their sacrifices in Jerusalem in times of famine, drought, war; for sins; during festivals. The temple of Solomon was a religious and political undertaking that deepened the relationship between the city of David and the people of Israel.[3]

No More Fighting

After the Ark was placed in the inner sanctuary of the Temple, the Holy of Holies, the practice of carrying it into battle forever ceased. From this time onward, the historical references concerning the Ark of the Covenant are few.[4]

Endnotes for Chapter 14

1.   C. H. Mackintosh writes:

> It [the Ark] was not always to be a traveller. "The
> afflictions of David," as well as the wars of Israel, were to
> have an end. The prayer was yet to be breathed and
> answered, "Arise O Lord, into thy rest: thou and the ark
> of they strength" (Ps. cxxxii. 8). This most sublime
> petition had its partial accomplishment in the . . . days of
> Solomon, when "the priests brought in the ark of the
> covenant of the Lord unto his place, into the oracle of the
> house, to the most holy place, even under the wings of the
> cherubims . . .
> When the moment arrived in which . . . the wanderings
> and wars of Israel were over, when the . . . house was
> completed . . . then the record of wilderness need and
> wilderness failure were unnoticed, and nothing remained
> save that which constituted the eternal foundation of the
> throne of the God of Israel, and all the earth (C.H.
> Mackintosh, *Notes on the Book of Exodus*, New York,
> Loizeaux Brothers, 1873, pp. 279-281).

2.   The figures of the cherubim were used for decorative
purposes: (1) they were embroidered on the veil separating the
Holy Place from the Holy of Holies and the curtains of the
Tabernacle (2) They were carved on the all the inner and outer
walls (1 Kings 6:29), the doors of the inner and outer
sanctuary (1 Kings 6:32,35), and the panels of Solomon's
Temple (1 Kings 7:29,36); and (3) carved on the walls on the
walls and doors of the Temple envisioned by Ezekiel 41:18-
20,25).

3.   Chaim Potok, *Wanderings*, New York, Alfred A. Knopf,
1978, p.114.

4.   A brief history of the Ark, up to this point, is succinctly
given by a seventeenth century Bible Commentary:

> As soon as Solomon had finished all the buildings of
> the Temple, and the utensils and furniture thereof, he
> resolved solemnly to dedicate and consecrate the same,
> and to bring up the Ark from the city of David, to place it
> therein.
> It will not be amiss to observe the several removals of
> the Ark of God; so famous in Scripture. The Tabernacle
> and the Ark being first made by Moses in the desert, were
> afterwards by Joshua set up at Shiloh, the 7th year after
> that the Israelites had passed through Jordan. This
> Shiloh was a city in the Tribe of Ephraim, and seems to

have been the same with Salem, where Melchisedeck reigned, and near to which John baptized. In this place the Ark continued 328 years, till the time that the Israelites carried it into their camp against the Philistines, who took it and sent it back . . . Upon its return into the Holy Land, it was placed in the house of Aminadab in Kiriath-jearim, where it continued 70 years, and then translated from thence to the House of Obed-Edom, where it abode only three months; at the end of which David transported it to Zion, which was the Citadel of Jerusalem. It seems likely also that at the same time, the Tabernacle, which had continued all this while at Shiloh, was set up in Gibeon, a city in the Tribe of Judah (*The History of the Old and New Testament*, Second Edition Corrected, London, 1699, p. 140).

CHAPTER 15

THE ARK IS MYSTERIOUSLY RETURNED TO THE TEMPLE

Solomon's magnificent Temple in Jerusalem brought Israel fame throughout the entire world. All, however, was not well. Even before Solomon's death, idolatry began to increase among the people. Time after time God had sent prophets to Jerusalem to warn the people of upcoming judgment, but their words fell on deaf ears.

Our story now moves forward some 350 years to a crucial time in Israel's history. Shortly after the death of Solomon, the nation of Israel was divided into two kingdoms: north and south. The ten northern tribes, called Israel, had their center of worship in Samaria. Constantly in idolatry, they were taken captive by the Assyrians in 721 B.C.

The two southern tribes, known as Judah, had Jerusalem as their capital. Though they experienced times of spiritual revival, idolatry was rampant. Both the Temple and the Ark had been neglected by the people. The judgment would soon be coming.

During this dark period, there were glimpses of light. One of them occurred in the reign of Josiah (621 B.C.)

Book of Law Found

The Book of the Law[1] had been lost through neglect of the holy things. It was found during the time of Josiah.

Now when they brought out the money that was brought out of the house of the Lord, Hilkiah the priest found the Book of the Law of the Lord given by Moses (2 Chronicles 34:14).

With the discovery and reading of the Book of the Law, King Josiah realized that Judah had ignored the commandments of the Lord. He ordered the Temple repaired and the renewed celebration of passover.

In the 18th year of King Josiah, the Temple was repaired, and the passover was celebrated. The priests and Levites were commanded to fulfill their duties for the occasion. Josiah then ordered that the Ark of the Covenant was to be placed in the Temple.

Then he said to the Levites who taught all Israel, who were holy to the Lord: 'Put the holy ark in the house which Solomon the son of David, king of Israel built. It shall no longer be a burden on your shoulders. Now serve the Lord your God and His people Israel' (2 Chronicles 35:3).

This mysterious command of Josiah is the last historical reference to the Ark of the Covenant.

Removed

Josiah ordered the Ark placed back into the Temple. The Scriptures do not tell us when and by whom it was removed. There has been much speculation as to when it was taken and where it was placed while outside of the Temple.

The Ark may have been removed during the reign of Manasseh, one of the worst kings in Judah's history.

He set up a carved image, the idol which he had made, in the house of God, of which God had said to David and to Solomon his son, 'In this house and in Jerusalem, which I have chosen out of all the tribes of Israel, I will put my name forever' (2 Chronicles 33:7).

The reign of Amon is another time the Ark could have been removed.

> But he [Amon] did evil in the sight of the Lord, as his father Manasseh had done for Amon sacrificed to all the carved images which his father Manasseh had made, and served them (2 Chronicles 33:22).

Some feel that the Ark was removed to keep it from being desecrated. The *Wycliffe Bible Commentary* says:

> In the dark days of Manasseh and Amon, the ark seems to have been removed by faithful Levites and carried away elsewhere for its protection.[2]

If the Ark had been previously removed it is surprising that nothing is said about it in Scripture. We are not told whether it was a helpful priest who removed it to keep it from being profaned or an idolatrous king to make room for his pagan idols.

There may be a simple explanation as to why the Ark was moved out of the Temple. It is possible that the Ark had been temporarily removed during the time Josiah was making repairs on the Temple. When the repairs were finished, the Ark was ordered returned.

We agree with the assessment of the *Speakers Commentary* that it is not possible to know why the Ark had been removed:

> It is impossible to say whether it had been cast out by Amon to make room for the idolatrous emblems with which he seems to have defiled the temple (2 Kings xii. 46) or had been temporarily removed by Josiah when he effected the necessary repairs.[3]

Whatever the case may be,[4] the Scripture records the command of Josiah to place the Ark back in the Temple.

Once the Ark was mysteriously returned to the Temple, it was no longer heard from. Its fate remains an enigma to this day.

Endnotes for Chapter 15

1. We have already seen (Endnotes for Chapter 2) that there
are various interpretations of what was contained in the Book
of the Law (Book of the Covenant) J. Barton Payne comments:

> At this point in the year 622, Hilkiah found the "Book
> of the Law." It is later called the "Book of the Covenant." (v.
> 30). . . It contains the curses (Deut 28) and it alone calls
> for a central sanctuary and was stored at the temple
> usually by the side of the ark (Deut 31:25,26) . . . The book,
> however, seems to have been misplaced during the
> apostate administrations of the previous kings,
> Manasseh and Amon, under whom the ark had been
> moved about (2 Chron 35:3) (J. Barton Payne, *The
> Expositors Bible Commentary*, Volume 4, General Editor
> Frank Gaebelein, Grand Rapids, Zondervan, 1988, p. 551)

There is a possible connection between the recovery of this
lost book and the returning of the Ark to the Holy of Holies.
Scripture tells us that the "Book of the Law" was later placed
by the side of the Ark.

> Take this Book of the Law, and put it beside the ark of
> the covenant of the Lord your God, that it may be thereas
> a witness against you (Deuteronomy 31:26).

2. The *Wycliffe Bible Commentary*, Chicago, Moody Press,
1962, p. 418

Calmet's Bible Dictionary says:

> The priests, unable to endure this profanation
> removed the ark and carried it from place to place to
> preserve it from the pollution and impiety of these
> princes. Josiah commanded them to bring it back to the
> sanctuary and forbade them to carry it, as they had
> hitherto done into the country (*Calmet's Dictionary of
> the Holy Bible*, Vol I, with Biblical fragments by the late
> Charles Taylor, London, Eighth edition, 1844, p. 190).

3. Cited by *Ellicott's Commentary on the Whole Bible*, edited
by Charles John Ellicott, Vol 3, 1 Kings-Esther, n.d.,

4. John Peter Lange notes another theory:

> Quite arbitrary is the hypothesis of some ancients
> that the ark was, in the days of the idolatrous kings,
> sometimes carried round the country as a means of
> strengthening the faith of the people, and Josiah now

forbids this custom in the present words (John Peter Lange, *Commentary on the Holy Scriptures*, Volume 7. p. 272).

C.J. Ball writes:

A third explanation takes the words in the sense of, "Let the Ark be, where it stands in its proper place. Do not give a thought to your ancient function of bearing it about. But set your mind upon present duties." This however is too artificial (C. J. Ball in *Ellicott's Commentary on the Whole Bible*).

CHAPTER 16

THE TEMPLE DESTROYED:
THE ARK IS GONE

Though the golden Ark of the Covenant had been placed back into the Holy of Holies during the reign of King Josiah, the days of the First Temple were numbered. Less that twenty years after the Ark was returned, Nebuchadnezzar, King of Babylon, began one of three separate sieges on the city of Jerusalem.[1]

Temple Destroyed

During the third siege of Jerusalem in 587 B.C. the armies of King Nebuchadnezzar destroyed both the city and its magnificent Temple. The Bible records that Nebuchadnezzar took the golden vessels with him to Babylon.

> And all the articles from the house of God, great and small, the treasures of the house of the Lord, and the treasures of the king and of his leaders, all these he took to Babylon. Then they burned the house of God, broke down the wall of Jerusalem, burned all its palaces with fire, and destroyed all its precious possessions (2 Chronicles 36:18,19).

What is not specifically mentioned is the Ark of the Covenant. It's fate is not recorded.

Nebuchadnezzar's Image

Some years after the destruction of Jerusalem and the pillage of the Temple, the Bible speaks of Nebuchadnezzar making a huge golden image of himself and then demanding that the people worship it.

> Nebuchadnezzar, the king made an image of gold whose height was sixty cubits and its width six cubits (Daniel 3:1).

Where did he get such an amount of gold? Is it possible that he used some of the golden vessels from the Temple to make this image? May these have included the Ark of the Covenant?[2]

Handwriting on the Wall

Another episode during this period involved the Temple vessels. Belshazzar, who ruled after Nebuchadnezzar, made a great feast in Babylon. During the feast, Belshazzar ordered that the holy vessels be brought to him.

> While he tasted the wine, Belshazzar gave the command to bring the gold and silver vessels which his father Nebuchadnezzar had taken from the temple which had been in Jerusalem, that the king and his lords, his wives, and his concubines might drink from them. Then they brought the gold vessels which had been taken from the temple of the house of God which had been in Jerusalem; and the king and his lords, his wives and his concubines drank from them (Daniel 5:2,3).

Belshazzar mocked the God of Israel by praising the gods of gold and silver. His blasphemy of the holy vessels could not go unpunished. It was in this context that the famous incident of the handwriting on the wall occurred.

> In the same hour the fingers of a man's hand appeared and wrote opposite the lampstand on the plaster of the wall of the king's palace; and the king saw the part of the hand that wrote. Then the king's countenance changed, and his thoughts troubled him, so that the joints of his hips were loosened and his knees knocked against each other (Daniel 5:5,6).

The old prophet Daniel was called in to interpret the message. He said to Belshazzar:

> And you have lifted yourself up against the Lord of heaven. They have brought the vessels of His house before you and your lords, your wives and your concubines, have drunk wine from them. And you have praised the gods of silver and gold, bronze and iron, wood and stone, which do not see or hear or know; and the God who holds your very breath in His hand and owns all your ways you have not glorified (Daniel 5:23).

The great city of Babylon fell that night and the blasphemous King Belshazzar was slain. The Babylonian kingdom, who had conquered Jerusalem, had itself been conquered by the Medes and the Persians. The holy vessels that had been taken from the Temple were now in their hands, and the fate of the Ark was still unknown.

Endnotes for Chapter 16

1. On the first siege Nebuchadnezzar took only the minor utensils. It was not until his third siege that he took all the vessels. Before the final siege, false prophets were telling the people that the Temple would not be destroyed. God's prophet, Jeremiah, spoke to the contrary (Jeremiah 27:18-22).

2. Though the theory has been advocated that Nebuchadnezzar used the gold from the Ark to build an idol of himself there is no evidence of this. As a trophy of war, the Ark would more likely be kept intact.

Humphrey Prideaux writes:

Nebuchadnezzar did put all the sacred vessels, which he carried from Jerusalem, into the House of his god at Babylon, that is unto the house or temple of Bel. For that is the name of the great god of the Babylonians. He is supposed to have been the same with Nimrod, and to have been called Bel from his dominion, and Nimrod from his rebellion. For both Bel or Ball, which is the same name, signifieth Lord (Humphrey Prideaux, *Old and New Testament Connected*, Part 1, Vol. 1, 10th edition, 1729, p. 142).

CHAPTER 17

THE SECOND TEMPLE PERIOD: NO ARK

Rightly, the city of Jerusalem had been judged for their idolatry. The Lord, however, is rich in mercy. Judgment is His strange work. The magnificent Temple, built by Solomon, had been destroyed and the people were in exile. Yet this would only be temporary. The people were soon returned to their land and a Second Temple was constructed.

The Return

Seventy years after their expulsion, the people returned to Jerusalem from the Babylonian captivity. The Temple restoration was their major focus of attention.

Hundreds of years earlier, the Prophet Isaiah had predicted that King Cyrus would give the command to restore the Temple.

Who says of Cyrus, 'He is My shepherd, and he shall perform all My pleasure,' even saying to Jerusalem, "You shall be built," and to the temple, "Your foundation shall be laid"(Isaiah 44:28).

Cyrus restoring the vessels of the Temple

A similar prophecy was made by Jeremiah.[1] The Chronicler ends his account with the fulfillment of this prophecy.

> Now in the first year of Cyrus king of Persia, that the word of the Lord spoken in the mouth of Jeremiah might be fulfilled, the Lord stirred up the spirit of Cyrus king of Persia, so that he made a proclamation throughout all his kingdom, and also put it in writing, saying, "Thus says Cyrus king of Persia: 'All the kingdoms of the earth the Lord God of heaven has given me. And He has commanded me to build a house at Jerusalem which is in Judah. Who is there among you of His people? May the Lord his God be with him and let him go up! (2 Chronicles 36:22,23).

In the same manner, the Book of Ezra begins with this prophecy's fulfillment.[2]

In 538 B.C. Cyrus declared that the return was for the purpose of rebuilding the Temple. Those who returned from the Exile were to be aided by the Jews remaining behind, as well as their Gentile neighbors. The Temple vessels taken for booty by Nebuchadnezzar were delivered to the treasurer for return to Jerusalem. A list of the Temple treasures is recorded.

> King Cyrus also brought out the articles of the house of the Lord, which Nebuchadnezzar had taken from Jerusalem and put in the temple of his gods; and Cyrus king of Persia brought them out of the hand of Mithredath the treasurer, and counted them out to Sheshbazzar the prince of Judah. This is the number of them: thirty gold platters, one thousand silver platters, twenty-nine knives, thirty gold basins, four hundred and ten silver basins of a similar kind, and one thousand other articles. All the articles of gold and silver were five thousand four hundred. All these Sheshbazzar took with the captives who were brought from Babylon to Jerusalem (Ezra 1:7-11).

As we see, there is a detailed list of the articles returned. Conspicuous by their absence are the sacred vessels of the Temple, the Golden Lampstand, the Table of Shewbread, the Altar of Incense, and the Ark of the Covenant. All of them had disappeared.

Articles Rebuilt

Upon the a royal decree, all the articles that were taken by Nebuchadnezzar were returned.

Also let the gold and silver articles of the house of God which Nebuchadnezzar took from the temple which is in Jerusalem and brought back to Babylon, be restored and taken back to the temple which is in Jerusalem, each to its place; and deposit them in the house of God (Ezra 6:5).

All those holy articles which were not returned were ordered rebuilt.[3] The one article that was not rebuilt was the Ark of the Covenant.

Temple Rebuilt Without Ark

The Second Temple was completed about 515 B.C. It was a smaller version of the original one built by Solomon.[4] The term "Second Temple" actually refers to two different structures. Later this Second Temple was expanded by Herod the Great.

About 20 B.C. Herod convened a national assembly announcing his plan to construct a new Temple. In his speech Herod explained how the Temple then standing lacked the sixty cubits of height that Solomon's Temple had. With the blessings of Rome, Herod would correct this situation.

He solved the space problem by doubling the size of the Temple Mount, building huge retaining walls that towered ninety feet above ground level.[5] The old Temple continued to be in regular use during the preparation. The daily sacrifices continued there during the time of Herod's rebuilding.

No Ark

During the time of the Second Temple (515 B.C to A.D. 70) the Ark was not present. This is confirmed by various sources.

For example, in 167 B.C. the Seleucid King Antiochus Epiphanes entered Jerusalem and desecrated the Temple. He removed the Table of Showbread, the Golden Altar, the Golden Lampstand and other costly things. When he entered the Holy of Holies he found it vacant. The account is recorded for us in First Maccabees.

On his return from the conquest of Egypt, in the year 143 [169 B.C], Antiochus marched with a strong force against Israel and Jerusalem. In his arrogance he entered the temple and carried off the golden altar, the lampstand with all its equipment, the table for the Bread of the Presence, the sacred cups and bowls, the golden censers, the curtain and the crowns. He stripped off all the gold plating from the Temple front. He seized the silver and gold vessels, and whatever secret treasures he found, and took them all with him when he left for his own country (1 Maccabees 1:20-24, New English Bible).

He did not find or take the Ark of the Covenant.

The Temple was restored three years later by Judas Maccabaeus. He built a new altar and made new hallowed vessels.

And they took whole stones according to the law and built a new altar according to the former. And they built up the holy places and the things that were within the temple, and they sanctified the temple and the courts. And they made new holy vessels, and brought in the candlestick, and the altar of incense and the table into the temple. And they put incense upon the altar, and lighted up the lamps that were upon the candlestick, and they gave light in the temple (1 Maccabees 4:47-50, Douay Version).

In this entire account of the Temple's desecration and subsequent restoration, there is no mention of the Ark.

Pompey

First century Jewish historian, Flavius Josephus, recorded that the Roman General Pompey also found the Holy of Holies empty when he entered in 63 B.C.[6] Nathan Ausbel notes:

Pompey was the first Roman who subdued the Jews. By right of conquest he entered their temple. It is a fact well known, that he found no image, no statue, no symbolical representation of the Deity: the whole presented a naked dome; the sanctuary was unadorned and simple. By Pompey's orders the walls of the city were levelled to the ground, but the temple was left entire.[7]

Josephus records that in his day, shortly after the time of Christ, the Ark was still missing. He wrote that the Ark was lost during the entire time of the Second Temple.[8]

The Jews agreed that there were five things that had been in the First Temple which were not in the Second: (1) The Ark of the Covenant (2) the Holy Spirit of Prophecy (3) the Urim and Thummim, (4) the Sacred Fire, and (5) the Shekinah Glory.

Foundation Stone

The Second Temple did not contain the Ark of the Covenant, but it was represented by a stone protruding some three fingers high off the ground called "the stone of foundation."[9] The foundation stone is the place where the Ark would have stood had it existed. On this stone, the High Priest sprinkled the blood of the sacrifice on the Great Day of Atonement. The blood had formerly been sprinkled on the Mercy Seat during the days of the Tabernacle and First Temple.

The Ark and the Life of Jesus

When Jesus of Nazareth came into the world, the nation of Israel was under the yoke of Rome. The Temple in Jerusalem was functioning, but without the Ark of the Covenant. The Holy of Holies was still without its only piece of furniture. Jewish scholar Alfred Edersheim wrote:

> Wherever a Roman, a Greek or an Asiatic might wander, he could take gods with him, or find rites kindred to his own. It was far otherwise with the Jew. He had only one Temple, that in Jerusalem; only one God, Him who had once throned there between the Cherubim, and who was still King over Zion. The Temple was the only place where a God-appointed, pure priesthood could offer acceptable sacrifices, whether for forgiveness of sin, or for fellowship with God.
> Here, in the impenetrable gloom of the inner-most sanctuary, which the High Priest alone might enter once a year—for most solemn expiation, had stood the Ark, the leader of the people into the land of Promise, and the footstool on which the Shechinah had rested.[10]

Jesus spoke of the glory having once been in the Temple.

He who swears by the temple, swears by it and by Him who dwelt in it (Matthew 23:21).

By using the past tense, Jesus implied that God had forsaken the Temple.[11]

The Bible states that God no longer manifested His visible presence there. Around 600 B.C., the prophet Ezekiel saw the glory leave the Temple and depart by the way of the Mount of Olives on the east of Jerusalem

And the glory of the Lord went up from the midst of the city and stood on the mountain, which is on the east side of the city (Ezekiel 11:23).

Destruction of Second Temple

The Second Temple was destroyed in A.D. 70 by Titus the Roman. The holy vessels of the Temple were taken by Titus and brought to Rome. First century writer and eyewitness to these events, Flavius Josephus, described them being paraded through the streets of Rome:

Most of the spoils were heaped up indiscriminately; but more prominent than all the rest were those captured in the Temple at Jerusalem. They consisted of a golden table weighing many talents, and a candelabrum also made of gold, but different in pattern from those we use in ordinary life. Its central shaft was fixed to a base, and from it extended slender branches arranged like the prongs of a trident, while a wrought lamp was attached to the end of each branch; these numbered seven, indicating the sanctity of that number to the Jews. After these—and last of all the spoils—was carried a copy of the Jewish Law. Then followed a large group carrying images of Victory, all fashioned of ivory and gold. Behind them Vespasian drove first, with Titus behind him while Domitian rode alongside in magnificent apparel and mounted on a horse that was itself a site worth seeing.[12]

The Ark is nowhere to be found among the items taken from the Second Temple by the Romans. Its fate remained unrecorded.

Endnotes for Chapter 17

1. Jeremiah predicted:

> And this whole land shall be a desolation and an astonishment, and these nations shall serve the king of Babylon seventy years. Then it will come to pass, when seventy years are completed, that I will punish the king of Babylon, and that nation, the land of the Chaldeans, for their iniquity,' says the Lord: 'and I will make it a perpetual desolation' (Jeremiah 25:11,12).

2. The Book of Ezra records the fulfillment:

> Now in the first year of Cyrus king of Persia, that the word of the Lord spoken by the mouth of Jeremiah might be fulfilled, the Lord stirred up the spirit of Cyrus king of Persia, so that he made a proclamation throughout all his kingdom (Ezra 1:1).

3. The Book of Ezra notes the King's command:

> Also the articles that are given to you for the service of the house of your God, deliver in full before the God of Jerusalem. And whatever more may be needed for the house of your God, which you may have occasion to provide, pay for it from the King's treasury (Ezra 7:19,20).

4. Many who saw the Second Temple wept:

> But many of the priests and Levites and head of the father's houses, who were old men, who had seen the first temple, wept with a loud voice when the foundation of this temple was laid before their eyes; yet many shouted aloud for joy (Ezra 3:12).

Humphrey Prideaux writes:

> And therefore had nothing else of the first Temple been wanting in the second but the Ark only this also would have been reason enough for the old men to have wept, when they remembered the first temple. Humphrey Prideaux, *Old and New Testament Connected*, Part 1, Vol. 1, 10th edition, 1729, p. 201).

Laetsch notes:

> The very fact that the returning exiles no longer possessed the Ark, was to be to them a lesson teaching

them that the complete dissolution of the Old Covenant was approaching (Theo. Laetsch, *Jeremiah*, St. Louis, Concordia Press, 1952, p. 56).

5. The only part of Herod's Temple that remains today is the western retaining wall, known as the "Western Wall" or the "Wailing Wall."

6. Josephus wrote:

Pompey went into it, and not a few of those that were with him also saw all that which was unlawful for any other men to see but only for the High Priest. There were in the Temple the Golden Table, the Holy Candlestick, and other pouring vessels, and a great quantity of spices; and besides these were among the treasure two thousand talents of sacred money; yet did Pompey touch nothing of all this on account of his regard to religion (Josephus *Antiquities*: 14:4:4).

This was confirmed by Cicero,

When he [Pompey] was conqueror, and had taken Jerusalem, did not touch any thing belonging to the temple (Cicero, *Oration for Flaccus*).

7. Nathan Ausbel, *Pictorial History of the Jews*, New York, Crown Books, 1953, p. 55.

8. Josephus stated:

But the inmost part of the Temple of all was twenty cubits. This was separated from the outer part by a veil. In this there was nothing at all. It was inaccessible and inviolable, and not to be seen by any; and was called the Holy of Holies (Josephus, *The Wars of the Jews*, 5:5:5).

9. The *Mishnah* says:

After the Ark was taken away, a stone remained there from the time of the Early Prophets, and it was called 'Shetiyah'. It was higher than the ground by three fingerbreadths (Yoma 5:2).

Leibel Reznick writes:

The rock was first uncovered by King David and the Prophet Samuel (Sota 48b). Some say the rock was in the very center of the Holy of Holies (Tosfos Yom Tov); others say it was near the western wall of the Holy of Holies

(Rambam, Bais HaB'chirah 4), and still others maintain that it was near the curtains separating the Kodesh (Holy Place) and the Holy of Holies (Tosfos, Baba Basra 25a). (Leibel Reznick, *The Holy Temple Revisited*, Northvale, New Jersey, Jason Aronson, Inc, 1990, p. 134).

The Gemara of Jerusalem (chap. 1) and that of Babylon both acknowlege that the Ark of the Covenant was lacking in the Second Temple. Jewish sage Abarbanel, (comments on Daniel 9) says it will be restored by the Messiah. Ezra, Nehemiah, Maccabees, and Josephus do not mention it as being in the Second Temple.

There are those, however, who believe the Ark was in the Second Temple:

But 40 years after this, at the time of the Dedication of the Temple, Solomon placed the Ark and the Brazen Altar there, where they continued 424 years, at which time Nebuchadnezzar took Jerusalem and burnt the Temple; which being foreseen by Jeremiah the Prophet, he took care to convey the Ark to Mount Pisgah, where he was assured by God that it should remain unknown till the return of the Children of Israel form the Bablylonish Captivity; which makes it more probable, that the said Ark was afterwards placed in the Second Temple, which was begun by Cyrus, and finished by Darius, Kings of Persia (*The History of the Old and New Testament*, Second Edition Corrected, London, 1699, p.140).

George Bush writes to the contrary:

Others say that it was indeed taken away by the Chaldeans (Babylonians), but was afterwards restored, and occupied its place in the second Temple; but the Talmud and some of the Jewish writers confess, that the want of the ark was one of the points in which the second Temple was inferior to that of Solomon; to which we may add that neither Ezra, Nehemiah, the Maccabees, nor Josephus, mention the ark as exant in the second Temple, and the last authority expressly says there was nothing in the sanctuary when the Temple was taken by Titus. It certainly does not appear in the Arch erected at Rome in honor of that conqueror, and in which the spoils of the Temple are displayed; although some writers have attempted to identify it with the table of shewbread which is there represented (George Bush, *Notes on the Book of Exodus*, Volume, 1, Boston, Henry A. Young & Co., 1841, p. 91).

10. Alfred Edersheim, *The Life and Times of Jesus the Messiah*, MacDonald Publishing Company, n.d. p. 7.

11. Some versions do not render Jesus' statement as past tense but rather present tense. For example

And he who swears by the temple swears by it and by the one who dwells in it (New International Version).

And he who swears by the temple,sear both both the temple and by Him who dwell in it (New American Standard Bible).

12. Flavius Josephus, *The Jewish War:* 5:5:5

William Knight recognized:

It is not exaggeration to say that the Fall of Jerusalem is the most significant national event in the history of the world. The fact that the Lord Himself connected it with His own passion is sufficient to establish its supreme importance (John ii,19). The destruction of the Temple was indeed involved in His death. That which had been in the past the shrine of the Presence of God among His people was necessarily doomed to final desolation when 'the more perfect Tabernacle' had been faithlessly and fatally violated (William Knight, *The Arch of Titus*, London, Religious Tract Society, 1896, p. 9).

CHAPTER 18

FROM THE SECOND TEMPLE UNTIL TODAY: THE ARK REMAINS LOST

With the Second Temple destroyed and the Jews scattered throughout the world, the city of Jerusalem was no longer the center for Jewish worship. Without a Temple, a High Priest, and a system of sacrifice, the Jews had to worship the Lord through other means. The loss of the Temple gave rise to the prominence of the synagogue.

After the Babylonian captivity in 539 B.C., a great number of synagogues sprang up. The term synagogue denotes a Jewish house of worship. The origin of the synagogues is unclear but many scholars feel that they originated during the Babylonian captivity. This was a time when the exiled Jews who had been forcibly removed from their Temple gathered in groups to read the Scriptures.

The New Testament records that Jesus taught in synagogues throughout Galilee. The Apostle Paul preached in synagogues in Damascus and refers to synagogues in every city he visited in Asia Minor.

The synagogues were widely used in New Testament times, but the central place of worship was still the Temple in Jerusalem while it remained standing.

With the destruction of the Second Temple, and the end to the state of Israel, the people scattered worldwide.

The Temple and the synagogue previously existed side by side in complementary roles. After A.D. 70 the synagogue became the central institution of Judaism and prayer became the central form of worship as there was now no sacrificial system.

Synagogues were now the only place of worship since Jerusalem had been lost to non-Jews. Abba Eban observes:

> By the fifth century the entire Roman world had become formally Christian, and no other faith was tolerated. Christianity was now the "Establishment." while the unconverted Jews remained the eternal dissidents, the perpetual minority. But from these five centuries they had carried away a new mobility and a new flexibility for their ideas and culture. These ideas and culture were no longer tied down to an Ark of the Covenant or to a Temple in Jerusalem. The Jews could now move forward in any direction, wherever books of the Bible and of the Talmud could be found.[1]

Synagogue Ark

The synagogues contained a chest or closet where the scrolls of the Torah and other sacred books were kept. The chest was known as the "Ark of the Torah." It was placed in an area shut off by a curtain from the rest of the building. The synagogue Torah arks, unlike the Ark of the Covenant, looked like a miniature building. They served as a symbolic representation of the former Temple in Jerusalem and of the Ark of the Covenant.

The Torah Ark is still a major architectural element in the synagogue, traditionally built into the eastern wall of the synagogue facing Jerusalem.

Lost Synagogue Ark Found

In the summer of 1981, an ancient synagogue ark was discovered by archaeologists Eric and Carol Myers. The discovery made in Nabratein in the upper Galilee caused a temporary worldwide sensation. Many confused their ancient synagogue ark with the original Ark of the Covenant. Of their experience they wrote:

> We will probably never stop asking ourselves why it was in the summer of 1981, rather than 1979 or 1983, that we uncovered a magnificent stone fragment from a lost synagogue ark. Had our discovery occurred in some other year, the world at large would probably never have

noticed. But because—by what strange coincidence we do not know—our ark fragment was unearthed during the summer of "Raiders of the Lost Ark," it attracted front-page media attention and we—comfortably accustomed to the life of obscure archaeologists—suddenly became minor international celebrities. . .

Too often the media tried to make the false connection between the Ark of the Covenant and the ancient synagogue ark we found. Some of the hundreds of newspaper articles even tried to give the impression that we found the Ark of the Covenant itself.[2]

The Myer's emphasized the importance of the synagogue ark.

It is now clear that our forebearers regarded their houses of worship and their communities . . . as the successors of the Temple of Jerusalem . . . The shrines they erected in their synagogues were conceived in the knowledge that they were to be the successors to the Biblical Ark of the Covenant. The Biblical Ark was the receptacle of the Covenant, which symbolized God's presence; the Torah Shrine of post-Temple days was the receptacle of the scrolls, God word preserved in Scripture. We did not find the original ark, but we did find one of its unique spiritual successors.[3]

Depictions of synagogue arks have also been found. At Capernaum there was a small frieze found showing a small columned structure, flanked by lions. A mosaic of a synagogue ark has also been found in Beth Alpha near Beth-Shean, south of the Sea of Galilee.[4]

Worship Today

Today Jewish worship is still conducted in the synagogue since there has not been a Temple in Jerusalem for over 1900 years. The Orthodox services themselves have changed little in 2,000 years. To this day, the synagogue is the central religious, social and educational institution in Judaism.

In most synagogues today, the ark is still placed in the wall of the building that is facing Jerusalem. It is usually positioned in such a way that it is visible from every part of the room. Congregation rise when this portion of the wall is opened, as it is considered symbolic of the Holy of Holies. The present synagogue arks are made of various materials including marble and carved wood. Some are highly ornamented.

The synagogue ark reminds the Jewish people of their past glory when the Ark of the Covenant stood in the Holy of Holies; first in the Tabernacle, and then in the Temple. Today, in its place, they have only representations of Israel's most sacred object for the Ark of the Covenant has mysteriously vanished.

The Mystery of the Ark's Disappearance

The Ark of the Covenant unexplainably disappeared from the pages of the Bible and history. Richard Friedman writes:

> There is no report that the Ark was carried away destroyed or hidden. There is not even any comment such as 'And then the Ark disappeared and we do not know what happened to it' or And no one knows where it is to this day'. The most important object in the world, in the biblical view, simply ceases to be in the story.[5]

Where did it go? Chaim Potok writes:

> No mention is made of the sacred ark, which had been in the temple since the days of Solomon. The humiliation of its loss may have been so painful it could not be shaped in words. We never hear of it again.[6]

From the time of Josiah, until the present-day, the Ark of the Covenant has disappeared from the face of the earth. Will it ever again appear? This question is the focus of the rest of the book.

Endnotes for Chapter 18

1.   Abba Eban, *Heritage: Civilization and the Jews*, New York, Summit Books, 1984, p. 94.

Religion writer John Noss gives further insight into the synagogue:

> The synagogues were controlled, in matters of doctrine and polity, by the scribes and Pharisees, but the local administration was in the hands of a council of elders, one of whom was elected the ruler of the synagogue and had charge of the religious services. He would be in a position to invite Jesus to speak in the synagogue. Another officer, the *chazzan* or attendant, was the synagogue's librarian, having in his care the rolls of the scriptures which were in the "ark" (John B. Noss, *Man's Religions*, Fourth edition, New York, Macmillan Company, 1969, p. 434 note).

2.   Eric M. Myers and Carol L. Myers, Finders of a Real Lost Ark, *Biblical Archaeological Review*, November/December 1981. pp. 25,26).

3.   Eric M. Myers and Carol L. Myers, ibid. p. 26.

The Myers also write:

> The pediment of the Holy Ark which we found in 1981, however, is the first and only part of a Torah Shrine to have survived from high antiquity. It is a kind of missing link. It dates from the third century A.D. a millennium and a half after the Ark of the Covenant (the original prototype) and a millennium before any extant medieval example. . .
> The entire Torah Shrine is called the "Holy Ark" or Aron Ha-Qodesh. This term only appears once in the Bible (in 2 Chronicles 35:3), but it has been used for the past 2,000 years to denominate the synagogue ark, symbolic descendent of the Ark of the Covenant (Myers, ibid. p. 29).

4.   See our pictures in center section of various synagogue arks. including the frieze at Capernaum and the floor at Beth Alpha. The Myers comment on the Beth Alpha mosaic:

> The mosaic floor from the synagogue at Beth Alpha contains many of the same elements as the Nabratein Ark: pitched roof, pair of lions on either side of the Ark, a shell motif in the center of the ark pediment, and an

eternal lamp hanging from the roof peak (Myers, ibid. p. 32).

The remains of a synagogue from the time of Ptolemy III (246-221 B.C.) has been found outside Alexandria. The Damascus museum contains the remains of a synagogue from about A.D. 200 removed from Dura-Europos the middle of the Euphrates. It has murals depicting the Ark and also has a likeness of a Torah shrine.

5.   Richard Elliott Friedman, *Who Wrote The Bible?* London Jonathan Cape, 1988, p. 156.

6.   Chaim Potok, *Wanderings*, New York, Alfred A. Knopf, 1978, p. 145.

The question we will now consider concerns what happened to the Ark of the Covenant. Was it lost? Has it been hidden? Has it been taken captive? What are the chances that it will ever be found? What about reports that it has been discovered?

We will now consider these and other important questions in the remainder of the book as we begin our search for the Lost Ark.

SECTION THREE

ARKEOLOGY-IN SEARCH OF THE LOST ARK

WAS THE ARK TAKEN BY FOREIGN INVADERS?

Was the Ark of the Covenant taken by foreign invaders? In our quest to discover what happened to the lost Ark, we will concentrate first on those nations who invaded Israel and took away certain holy vessels from the Temple. Three times this happened to Solomon's Temple as scholar Menahem Haran notes:

> There is evidence of foreign kings penetrating the Solomonic temple at various periods. There were three such invaders (Pharaoh Shishak [Egypt] 1 Kgs. 14:26), Jehoash of Israel (2 Kgs. 14:14), and Nebuchadnezzar of Babylon . . . Small wonder, therefore that some scholars have linked the disappearance of the Ark and the cherubim with one of these invasions, in particular with one of the first two.

We add a fourth nation to the list—Rome. When the Second Temple was destroyed by the Romans they also took some of the holy vessels and brought them to Rome.

Each of these four nations, at various times, plundered the Temple in Jerusalem and took out certain Temple vessels. We will now consider the possibility that one of these foreign invaders took with them the Ark of the Covenant.

CHAPTER 19

DID THE EGYPTIANS
STEAL THE ARK?

One suggested nation that may have taken the Ark of the Covenant is Egypt. This is the view that was portrayed in the movie "Raiders of the Lost Ark." Indiana Jones suggested that the Ark was removed by Pharaoh Shishak of Egypt in 926 B.C. and brought to the city of Tanis where a sandstorm, lasting an entire year, buried the city. The plot of the movie concerns the discovery of Tanis and the finding of the lost Ark. This idea made for the most exciting movie one could imagine to see with the forces of good, embodied in the person of Indiana Jones, fighting the forces of evil, represented by the Nazis.

There are those who genuinely hold this view:

The historic importance of the Ark ceased after Temple times. One view is that when Pharaoh Shishak carried off Rehoboam, King of Judah, into Egypt, he also took along the Ark as a trophy of war. From that time on it disappeared from Jewish life.[1]

Temple Plundered

King Solomon had been dead only five years when the Temple and its sacred items were plundered. The nation had been divided into the northern kingdom of Israel and the southern kingdom of Judah. Judah was the weaker of the two.

In the fifth year of the reign of Reheboam, Solomon's successor, Pharaoh Shishak (Sheshonk I) of Egypt invaded Israel and Judah. Shishak was the ruler of the 22nd Dynasty (ca. 945-924 B.C.).

The Bible gives the account of Shishak's siege in the following manner.

> And it happened in the fifth year of King Rehoboam, that Shishak king of Egypt came against Jerusalem, because they had transgressed against the Lord, with twelve hundred chariots, sixty thousand horsemen, and people without number who came to him out of Egypt— the Lubim and the Sukkiim and the Ethiopians. And they took the fortified cities of Judah and came to Jerusalem. Then Shemiah the prophet came to Rehoboam and the leaders of Judah, who were gathered together in Jerusalem because of Shishak, and said to them, "Thus says the Lord: 'You have forsaken Me, and therefore I also have left you in the hand of Shishak,' " So the leaders . . . and the king humbled themselves; and they said, "The Lord is righteous." Now when the Lord saw that they humbled themselves, the word of the Lord came to Shemiah saying, "They have humbled themselves; therefore I will not destroy them, but I will grant them some deliverance. My wrath shall not be poured out on Jerusalem by the hand of Shishak. Nevertheless they will be his servants, that they may distinguish My service from the service of the kingdoms of the nations. So Shishak king of Egypt came up against Jerusalem, and took away the treasures of the house of the Lord and the treasures of the king's house; he took everything. He also carried away the gold shields which Solomon had made (2 Chronicles 12:2-9).

Returning to Egypt, Shishak built a temple to his god Amon (Amun) at Karnak. Shishak's own record of his campaign is inscribed on the south wall of this great Temple. The record included a list of the walled cities of Judah as well as images of the captured Israelites that were taken back to Egypt as slaves. He is described as presenting 156 cities of Palestine to his god Amon.

Shishak's gold masked mummy was found in Tanis in 1939[2] in a sarcophagus (burial vault) of silver encased in solid gold (possibly some of Solomon's gold which he had taken from Jerusalem).

Took the Ark?

The possibility that the Egyptians stole the Ark of the Covenant is, however, highly unlikely when the facts are examined. It is true Pharaoh Shishak came up against Jerusalem:

> Now it came about in the fifth year of King Rehoboam, that Shishak the king of Egypt came up against Jerusalem. And he took away the treasures of the house of the Lord and the treasures of the king's house, and he took everything, even taking all the shields of gold which Solomon had made (1 Kings 14:25,26).

It is mentioned that he took away all the valuable articles in the Temple, however, no one article is specifically detailed. We read in 2 Chronicles 13:11 that the Golden Lampstand, the Menorah, as well as the Table of Showbread were still being used in the Temple after the invasion.

> And they burn to the Lord every morning and every evening burnt sacrifices and sweet incense; they also set the showbread in order on the pure table and the lampstand of gold with its lamps to burn every evening (2 Chronicles 13:11).

This mention of the Lampstand and the Table of Showbread occurred shortly *after* the invasion of Shishak, giving inference that he did *not* get all of the valuable artifacts connected with the Temple. The Menorah weighed over fifty pounds[3] and was made of pure gold.

> He also made the lampstand of pure gold; of hammered work he made the lampstand. Its shaft, its branches, its bowls, its ornamental knobs, and its flowers were of the same piece . . .
> Of a talent of pure gold he made it with all its utensils (Exodus 37:17,24).

As the Menorah would have been an obvious prize, this seems to indicate that Shishak did not get any of the vessels that were in the Holy Place or the Holy of Holies. As we will see in our next chapter, what Shishak actually took were only the holy vessels in the Temple treasury, not in the Temple proper.

Existed Later

As we have already mentioned, the Scripture attests to the fact that the Ark was still in existence at the time of Josiah (about 620 B.C.), hundreds of years after Shishak's invasion.

He also said to the Levites who taught all Israel and who were holy to the Lord, 'Put the holy ark in the house which Solomon the son of David king of Israel built; it will be a burden on your shoulders no longer. Now serve the Lord your God and His people Israel' (2 Chronicles 35:3).

This being the case, the theory that Shishak took the Ark to Egypt in 926 B.C. seems to be ruled out by the Scriptures.

Hezekiah

Some have alleged that the Ark was removed to Egypt during the reign of King Hezekiah (around 700 B.C). While Hezekiah was ruling in Judah, the Assyrian army was advancing toward Jerusalem destroying cities on the way. Many of the inhabitants of these toppled cities took refuge in Jerusalem.

Fearing for his safety and that of the city of Jerusalem, Hezekiah sent messengers to the Assyrian king asking him to forgive their rebellion. The Assyrian King Sennacherib demanded 300 talents of silver and 30 talents of gold from Hezekiah. The Scripture tells us that Hezekiah removed the golden ornaments of the Temple to meet the demand.

This, however, was not enough. When Sennacherib received the payment, he wanted more. The Assyrian army was then dispatched to Jerusalem.

Hezekiah hoped that the Lord would somehow intervene. The prophet Isaiah assured him that Assyria would not conquer them.

Isaiah's prediction came true. The Assyrians heard that the Egyptian army was advancing on them. They left Jerusalem and hurried south to do battle.

Paid with Ark?

Some have suggested that the Ark of the Covenant was among the items of gold that Hezekiah paid to the Assyrians. This would have placed the Ark in the hands of the Assyrians. With the defeat of Assyria by Egypt, the

Ark, it is contended, went back to Egypt with the conquering army.

It is not stated, however, in the Scripture that Hezekiah gave the Ark to the Assyrians. It was only the golden ornaments of the temple that were used to pay the tribute. Furthermore, there is no record of the Ark ever having been in Egypt. Hence, this theory does not seem to have any plausibility of being true.

Add to this the reference of the Ark still being in existence during the time of Josiah, the Egyptian connection falls flat.

We need to find a better answer as to what happened to the Ark of the Covenant.

Endnotes for Chapter 19

1. Nathan Ausbel, *Pictorial History of the Jews*, New York, Crown Books, 1953, p. 34.

2. The movie *Raiders of the Lost Ark* was set in the same time frame as this discovery.

3. A talent of gold weighed about 75 pounds.

Concerning Shishak's march on Jerusalem C. J. Ball notes:

There is no notice of any sack of Jerusalem, nor as in later cases, of any destruction of the Temple, or even plunder of its decorations. The record seems to imply surrender to those cities and its treasures. The idea sometimes advanced, that, like the capture of Rome by the Gauls, the invasion of Shishak destroyed all ancient monuments and archives, has therefore no historical support from this passage; and with it many conclusions derived from it . . . must pass away (C. J. Ball *Ellicott's Commentary on the Whole Bible*, edited by Charles John Ellicott, Vol 3, 1 Kings-Esther, n.d., p. 70).

James Montgomery adds:

It is generally recognized for the other cities which Shishak "took", that it was rather their tribute he received; so Jerusalem was not actually taken, but the king would have paid a sumptuous indemnity in specie and *objects d'art*, like the gold shields (J. A. Montgomery, *The Book of Kings*, Edinburgh: T&T Clark, 1951, p. 270).

Therefore the idea of the Ark in Tanis, the theme of *Raiders of the Lost Ark*, does not have much merit:

In the movie, the ark was supposedly carried away from Jerusalem by invading Egyptians and hidden in the ancient North African city of Tanis. But biblical archaeologists find that scenario unlikely. . . It's improbable that the ark would have been taken to Egypt, said [Old Testament specialist William] LaSor. Jews wouldn't have fled to Tanis, which according to their tradition, is one of the cities they built during their years of slavery. Also if the Jewish priests were trying to hide their precious objects from the enemy, they wouldn't have taken it that far to hide, LaSor said (Laurinda Keys, In Search of the Real Lost Ark, Associated Press, 1981).

CHAPTER 20

DID JEHOASH TAKE THE ARK TO ISRAEL?

When King Solomon built the magnificent Temple in Jerusalem that housed the Ark of the Covenant, the nation was prospering. The wisdom and wealth of Solomon was known to the ends of the earth. Though he was blessed by God, Solomon acted foolishly in his later years by marrying foreign wives. These wives brought their pagan gods with them to Jerusalem. Altars were built to these gods within sight of the Temple. God would not allow this sin to go unpunished.

As already mentioned, a few short years after Solomon's death, the kingdom was divided between north and south. Although Israel and Judah were once united, from time to time they had cause to war with each other. The Bible records that on one such occasion the "Temple vessels" were taken. The account is given to us in both Kings and Chronicles:

> Then Jehoash king of Israel, captured Amaziah, at Beth Shemesh; and he went to Jerusalem, and broke down the wall of Jerusalem from the Gate of Ephraim to the Corner Gate—four hundred cubits. And he took all the gold and silver, all the articles that were found in the house of the Lord, and in the treasure of the king's house, and hostages, and returned to Samaria (2 Kings 14:13,14).

> And he took all the gold and silver, all the articles that were found in the house of God with Obed-Edom, the treasures of the kings house, and hostages and returned to Samaria (2 Chronicles 25:24).

There have been those who have suggested that the Ark of the Covenant was among those Temple vessels taken by Jehoash (Joash), King of Israel. The Ark, it is contended, was then brought back to Samaria and nothing further was ever heard of it. L. Elliot Binns writes:

> Various suggestions have been put forward to account for the disappearance of the ark. It may have perished in some invasion. Perhaps it was taken to Jerusalem by Joash, King of Israel, in 785 B.C. when he carried off the temple treasures (2 K. xiv. 14). He may have felt, as Cheyne suggests (Enc.Bib. 306), that he was reclaiming 'the long-lost treasure of the Ephraimitish sanctuary at Shiloh.' If this suggestion is a sound one, and on the face of it there is nothing against it beyond the failure of the Biblical writers actually to mention it, it may be that the ark finally disappeared with the destruction of Shiloh referred to in vii. 12. The possession of the ark by the Southern Kingdom may have been a sore point with the men of Israel.[1]

There are three basic problems with the theory that Jehoash took the Ark when he plundered the Temple.

First, there is no reference in Scripture that the Ark was taken during this siege by Jehoash. It seems incredible that the Bible would not mention the capture of the Ark, particularly when it was Israel, the northern kingdom, fighting Judah, the southern kingdom. Since the Scripture had earlier recorded the Ark's capture between Israel and the Philistines (1 Samuel 6), we would assume it would have also documented another capture if it had occurred. The fact that the Scripture does not mention the Ark among the vessels taken gives weight to the argument that it was not taken at that time.

Temple Treasury

Second, this raiding of the Temple did not seem to reach the Holy of Holies. It is possible that the items were taken from the Temple treasury, and not from the Temple proper.[2] Scholar Menahem Haran notes that there were other vessels connected with the Temple that were deemed holy.

Vessels were kept in the Jerusalem temple not only in the court and in the sanctums, but also in the temple treasuries. These treasuries were always mentioned cojointly with the kings house' and seem to be similar in nature. The vessels in the temple treasuries were also deemed holy, though they were certainly less sacred than those housed in the temple sanctums. . .

Shishak and Jehoash did not even enter the temples outer sanctum, certainly not the inner one; . . .

The invasions of Shishak and Jehoash have, therefore, nothing to do with the temple sanctums, and it would be entirely inaccurate to associate them with the disappearance of the ark and the cherubim. These invaders did no more than what the kings of Judah sometimes ventured to do themselves.[3]

If Haran's argument is valid, then the Ark would not have been the object of Israel's plunder.

Finally, we have the statement in 2 Chronicles 35:3, mentioned previously, that the Ark had been returned to the Temple during the time of Josiah. This event occurred hundreds of years after the Ark was supposedly taken by Jehoash, never to be heard of again.[4]

Though the plundering of the Temple by Jehoash has been thought to include the Ark, the evidence for this is lacking.

Endnotes for Chapter 20

1. L. Elliott Binns, *The Book of the Prophet Jeremiah*, London, Methuen and Company, Ltd. 1919, p. 35.

2. C. J. Ball notes:

>   This expression seems to hint there was not much treasure to carry off (C. J. Ball in *Ellicott's Commentary on the Whole Bible*, edited by Charles John Ellicott, Vol 3, 1 Kings-Esther, n.d., p. 447).

3. Menahem Haran, *Temples and Temple-Service in Ancient Israel*, Oxford, Claredon Press, 1978, p. 285.

The Judean Kings were in the habit of filling and emptying their treasure houses. King David dedicated much of the spoil he obtained to the Lord (2 Samuel 8:7,12). These items, including gold, silver, and bronze vessels, were put in the Temple treasury by Solomon.

>   Thus all the work that King Solomon had done for the house of the Lord was finished; and Solomon brought in the things which his father David had dedicated: the silver and gold and the furnishings. And he put them in the treasuries of the house of the Lord (1 Kings 7:51).

Most of the treasure that was placed in the Temple came from gifts from the Kings of Judah. From their spoils of war, as well as from other sources, the kings of Judah kept the treasury full.

As discussed in the last chapter, the Temple treasury was emptied by Pharoah Shishak. Later Kings of Judah, Abijam and Asa made up some of the loss and replenished the treasury.

>   He [Asa] brought into the house of the Lord the things which his father had dedicated, and the things which he himself had dedicated: silver and gold and utensils (1 Kings 15:15).

Unfortunately, Asa emptied the treasure house to pay King Ben Hadad of Damascus. The Temple was then again filled with gifts from other kings of Judah including Jehoshaphat and Ahaziah.

4. One could argue that Jehoash did take the Ark at that time and that it was brought back to Jerusalem some years later with the Bible recording neither the capture nor the return. This supposition seems highly unlikely.

CHAPTER 21

DID THE BABYLONIANS TAKE THE ARK?

Since the last Biblical mention of the Ark was shortly before the destruction of Jerusalem by the Babylonians, it is possible that the Ark was carried off to Babylon.

The story of the Babylonians and the Temple treasures go back some one hundred years before Jerusalem and the temple were destroyed.

Israel was forced to pay tribute to Babylon, and King Hezekiah made a tragic mistake by showing Merodach Baladan, the ambassador from Babylon, the temple's treasures:

And Hezekiah was pleased, and showed them all his treasure house, the silver and the gold and the spices and the precious oil and his whole armory and all that was found in his treasuries. There was nothing in his house, nor in his dominion, that Hezekiah did not show them. Then Isaiah the prophet came to King Hezekiah and said to him, 'What did these men say, and from where have they come to you?' And Hezekiah said, 'They have come to me from a far country, from Babylon.' And he said, 'What have they seen in your house?' So Hezekiah answered, 'They have seen all that is in my house, there is nothing among my treasures that I have not shown them.' Then Isaiah said to Hezekiah. 'Hear the word of the Lord of hosts.' 'Behold, the days are coming when all that is in your house, and all that your fathers have laid

up in store to this day shall be carried to Babylon;
nothing shall be left! says the Lord' (Isaiah 39:2-6).

This prophecy indicates that nothing shall be left in
the Temple. The precious vessels shall be taken to Babylon.
This being the case, it is possible that the Ark was taken to
Babylon along with the other treasures from the Temple
when the Temple was destroyed. Nineteenth century
scholar, George Bush writes:

> It seems that the ark, with the other precious things of
> the Temple, became the spoil of Nebuchadnezzar, and was
> taken to Babylon; and it does not appear that it was
> restored at the end of the captivity, or that any new one
> was made.[1]

After the inhabitants of the kingdom of Judah were
taken to Babylon, Nebuchadnezzar, the Babylonian King,
put some of their treasures in his Temple.

> And the Lord gave Jehoiakim king of Judah into his
> hand, with some of the articles of the house of God, which
> he carried into the land of Shinar to the house of his god;
> and he brought articles into the treasure house of his god
> (Daniel 1:2).

It is interesting to note that Daniel tells us that
Nebuchadnezzar only took some of the vessels with him.
This may infer that the Ark was not among the sacred
vessels taken to Babylon.

Neither Daniel nor any of the prophets that lived
during the period of the Babylonian Captivity mentioned
the Ark of the Covenant being taken by Nebuchadnezzar.

The Old Testament, as well as first century writer
Flavius Josephus, informs us that all the vessels taken to
Babylon were returned to Jerusalem before the Second
Temple was completed.

2 Esdras

The apocryphal book of 2 Esdras does mention the Ark
being taken to Babylon.[2] It records the people lamenting at
the plunder of the holy vessels, including the Ark.

> You see how our sanctuary has been laid waste our
> altar demolished, and our temple destroyed. Our harps
> are unstrung, our hymns silenced, our shouts of joy cut

short; the light of the sacred lamp is out, and the ark of our covenant has been taken as spoil (2 Esdras 10:21,22).

Since 2 Esdras was written some 600 years after the destruction of the Temple, the historical accuracy of this reference is doubted. There is no other record of the Ark being brought to Babylon. It is not listed in the items taken nor in the items returned. Though the Ark could have been carried there by Nebuchadnezzar's armies, it is strange that nothing from Biblical or Babylonian sources records this. Some of the later Jewish writers believed the Ark went to Babylon as Menahem Haran notes:

Talmudic sages also held that the ark was taken along into the Babylonian exile but this . . . was based on nothing more than midrashic inferences.[3]

Some scholars believe Nebuchadnezzar only took the vessels of the outer court. Writing about Nebuchadnezzar, Menahem Haran states:

It seems, however that he [Nebuchadnezzar] was the first to penetrate the Temple, that is, to enter the outer sanctum. Of him alone it is said that he cut in pieces all the vessels of gold which Solomon, king of Israel had made in the Temple. Thus the vessels of the treasures were taken by him as they were while those of the Temple underwent deformation, their precious metals only serving as war booty . . . It seems likely that he took only the vessels of the Temple court.[4]

Conclusion

There is no solid historical evidence that the Ark was ever taken to Babylon by King Nebuchadnezzar. The Biblical writers living at that time, Daniel, Jeremiah, and Ezekiel, do not mention it. Neither do the books of Kings and Chronicles. Babylonian history is also silent as to the fate of the Ark. There is no known claim in Babylonian chronicles of the capture or destruction of the Ark. We only have the testimony of the apocryphal book of 2 Esdras which was written long after the fact.

Though some of the later Jewish interpreters thought the Ark was captured by the Babylonians, there is no documentation of this. Thus there is not much solid evidence that the Ark was taken to Babylon.

Endnotes for Chapter 21

1. George Bush, *Notes on the Book of Exodus*, Volume, 1,
Boston, Henry A. Young & Co., 1841, p. 91.

2. Esdras was written at the end of the 1st century A.D.
M.A. Knibb writes:

> This is a Jewish apocalypse, probably composed in
> Hebrew and dating from toward the end of the reign of the
> Emperor Domitian (A.D. 81-90) . . .
> The mention of the Ark is an historical allusion
> appropriate to the supposed setting of 2 Esdras 3-14 in
> the sixth century B.C., not to its actual setting at the end
> of the first century A.D. The Ark was apparently
> destroyed at the time of the destruction of Jerusalem in
> 587 B.C., if not earlier, and in any event nothing is known
> of it after this date . . .
> In the case of the vessels, however, the author was
> probably thinking of their seizure by Titus in his own day.
> (M.A. Knibb, *The First And Second Books of Esdras*,
> Cambridge, At the University Press, 1979, pp. 76,
> 222,223).

3. Menahem Haran, *Temples and Temple-Service in Ancient
Israel*, Oxford, Claredon Press, 1978, p. 285.

4. Haran ibid. p. 285.

Edwin Yamauchi wrote:

> Conquerors customarily carried off the statues of the
> gods of conquered cities. The Hittites took the statue of
> Marduk when they conquered the city of Babylon. The
> Philistines took the ark of the Jews and placed it in the
> temple of Dagon (1 Sam 5;2). As the Jews did not have a
> statue of the Lord, Nebuchadnezzar carried off the temple
> goods instead. The Hebrew of 2 Kings 24:13 indicates that
> he cut up the vessels of gold, no doubt the larger ones, to
> facilitate their transportation (cf. 2 Kings 25:13; Jer
> 52:17) (Edwin Yamauchi, *The Expositors Bible
> Commentary*, Volume 4, Frank C. Gaebelein General
> Editor, Zondervan, Grand Rapids, 1988, p. 604).

CHAPTER 22

WAS THE ARK TAKEN BY THE ROMANS?

Did the Romans take the Ark of the Covenant when they destroyed the city of Jerusalem in A.D. 70? Though there are those who contend the Ark was in the Second Temple, convincing evidence is lacking.

Procession

After the Second Temple was destroyed, the victorious Romans paraded their spoils before their people. Flavius Josephus described a procession of hundreds of Jewish prisoners as they marched through Rome. He mentioned the vast wealth from Jerusalem that was deposited in Rome's Temple of Peace. This includes the Golden Table where the Bread of Presence was kept, the Menorah—the Golden seven-branched Lampstand, trumpets and cups, as well as scrolls of the law. These vessels were constructed during the time of the cleansing of the Temple by Judas Maccabaeus in 164 B.C. Less than 250 years after their construction, they were taken into captivity.

This procession was memorialized in stone on the famous Arch of Titus. What is missing from the Arch of Titus and from Josephus' description of the procession is the Ark of the Covenant.

Arch of Titus Vespasianus

Arch of Titus

The Arch of Titus was built in honor of Titus Vespasian, conqueror of Jerusalem and later Emperor of Rome. Erected after his death, the Arch of Titus commemorated this great victory.[1]

Though some writers have claimed the Arch of Titus depicted the Ark, scholar William Knight says they were mistaken.

Nothing is said of the Ark of the Covenant, which Pitiscus and others say was carried in the procession; probably mistaking this Table for the Ark, as has been done by many writers. For Jewish authorities are generally agreed that there was no Ark in the second Temple. Josephus says there was nothing at all in the Holy of Holies in his time. Pompey, upon entering, found it utterly empty: a circumstance which Lucan is supposed to refer to, when, in speaking of Judea's subjection to his hero, he calls her the worshipper of an unknown God.[2]

Was Another Ark Made?

There have been those who have suggested that after the original Ark of the Covenant was lost around the time of the Babylonian captivity, another Ark was made and placed in the Second Temple. The Ark, as we have seen, was lost as well as were all the sacred vessels: the Golden Lampstand, the Table of Showbread and the Altar of Incense. We know that all of these items (except the Ark) were rebuilt for the Second Temple. If the Jews built another Golden Lampstand, Table of Showbread and the Altar of Incense, why not another Ark of the Covenant? This suggestion comes from two of the most learned scholars of the seventeenth century, John Lightfoot and Humphrey Prideaux. Prideaux wrote:

For in the second Temple there was also an Ark made of the same shape and dimensions, with the first and put in the same place. But though it was substituted in its stead . . . yet it had none of its Prerogative or Honours conferred upon it. For there were no Tables of the Law, no Aaron's Rod, no pot of Manna in it, no appearance of the Divine Glory over it, no Oracles given from it.[3]

According to Prideaux, this second "ark" would have been empty of any of the original contents and would have not been surrounded by the Divine glory of God.

Though the Jewish writers living at the time of the Second Temple deny the Ark was present, Prideaux reckoned that the Ark was necessary for their worship:

> That there was any Ark in the second Temple, many of the Jewish writers do deny, and say that the whole service on the great day of Expiation was performed in the second Temple, not before the Ark but before the stone, on which the Ark stood in the first Temple. But since on their building of the second Temple they found it necessary for the carrying on of their worship in it to make a new Altar of Incense, a new Shew-bread Table, and a new Candlestick, instead of those which the Babylonians had destroyed, though none of them could have been consecrated, as in the first Temple, there is reason to believe, that they made a new Ark also.[4]

He argues that they must have made a new Ark since all the other furniture in the Temple revolved around the Ark in the Holy of Holies. Without the Ark, all the other furnishings were meaningless. Prideaux writes:

> Since the Holy of Holies, and the Veil that was drawn before it, were wholly for the sake of the Ark, what need had there been of these in the second Temple, if there had not been the other also?[5]

This position has not won many converts. Some have suggested that there may have been some type of receptacle for the Law in the Holy of Holies. John Lawson and John M. Wilson write:

> It is not unlikely that there may have been in the second temple, as is found still in all Jewish synagogues, an ark or coffer in which is kept a copy of the Hebrew scriptures in the form of an ancient roll. One great presumption against the existence of an ark of the covenant in the second temple is the striking fact that, in the representation of the temple furniture which is sculpted on the triumphal arch of Titus, still to be seen at Rome, there is no figure of an ark.[6]

Prideaux, on the one hand, admitted that the Arch of Titus did not *depict* the Ark. He believed the Table carved on the Arch was the Table of Shewbread, not the Ark.

Relief on the Arch of Titus

Close-up of Table on relief of Arch of Titus

It plainly appears to have been the Shew-Bread Table, especially from the two cups on top of it. For two such cups filled with Frankincense were always put upon the Shew-bread Table, but never upon the Ark.[7]

On the other hand, he believed the Arch of Titus did give silent testimony to the Ark's existence. His reasoning was as follows:

Josephus, who was present during the procession, testified of three objects being carried by the Romans, first, there was the table of Showbread, Second, the Golden Lampstand, and third, the Law. The first two items are depicted on the Arch in the same order, the last item is not found on the Arch, possibly because they ran out of room.

Also depicted on the Arch are three title boards. The purpose of the title boards was to describe for the multitudes watching what the objects were and where they were taken from. There is a title board before the Table of Showbread, there is a second title board before the Golden Lampstand. There is a third title board depicted but there the Arch ends and we do not know what this third one was explaining. Flavius Josephus called it the Law. Prideaux reckoned it was not some ordinary copy of the Law, of which there were many, but rather a sacred copy of the Law, that had been kept in the Temple. Prideaux concluded that the only container that could house such a sacred copy of the Law was the Ark. Hence a replica of the Ark must have existed during the time of the Second Temple. Just what happened to this "copy" of the Ark, we are not told.

William Knight shows that the third object on the Arch was known at one time.

There is one above the Table, another near the Candlestick, and a third, which must have indicated the Book of the Law; which, however, is no longer visible. Villapanda thinks that the Book was ommitted, as a less imposing object than the other spoils. Prideaux suggests that it was not inserted for want of sufficient space to introduce it, together with the coffer in which it was kept. Dr Cardwell seems to think the book was nothing more than a tablet of gold, or of some other metal, inscribed with some portions of the Divine Law; of which, he says, there were many in the Temple, and one more important than the rest, which had the Ten Commandments engraved upon it. None of these conjectures is satisfactory. . . Biondo or Blondus [who lived in early part of the 15 century] . . . for many years the popes secretary tells us in his work *De Roma Triumphante*, that the Book of the Jewish Law was extant in his time amongst the marble sculptures on the Arch, together with the golden Table and Candlestick: and it is a curious circumstance which may account in some measure for the doubts and conjectures above, that in the later editions of Biondo's work this notice of the sculptured spoils is wanting.[8]

Prideaux's logic does not fit with the known facts. *Smith's Bible Dictionary* comments:

> Prideaux's argument that there *must* have been an ark in the second Temple is of no weight against express testimony, such as that of Josephus . . . and Tacitus . . . confirmed by the Rabbins, who state that a sacred stone called by them a stone of drinking, stood in its stead; as well as by the marked silence of those apocryphal books which enumerate the rest of the principle furniture of the sanctuary as present.[9]

Conclusion

The idea that the Ark was in the Second Temple and then later taken to Rome does not have any solid historical basis. Neither does the idea of a second Ark having been constructed. All the reliable records that come down to us say the Ark was not to be found in the Second Temple. Its disappearance occurred before the Second Temple was constructed. We, then, must look elsewhere for the final destination of this sacred object.

Endnotes for Chapter 22

1.   The arch of Titus was erected after the death of Titus Vespasian, conqueror of Jerusalem who later became emperor of Rome. William Knight writes:

> As to the precise date of the erection of the Arch of Titus we have no information. But if not the first it was one of the earliest of those twenty arches with which Rome was once adorned. . . . it was the practice of Romans in very early times to erect arches to commemorate their victories. . . The Arch of Titus is said to have had originally two inscriptions . . . one of these inscriptions is still legible . . . From this inscription it appears that the arch was erected to Titus by the Senate and the people, but that it was not erected till after he became emperor . . . nor was it erected till after his death (William Knight, *The Arch of Titus*, London, Religious Tract Society, 1896, pp.64,65).

Knight also writes:

> The sculptures on the other side of the Arch represent the spoils which were taken from the Temple. They are borne aloft by Roman soldiers, not by Jewish captives, as some writers represent them; for they are crowned with laurel, and they have in their hands the short and pointless spears that had been given them when they started (Knight, ibid. p. 84).

2.   William Knight, ibid. p. 84.

3.   Humphrey Prideaux, *Old and New Testament Connected*, Part 1, Vol. 1, 10th edition, 1729, p. 207.

4.   Prideaux, ibid. p. 208.

5.   Prideaux, ibid. p. 209.

6.   John Lawson and John M. Wilson, *A Cyclopaedia of Biblical Geography, Biography, Natural History, and General Knowledge*, Vol 1, Aaron to Egypt, Edinburgh, A Fullarton & Co., 1867, p. 184.

7.   Prideaux, ibid. p. 209.

8.   Knight, ibid. pp. 85,86.

9.   *Dr. William Smith's Dictionary of the Bible*, Revised and edited by Ezra Abbot, Vol 1, 1872, p. 156).

INTRODUCTION

HAS THE ARK BEEN FOUND?

We have reviewed four possible destinations of the Ark and found none of them very convincing. The idea that some foreign invader whisked the Ark away has no solid historical basis.

If the Ark was not taken away by a foreign power then what are the other possibilities that we face? The Ark could have been removed from the Holy of Holies by friendly hands who did not want to see it become the war spoils of some unfriendly nation.

Along this line, many theories have arisen as to what happened to the Ark of the Covenant. Three popular ones include: hidden by Jeremiah on Mt. Nebo in Jordan, taken away to Ethiopia by Solomon's son Menelik, or hidden in some secret place beneath the Temple Mount in Jerusalem. All of these have a long tradition of being the hiding place of the Ark.

Furthermore, since 1981, there have been claims that the Ark has actually been discovered in each of these spots! Each of these claims have, in turn, received international attention.

We are now going to look at each of these possible resting places for the Ark and determine which, if any, could lay claim to the its possible whereabouts.

CHAPTER 23

HAS THE ARK BEEN FOUND ON MOUNT NEBO?

In 1981, the world was entertained with the extraordinarily successful adventure film, "Raiders of the Lost Ark." Several months after the film's release, and while the Ark of the Covenant was still on the minds of millions of people, news came out that an American, Tom Crotser, had found the lost Ark in the country of Jordan. Worldwide attention was given to this claim. With seemingly perfect timing, the Ark, which had been missing for over 2,500 years, was discovered soon after the film's release. The excitement over the Ark's discovery, however, died down rather quickly when serious questions arose as to whether Tom Crotser had actually found the long lost Ark.

The story of the Ark being hidden in this area of the world takes us back to the time before the Ark was lost.

Ancient Tradition

There is an ancient tradition that the Ark of the Covenant was taken by the prophet Jeremiah, and hidden in a cave in Moab. Knowing the Babylonians were about to destroy both the city of Jerusalem and the Temple, Jeremiah, it is said, hid the Ark to keep it from being captured. In the Apocryphal book of 2 Maccabees we read the following:

The records show that is was the prophet Jeremiah who ordered the exiles to hide the fire, as has been mentioned; also that, having given them the law, he charged them not to neglect the ordinances of the Lord, or be led astray by the sight of gold and silver with all their finery. In similar words he appealed to them not to abandon the law. Furthermore, this document records that, prompted by a divine message, the prophet gave orders that the Tent of Meeting and the ark should go with him. Then he went away to the mountain from the top of which Moses saw God's promised land. When he reached the mountain, Jeremiah found a cave-dwelling; he carried the tent, the ark, and the incense-altar into it, then blocked up the entrance. Some of his companions came to mark out the way, but were unable to find it. When Jeremiah learnt of this he reprimanded them. 'The place shall remain unknown,' he said 'until God finally gathers his people together and shows mercy to them. Then the Lord will bring these things to light again, and the glory of the Lord will appear with the cloud, as it was seen both in the time of Moses and when Solomon prayed that the shrine might be worthily consecrated' (2 Maccabees 2:1-8).

This account in 2 Maccabees claims to have been drawn from previous documents. According to this reference, Jeremiah hid the Ark of the Covenant in a secret place until the "last days." In this reference the Tabernacle, the Ark and the Altar of Sacrifice are classed together. We do know that Jeremiah was taken to Tanis in Egypt, after the fall of Jerusalem, by a remnant of the Jews (Jeremiah 42:1-43:7). It is possible, therefore, that he hid the Ark in a cave along the way.

But the source of this report, 2 Maccabees, contains some legendary material and quite possibly the story of the Ark is in that category as well.[1] While 1 Maccabees is a very reliable source of historical information, 2 Maccabees contains many questionable elements. This alone makes the report suspect. It is, however, an ancient description of what happened to the Ark and hence it cannot be ignored.

Burial Place of Moses

The Mount Nebo area, or Mt. Pisgah, where the Ark is supposed to have been hidden, was the burial place of Moses.[2]

> Then Moses went up from the plains of Moab to Mount
> Nebo, to the top of Pisgah, which is across from Jericho,
> And the Lord showed him all the land of Gilead as far as
> Dan . . . So Moses the servant of the Lord died there in the
> land of Moab, according to the word of the Lord. And He
> buried him in a valley in the land of Moab opposite Beth
> Peor; but no one knows his grave to this day
> (Deuteronomy 34:1,5,6).

The exact burial place of Moses has never been found
and is subject to much debate.

Modern-Day Searches

The account recorded in 2 Maccabees has, over the
years, led people to explore the Mt. Nebo region. This
mountain is located in present-day Jordan, some thirty five
miles southwest of Amman. Mt. Nebo is in the Abarim
Mountains, a range which runs in a general north and
south direction about ten miles east of the most northern
part of the Dead Sea. Mt. Nebo rises to about 4,000 above the
Dead Sea making it about 2,700 feet above Sea Level.

The tradition of searching on Mt. Nebo goes back, at
least, to the beginning of this century. Enter a colorful
character by the name of A.F. Futterer. Futterer, dubbed the
"Golden Ark explorer," was somewhat of an eccentric. He
looked for the Ark in the Mt. Nebo region in the 1920's.
Futterer recorded his reasoning for looking for the Ark in
that area.

> I acquainted myself with the Ark's complete history. In
> the year 1594 B.C.E. Moses made the Golden Ark at Mt.
> Sinai. . . 981 years later Prophet Jeremiah hid it near the
> tomb of Moses on Mt. Nebo (about 613 B.C.E.). Both
> Moses and Jeremiah were Levites, the only tribe of people
> allowed by God to handle God's sacred Ark. . .
> During this period of 981 years the wanderings of the
> Ark covered approximately 700 miles of territory in
> twelve prolonged stopping places. . . beginning in the
> center of the Arabian deserts (Petra) and finishing upon
> old Mt. Nebo from whence the Ark has never been taken
> since Jeremiah hid it. In fact, Jeremiah prophesied that it
> would remain there until God gather His People Israel
> back into Palestine, which gathering began quite recently
> since the world war when Lord Allenby took Jerusalem
> from the Turk in 1917. This gave me my first inspiration
> to go to Palestine and search for the Ark, though I have
> had it in my mind for twenty-five years.[3]

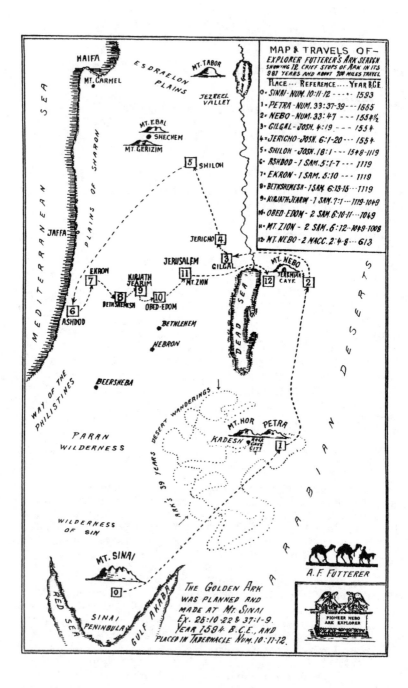

MAP & TRAVELS OF —
EXPLORER FUTTERER'S ARK SEARCH
SHOWING 12 CHIEF STOPS OF ARK IN ITS
981 YEARS AND ABOUT 700 MILES TRAVEL

PLACE --- REFERENCE .... YEAR B.C.E.
0 - SINAI - NUM. 10:11-12 - - - - 1593
1 - PETRA - NUM. 33:37-39 - - - 1555
2 - NEBO - NUM. 33:47 - - - 1554½
3 - GILGAL - JOSH. 4:19 - - - 1554
4 - JERICHO - JOSH. 6:1-20 - - - 1554
5 - SHILOH - JOSH. 18:1 - - - 1548-1119
6 - ASHDOD - 1 SAM. 5:1-7 - - - 1119
7 - EKRON - 1 SAM. 5:10 - - - 1119
8 - BETHSHEMESH - 1 SAM. 6:13-15 - - - 1119
9 - KIRJATH-JEARIM - 1 SAM. 7:1 - - - 1119-1049
10 - OBED-EDOM - 2 SAM. 6:10-11 - - - 1049
11 - MT. ZION - 2 SAM. 6:12 - 1049-1008
12 - MT. NEBO - 2 MACC. 2:4-8 - - - 613

HAIFA
MT. CARMEL
ESDRAELON PLAINS
MT. TABOR
JEZREEL VALLEY
MT. EBAL
SHECHEM
MT. GERIZIM

MEDITERRANEAN SEA
PLAINS OF SHARON
JAFFA

5 SHILOH

JERICHO 4
3 GILGAL
JERUSALEM
11 MT. ZION
EKRON
7
KIRJATH JEARIM
9
6 ASHDOD
8 BETHSHEMESH
10 OBED-EDOM

MT. NEBO
12 JEREMIAH CAVE
2

BETHLEHEM
HEBRON

DEAD SEA

ARABIAN DESERTS

WAY OF THE PHILISTINES

BEERSHEBA

PARAN WILDERNESS

ARK'S 39 YEARS DESERT WANDERINGS

MT. HOR PETRA
KADESH
ROCK CAVE CITY
1

WILDERNESS OF SIN

MT. SINAI

0

RED SEA

SINAI PENINSULA

GULF AKABA

A. F. FUTTERER

THE GOLDEN ARK
WAS PLANNED AND
MADE AT MT. SINAI
EX. 25:10-22 & 37:1-9.
YEAR 1594 B.C.E. AND
PLACED IN TABERNACLE NUM. 10:11-12.

PIONEER NEBO
ARK EXPLORER

Why Buried at Mt Nebo?

Futterer believed there were good reasons why Jeremiah hid the Ark where he did.

Jeremiah, being a Levite prophet, foresaw the disaster coming to the Jews and to Jerusalem (the destruction) and to the sacred vessels of the Temple, therefore he most naturally and sacredly hid them from the coming Babylonians. Jeremiah knew the entire Ark's history and knew well all about Levite Moses who had made it and he knew where Moses was (the old Ark maker and law giver), and for the Ark's sake, Jeremiah was told by God to climb the same mountain where Moses climbed up and saw the promised land and died and there God said to bury the Ark which Jeremiah did by selecting a cave as near as possible to the place where Moses was buried or perhaps in the same cave.[4]

Futterer's two year search led him to believe he had discovered the cave that held the Ark of the Covenant along with the Golden Lampstand (Menorah), the Golden Table of Showbread, and the actual tent of the Tabernacle. Futterer reckoned if he did find the Ark, he could not move it. He felt it necessary that only a member of the tribe of Levi should carry the Ark as ordered in the Bible.

In his book, *Palestine Speaks*, written in 1931, Futterer wrote of his experience of tracking down the Ark in the Holy Land.

I believe that the Golden Ark of the Covenant, the world's greatest and most valuable antique relic of all history, has been trailed to its lair (in my two years recent research work in the Holyland)—trailed to its last hiding place on Mt. Nebo where Jeremiah hid it about 2544 years ago. In verification of this I offer both the historical and as well as prophetic data.

I have collected convincing evidence enough to make it hard not to believe that the Ark will return to old Jerusalem. The return of the Ark would stagger the world; may change the belief of millions of people of all nations for the better; be the greatest blow skeptics ever received; and perhaps be the greatest modern proof of the authenticity of Holy Writ. The tablets of Sinai written 3535 years ago, now in the Ark, may bring to this whole world a feeling akin to Belshazzar, King of Babylon, on the night when he too saw God's "Handwriting" upon the walls of that famous city before its consummation, which made the King and all his nobles tremble with fear when that terrible warning: "Thou are weighed in the balances and found wanting" stared them in the face.[5]

Feeling he had discovered the Ark's location, Futterer attempted to solicit funds for a return trip to Mt. Nebo. The magazine *Biblical Archaeological Review* wrote:

> In a pamphlet Futterer published in 1927 he reports squeezing into a cave leading to a long vault or corridor with "hieroglyphics" on the walls. At the end of the corridor he found two locked doors. Futterer took note of the "hieroglyphics" and when he returned to Jerusalem, "a Hebrew scholar" deciphered his "hieroglyphic" signs "numerically." The numerical value of the signs (apparently they were interpreted as Hebrew letters which also have numerical values) totaled 1927, according to Futterer. He interpreted this to mean he would discover the Ark of the Covenant in 1927. After uncovering the Ark he planned "to build a Tourist Resort here out of these already prepared stones of old ruins." Futterer's pamphlet solicited funds for his project: "What will you give to see the lost Ark restored to Jerusalem?" he asked. Will you help us materially?[6]

It is also reported that the deciphered markings read "Herein lies the Golden Ark of the Covenant." Attempts by Futterer to return to his discovered cave were thwarted by the British government. He was granted a permit by the government to search the area but his permit was given with the understanding that he would not attempt any archaeological digs. Futterer died without finding the Ark of the Covenant, but his search on Mt. Nebo would not be the last.

Tom Crotser

The quest of Futterer to find the Ark in the mountains of Jordan was continued by an American named Tom Crotser. Tom Crotser had been looking for the Ark of the Covenant for some sixteen years, initially focusing his search in Syria. Based upon information he had found in several old manuscripts, he believed Hyropolis, in northern Syria, was one possible location. After reading, however, from the 2 Maccabees, *Palestine Speaks*, and the writings of explorer Peter the Iberian, Crotser concluded the Ark was in Jordan.

Tom Crotser directed the "Institute for the Restitution of All Things." The Institute interpreted the "restitution of all things" as referring to five particular objects that must be discovered before Christ's return. They claim to have previously found the first four: the City of Adam, the stone Cain used to kill Abel, the Tower of Babel, and Noah's Ark. The only missing thing that remained for them to discover was the Ark of the Covenant.

The Quest for the Ark

Believing he knew approximately where the Ark was located, Crotser tracked down a student of the late Futterer, a retired minister named Clinton Locy. Locy was the keeper of Futterer's papers. Crotser obtained from Locy a sketch of the area that Futterer had made where he found the inscription concerning the Ark. According to Futterer, this inscription was discovered on a secret passageway, blocked by a cement wall, which Futterer did not attempt to remove.

Armed with the sketch, Crotser and three associates went to Jordan in 1981 to find the lost Ark. First, the group had to pay a visit to the Franciscan monastery on top of Mount Nebo because the property on the mountain belongs to them. A permit to photograph, but not to dig, was granted by the director of the Monastery. They also obtained a permit to photograph from the military commander.

Crotser and his three companions stayed four days, spending nights in sleeping bags, while investigating the area and taking pictures. On Mt. Pisgah, they found an opening to a cave that seemingly matched the one in Futterer's sketch.

Ark Found?

On October 31, 1981, at 2:00 am, Crotser and his group returned to the cave. They removed a tin sheet which was covering the opening and then traveled some six hundred feet in a narrow passageway which was about four to six feet wide and seven feet high. Two walls had to be broken in the passageway to allow the explorers to continue.

Reaching the end of the passageway they came to a third wall. They cut an opening in that wall and found themselves in a small chamber, about seven feet by seven feet. Inside this chamber they shined their flashlights upon a gold colored object which they believe was the Ark of the Covenant. Lying next to the object were poles that Crotser said matched the description of the ones which were to carry the Ark.

Not wishing to touch the "ark" because of its holy character, the group took some 200 photographs. They did, however, measure the object. Its size was sixty-two inches long, thirty-seven inches high and thirty-seven inches wide. They did not attempt to remove it from its restingplace because they did not want to get in trouble with the Jordanian authorities. Furthermore, it would have been impossible to carry the object back through the tunnel because of the lack of room in the passageway.With photographs in hand, Crotser would now tell the outside world of his discovery of the Ark.

Unhappily, Crotser could not get either the Jordanian or Israeli authorities interested in his find. The story was reported in the Jerusalem *Post* on November 22, 1981 but not given much credence.

Upon returning to Kansas, Crotser gave his story to a local UPI reporter named Darrell Day. The next day, the story of the discovery of the Ark of the Covenant went out over the main news wire of UPI to newspapers all over the United States. Crotser immediately received worldwide attention as the man who found the lost Ark.

Scholars Say No

Because of the publicity Crotser received, the magazine Biblical Archaeology Review sent Dr. Siegfried Horn to interview Tom Crotser concerning his claim that he had found the Ark. Horn, a highly respected archaeologist, had spent sixteen years excavating some four miles northeast of Mt. Nebo. *Biblical Archaeology Review* reported the following of what transpired:

> Horn was asked to go to Winfield by a group who knew of his scholarly reputation and standing, and who wanted a respected authority to examine Crotser's claims. Horn, confident that Crotser had not found the Ark of the Covenant, nevertheless agreed to go not only because of the intense interest aroused by the UPI story but also because Horn felt that the best way to handle such claims was to examine the evidence and then report what artifacts Crotser had erroneously identified as the Ark of the Covenant.[7]

Whether or not Crotser had found the lost Ark, it is unfortunate that Horn prejudged his claims before he had examined the photographs.

Horn did go to Winfield Kansas to visit Crotser.After explaining the details of his journey, Crotser showed Horn the slides he had taken. They further convinced Horn that Crotser had not found the Ark.

All but two of Crotser's two hundred color slides had turned out very badly. *Biblical Archaeology Review* reported that:

> Of the two that registered images, one is fuzzy but does depict a chamber with a yellow box in the center. The other slide is quite good, according to Horn, and gives a front view of the box. . .
>
> The front of the box appeared to be covered with a sheet of bronze, containing a pattern of small holes. Around the edges and down the middle are metal strips with a diamond pattern. Although Horn is not certain, the diamond-(and triangular-) shaped pattern may have been punched out of the strips. In any event, the strips are lighter yellow than the underlying metal sheet. The regularity of the patterns indicated to Horn that the metal was machine worked.
>
> In the upper right hand corner of the face of the box was a nail with a modern looking head.
>
> Horn concluded: "I do not know what the object is, but the pictures convinced me that it was not an ancient artifact but of modern fabrication with machine produced decorative strips and underlying metal sheet.[8]

Horn was then to proceed to Mt. Nebo to identify what Crotser had discovered. The trip however, was cancelled. It seems that publicity surrounding Crotser's illegal digging on the mountain caused Jordanian authorities to cancel excavation permits for 1982. *Biblical Archaeology Review* reported:

> One of the major reasons for withdrawing the 1982 excavation permit . . . was the illegal excavation, subsequently highly publicized, of a group of Americans— Tom Crotser and his associates—looking for the Ark of the Covenant. Several reliable sources, including a professor of archaeology at the University of Jordan, have confirmed that Crotser's expedition was a key element in the Jordanian decision.
>
> It is difficult for Americans to understand the Jordanians government decision. There seems to be little relationship between the crime and the punishment. It is well-known, however that the Jordanians do not want any Biblical discoveries made in Jordan. This policy

became even firmer in the summer of 1982 after the Israeli invasion of Lebanon.[9]

The group was also rejected a permit to dig in 1983. To this day, no one knows for certain what Tom Crotser found in that cave in Jordan.

Some feel that this adds to the credibility of Crotser's findings. Bible teacher Anish Shorosh writes:

> Why would the popular *Biblical Archaeological Review* magazine take four pages of its May-June issue, 1983, to question the discovery of the Ark if there is nothing to it? The article was written with no direct involvement between the magazine's staff and Crotser. He told me that no one came to see him except Dr. Seigfried Horn, a Seventh Day Adventist professor who never even mentioned the magazine as his sponsor for the interview. Moreover, Dr. Horn was even misquoted by the magazine. A very unscientific approach to the subject was most obvious. . . What more evidence does one want than seeing the picture of the very object the four explorers found in the cave?[10]

Biblical Archaeology Review noted:

> Anyone assessing Tom Crotser's claim that he has found the original Ark of the Covenant in all its gilded glory must surely exercise caution in light of Crotser's additional claims to have previously located the Tower of Babel, Noah's Ark, the City of Adam, and the great stone of Abel, where the son of Adam was killed.[11]

The assessment of scholars to Crotser's find has been universal—they don't believe he found the Ark of the Covenant.

Different Looking

One problem with the "ark" Crotser found is that it did not look like anyone's conception of the sacred object. What it did have, which no one expected, were "front sliding doors." What it did not have, was the Mercy Seat and the cherubim. Crotser did report seeing gauze-covered packages in the corner tied with leather thongs. Though he and his group did not open the packages, Crotser speculated the cherubim may have been inside.

Crotser also suggested that the Ark may have been altered over the years. Bible teacher Anish Shorosh, who viewed Crotser's photographs, wrote:

> As to the design, it kind of looked different from what anyone pictured in his mind. Personally, I did not expect what I saw of the design. To say it is modern and possibly sheet metal is to call Tutankhamun's mask a fake because it looks so new and colorful.[12]

Bringing the Ark Back

Undaunted by scholarly rejection, Crotser reckoned there was only one man in the world who had the power to bring the Ark from Jordan to Jerusalem, Jewish financier David Rothchild. Rothchild, Crotser believed, was the only person who could finance the delivery of the Ark from Jordan to Israel. Crotser stated he would not publicly release the photographs until David Rothchild responded. Rothchild, however, never did respond and the photographs were never released.

Christ's Coming Calculated

In 1982, Crotser spoke of his calculations of the soon coming of Christ.

> Their purpose [Crotser and his associates] in these excavations and searches is to unveil five objects which they believe must be discovered before Christ returns in the fall of 1988. Those objects are the city of Adam, Stone of Abel, Ten Commandment tablets, Ark of the Covenant, and the tower of Babel. The group maintains that Noah's Ark is also an important discovery.
>
> They claim it is very complicated to explain their scientific calculations for Christ's return. "However, we feel as the time grows nearer, we'll know more, just as it was in Noah's day. He knew 120 years before the Great Flood, but just seven days before the Lord told him to get his family into the Ark. And as the time drew nearer, he knew precisely when it would transpire.[13]

Croster's "scientific calculations" of Christ returning in 1988, like so many others, have proved to be wrong.

Cover Up?

Some saw the rejection of Crotser's find as a cover up such as Anish Shorosh who said:

> Logically, one would have to conclude that the find is trustworthy, based upon the reaction of the government of Jordan to the rumor. The Jordanian Prime Minister's office, mind you, not the Department of Antiquities, ordered all archaeological excavations halted from the time the rumor started. Why? Apparently, Jordanian authorities are convinced that the Ark is really on Mount Nebo in Jordan. However they are justifiably fearful of losing it because Israel would certainly attempt to reclaim it at any cost.[14]

Museum

Crotser set up a small museum in Winfield, Kansas where he displayed a picture of the Ark. Dr. Anish Shorosh described Crotser's museum.

> The central object in the small museum is the papier-mache cave with a window. When you bend down to look inside the window the picture of the golden Ark is seen in a spectacular manner. Since the cave-like exhibit is dark and the slide projected from the back of the screen which you are looking at is bright, the golden box seems to glow. It is a marvelous sight indeed. No nails can be seen anywhere in the box as the Biblical Archaeology Review Magazine reported. The flash light from the camera, when the picture was taken, does show the reflection of several dots which can be construed as tips of modern nails. However, subsequent slides which Mr. Crotser graciously showed us dispelled any doubts that the golden box was all gold.[15]

Crotser and his museum are no longer in Winfield, Kansas.[16]

Believed to be True

Many people believed Crotser's report to be true. Shorosh writes:

> The pictures flashed in the cave did not all come out, nevertheless, I personally saw enough of the slides to believe that what those four men beheld in the cave was definitely the fantastic Golden Ark of the Lord. . .

The exciting discovery of the Ark of the Covenant on Mount Nebo in Jordan, is by and large a fact which time will reveal to be true. A controversy or even a war may erupt between Jordan and Israel over the ownership of the Ark very soon if someone does not remove the sacred vessel.[17]

The magazine *Biblical Archaeology Review*, however, took a dim view of Crotser's find.

In the meantime, we still cannot report what it was Tom Crotser photographed at 2:00 a.m. on the night of October 31, 1981. As soon as we find out, we'll let you know. But rest assured, it was not the Ark of the Covenant.[18]

Conclusion

We do not know if the account in 2 Maccabees of Jeremiah's hiding the Ark is historically valid. One may ask, "If Jeremiah had hidden the Ark on Mt. Nebo why wasn't it restored and used in the Second Temple?" There is no record of anyone looking for it in ancient times. Those who believe Jeremiah hid the Ark usually say the site was so well-hidden, that no one could find it. Jeremiah, according to 2 Maccabees, kept the location secret, waiting for it to be revealed in the last times.

Tom Crotser's "find" certainly does not appear to be the genuine Ark of the Covenant. Only time will tell if the Ark does remain in the area of Mt. Nebo.

Endnotes for Chapter 23

1. On the date of and reliability of 2 Maccabees, John R. Bartlett writes:

> The book may belong anywhere in the last 150 years B.C. . . .
> The more obvious liking the author of 2 Maccabees with the author of 1 Maccabees, for legendary material and theological explanation has tended to make modern scholars value 1 Maccabees more highly as a historical source. But it has become clear that 2 Maccabees does contain much genuine and valuable material . . . (John R. Bartlett *The First and Second Books of Maccabees*, Cambridge, At the University Press, 1973, pp. 215,217).

> The legend that Jeremiah had hidden the Tabernacle and Ark in a cave that they might later be restored in the latter days, presents a singular contrast to the higher thoughts of the prophet (*Ellicott's Commentary on the Whole Bible*, edited by Charles John Ellicott, Vol 3, 1 Kings-Esther, n.d., p. 20).

2. Regarding Mt. Pisgah, Earl S. Kallard writes:

> Pisgah might not be a proper noun; (pisgah) means "cleft," "ridge," or "range." The top of pisgah might mean the highest point of the ridge of mountains rising in Moab east of the Dead Sea (Earl S. Kallard, Deuteronomy, The Expositors Bible Commentary, p. 234).

> Mount Suagha is the Arabic name for Pisgah. It means "the Mount of Goldsmiths." It has been supposed that the story of it being the hiding place of the Golden Ark could have been behind this unusual name.

3. A.F. Futterer, *Palestine Speaks*, Los Angeles, Calif. A. F. Futterer, 1931, 537,539.

4. Futterer, ibid. 543, 544.

5. Futterer, ibid. 536, 537.

6. Tom Crotser Has Found the Ark of the Covenant—Or Has He? *Biblical Archaeology Review*, (BAR), May/June, 1983, p. 67.

7. BAR, ibid. p. 68.

8. BAR, ibid. pp. 68,69

9. BAR, ibid. p. 68.

10. Anish A. Shorosh, *The Exciting Discovery of the Ark of the Covenant*, Winona, MN, Justin Books, 1984, p. 17.

11. BAR, ibid. p. 66.

12. Shorosh, ibid. p. 26.

13. Doug Wead, David Lewis, and Hal Donaldson, *Where is the Lost Ark*, Minneapolis, Bethany House Publishers, 1982, pp. 80,81.

Shorosh, who believed that Crotser had discovered the Ark, had his own predictions as to the Second Coming of Christ. He wrote:

> It seems to me that from age 40-50 the years of declension, destruction, and death will begin 1988-1998, concluding with the Second Coming of Jesus. The Rapture may happen from now [1984] till 1988 with His return 7-10 years later (Shorosh, ibid. p. 38).

This gives us another example on how we should be careful in trying to calculate Christ's coming.

14. Shorosh, ibid. pp. 19,20.

15. Shorosh, ibid. pp. 25,26.

16. After unsuccessful attempts in 1992 to contact Crotser, the author called the Chamber of Commerce in Winfield, Kansas. He was told that Crotser and his group had moved out several years previously and no one was certain of there whereabouts.

17. Shorosh, ibid. pp. 28,46.

18. BAR, ibid, p. 69.

Louis Rapoport notes the response to Tom Crotser's discovery:

> No archaeologist took the report seriously—the dimensions of the "ark" were all wrong, according to Biblical references and the whole matter seemed spurious . . . Israeli rabbi's also dismissed the report, as did the small Samaritan community, which claims the ark is in its possession on Mount Gerizim near the West Bank town of Nablus (Louis Rapoport, The Mystery of the Real Lost Ark, *Jewish Digest*, September, 1982, p. 26).

CHAPTER 24

WAS THE ARK TAKEN TO ETHIOPIA?

With the disappearance of such a famous object as the Ark of the Covenant, unique explanations have arisen as to where the holy object is now located. One ancient theory as to what happened to the Ark involves the tiny country of Ethiopia. It has been alleged that sometime in the past, the Ark of the Covenant was taken from Israel and spirited away to Ethiopia. As we will see, the Ethiopian connection takes two forms. The traditional Ethiopian account, handed down in various versions, asserts that the Ark was taken by Menelik I, the alleged offspring of Solomon and the Queen of Sheba. The genuine Ark of the Covenant was replaced with a bogus ark which was placed in the Holy of Holies. The real Ark was brought to Ethiopia where it resides to this day.

A more recent theory rejects this account as being unhistorical, yet contends the Ark did make its way to Ethiopia, but later in history. British author Graham Hancock gained international publicity by claiming that he had actually traced the Ark to its location—a tiny chapel in Axum, Ethiopia.[1] Upon close examination, we will find that neither of these theories has much to support them.

Queen of Sheba

The Ethiopian story takes us back to the time of Solomon. The Bible says that the Queen of Sheba heard of the fame of Solomon and paid him a visit:

Now when the queen of Sheba heard of the fame of Solomon concerning the name of the Lord, she came to test him with hard questions. She came to Jerusalem with a very great retinue, with camels that bore spices, very much gold, and precious stones; and when she came to Solomon, she spoke with him about all that was in her heart. So Solomon answered all her questions; there was nothing so difficult for the king that he could not explain it to her (1 Kings 10:1-4).

She was duly impressed:

Then she said to the king, 'It was a true report which I heard in my own land about your words and your wisdom. However I did not believe the words until I came and saw it with my own eyes; and indeed the half was not told me. Your wisdom and prosperity exceed the fame which I heard (1 Kings 10:6,7).

The Queen then gave gifts:

Then she gave the king one hundred and twenty talents of gold, spices in great abundance, and precious stones. There never again came such abundance of spices as the queen of Sheba gave to King Solomon (1 Kings 10: 10).

Solomon, in turn, gave the Queen all her desire:

And King Solomon gave the queen of Sheba all she desired, whatever she asked, . . . So she returned and went to her own country, she and her servants (1 Kings 10:13).

Some have interpreted this passage to mean that part of her desire was to bear Solomon's child. The story, still told in Ethiopia today, is that the Queen *did* conceive a son by Solomon and named him Menelik.

According to Ethiopian tradition, the son of Solomon and Sheba was Menelik I—or Ibn al-Hakim, "son of the wise man." Today it is still believed in Ethiopia that the royal line "descends without interruption from the dynasty of

Menelik I, son of the queen of Ethiopia, the Queen of Sheba, and King Solomon of Jerusalem."

Menelik's Visit

The story of Menelik is told in a variety of versions, both written and oral. The earliest written form, called the *Kebra Nagast*, (*The Book of the Glory of Kings*) dates from the thirteenth century.

According to one version of the story, Menelik, who was twenty at the time, paid an unannounced visit to his father Solomon in Jerusalem. Solomon who had not realized he had fathered this child through the Queen of Sheba, accorded him great honor. After staying for a year, he decided to go back home to Ethiopia.

Menelik, as the story goes, was given a present as he was leaving Jerusalem to go back to Ethiopia—a replica of the Ark of the Covenant. At his going away party, when the priests had become intoxicated, Menelik substituted the bogus ark for the real thing, all unbeknownst to the priests. With the help of certain other priests, he returned to Ethiopia bringing back the one, true, Ark of the Covenant.

Menelik, it is said, took the Ark because he was concerned about the spiritual state of Israel. The Ark would be returned when Israel turned back to the Lord. Unfortunately, they never did and the Ark remains to this day in Ethiopia.

Another version of the story has Azarius, the son of the High Priest Zadok, taking the Ark and only telling Menelik of his theft while they were on their way back to Ethiopia. Whatever the case may be, it is agreed that the real Ark made its way to Ethiopia, never to return.

The *Kebra Nagast* records the procession glided above the ground with the returning Ark.

> And they loaded the wagons, and the horses and the mules in order to depart . . . And as for the wagons, no man hauled his wagon . . . and whether it was men, or horses or mules or loaded camels, each was raised above the ground to the height of a cubit; and to all those who rode upon beasts were lifted up above their backs to the height of one span of a man, and all the various kinds of baggage which were loaded on the beasts, as well as those who were mounted on them, were raised up to the height of one span of a man, and the beasts were lifted up to the height of one span of a man. And everyone traveled in the

wagons . . . like an eagle when his body glideth above the wind.[2]

Solomon was later chastised for allowing the sacred object to be whisked away by his illegitimate son. The *Kebra Nagast* reads:

> Thy son hath carried away the Ark of the Covenant, thy son whom thou hast begotten, who springeth from an alien people into which God hath not commanded you to marry, that is to say from an Ethiopian woman, who is not of thy colour, and is not akin to thy country, and who is moreover black.[3]

Evidence

It would seem on the surface that this story could be dismissed out of hand as mere legend. There are, however, a few interesting facts that prevent us from doing this.

First, there is a long held Ethiopian belief that they can trace the ancestry of their kings back to Solomon. For example, the late Ethiopian leader, Haile Selassie, was given titles belonging to the Davidic kings such as the "The Lion of the Tribe of Judah."

Second, there are many Ethiopians who practice their own form of Judaism. Known as "Falashas," they practice Jewish customs, and have traces of Hebrew mixed in with their language. Their unique brand of Judaism has certain forms that resemble the Judaism practiced at the time of Solomon. Other Jewish practices that were added after Solomonic times have not been incorporated by the "Falashas." This, they contend, demonstrates their direct connection with Solomon.

Solomon was also well known for having many wives and concubines. It is, therefore, not out of the question that he would have fathered a child through the Queen of Sheba. Furthermore, there is a long standing tradition that the Queen of Sheba was converted to the God of Israel after visiting Solomon. According to the *Kebra Nagast*, the Queen of Sheba said to Solomon:

> From this moment I will not worship the sun, but will worship the creator of the sun, the God of Israel . . . because I have found favor with thee, and before the God of Israel, my Creator.[4]

In addition, every Christian church in Ethiopia has a room similar to the Holy of Holies of the Jewish Temple. In this room a *tabot* is kept. The tabot is a wooden carving or stone slab representing the contents of the Ark—the Ten Commandments. The purpose of keeping this replica is to remind the people that the original Ark of the Covenant is in their country.

Finally, and most important, there is a chapel in the city of Axum where the Ark of the Covenant supposedly resides. The ark is only seen by the selected guardian. The only time the "ark" has been taken out of this chapel is at the time of a yearly celebration called Timkat.

Though the tradition of the Ark being brought to Ethiopia goes back centuries, the evidence of its genuineness is lacking.

Problems

The idea that the Ark was taken to Ethiopia by Menelik I, has insurmountable problems, the first being geography. The geographical location of Sheba, the home of the Sabean people, is debated. Most scholars, however, believe that it was in southwest Arabia, in the region of present day Yemen,[5] and not Ethiopia. Hence, the location of Sheba does not seem to match up with Ethiopia.

There is even a bigger problem with Ethiopia being the home of the Queen of Sheba. All historians agree that at the time of Solomon, 960 B.C., there were no large settlements in the country of Ethiopia. The Queen of Sheba is represented as ruling an empire, but no empire existed in Ethiopia during Solomonic times.

Graham Hancock, who at first attempted historical confirmation of the *Kebra Nagast*, had to admit that it was legendary. He writes:

> Several authorities make much of the fact that in Solomon's time—a thousand years before Christ—Ethiopia had not possessed any real civilization of its own and certainly had not boasted an urban society capable of producing so illustrious a monarch as the Queen of Sheba. Indeed the consensus was that enlightenment had not even begun to dawn in the Abyssinian highlands until about the sixth century BC and had not reached any level of sophistication until some four hundred years after that. Neither could this period of progress be regarded as an Ethiopian achievement: instead the catalyst had been an influx of Arab tribesmen whose 'superior qualities' had revolutionized the sluggish culture of the native inhabitants. . .

In short, Ethiopic civilization was not only much more recent than the Axumite legends implied but also had been borrowed from elsewhere. In their heart of hearts, furthermore, most Ethiopians knew this to be true and felt deeply insecure about their heritage. Indeed one standard work went so far as to suggest that the *Kebra Nagast* was popular because it filled a deep psychological need on the part of the Abyssinians 'to prove their ancient origins.'[6]

Hence the story of the Ark being taken to Ethiopia at the time of Solomon is historically improbable.

In addition, the idea that Solomon had a son through the Queen of Sheba, wherever she came from, has no historical basis. Geoffrey Grogan writes:

> The Jewish romantic legend that the queen desired and received a son fathered by Solomon is unsubstantiated, as the Ethiopic tradition that the royal Abyssinian line was founded by the offspring of Solomon and the queen of Sheba.[7]

Certainly there is nothing in Scripture to verify this story. Even granting Solomon and the Queen of Sheba conceived a son, there is nothing in the Bible that records this son's visit to Jerusalem, let alone having a replica of the Ark constructed for him.

The main problem with this theory is that the Ark is mentioned as being in the Temple some three hundred years *after* the time of Solomon (2 Chronicles 35:3). The Scriptures would have to be incorrect if previously it had been taken to Ethiopia.

The theory that Menelik I, the son of Solomon and the Queen of Sheba, took the genuine Ark to Ethiopia has no Biblical or historical basis.

Theory of Graham Hancock

Recently, there has been a new twist on the Ethiopian connection by British journalist Graham Hancock. Hancock had been working on a book sponsored by the Ethiopian government when he heard the story of the Ark residing at Axum. After some preliminary investigation, including an attempt to view the "ark," he dismissed the Ethiopian account as pious legend. Only later, after considerable research, did he come to embrace the idea that the Ark does reside in Ethiopia.

Hancock rejects the Ethiopian story that Menelik I brought the Ark from Jerusalem. He does believe the Ark was taken from the Temple in Jerusalem, but he asserts that this occurred during the time of Manasseh, hundreds of years after the reign of Solomon. The Ark, he contends, was then transferred to a Jewish garrison at Elephantine Island in the upper Nile of Egypt. From there it was brought to Tana Kirkos Island in Ethiopia's Lake Tana, the source of the Blue Nile. Finally, it was brought to a stone chapel in Axum Ethiopia where it remains to this day.

It is interesting to note that Hancock wanted to verify the historicity of the Ethiopian story that tells of the Ark's journey. He, however, realized it could not be historically verified. Undaunted, he then felt that it was more a metaphor than genuine history. He wrote:

> I had looked for alternative resting places for the Ark, but none of those that legend or tradition offered had seemed in the least bit likely. I had looked for proofs that the relic might have been destroyed, but no such proofs existed. I had established that the Kebra Nagast's claims about Solomon, Sheba and Menelik could not literally be true—only to discover these same claims might well serve as a complex metaphor for the truth. Certainly, the Ark of the Covenant could not have gone to Ethiopia in the era of Solomon; but it was entirely plausible that it might have made the journey later, at the time of the destruction of the Jewish Temple that had stood on the island of Elephantine in the upper Nile.[8]

Manasseh

Hancock believes the Ark was taken out of the Temple during the time of Manasseh. This however, brings up the problem of the mention of the Ark in 2 Chronicles 35:3, after the time of Manasseh. Hancock found this passage actually provided support to his thesis.

> It was immediately obvious to me that these few short verses . . . were of vital importance to my quest. Why? Quite simply because Josiah would have had no need to ask the Levites to put the Ark in the Temple if it had already been there.[9]

Hancock does not believe the Ark was returned per Josiah's request.

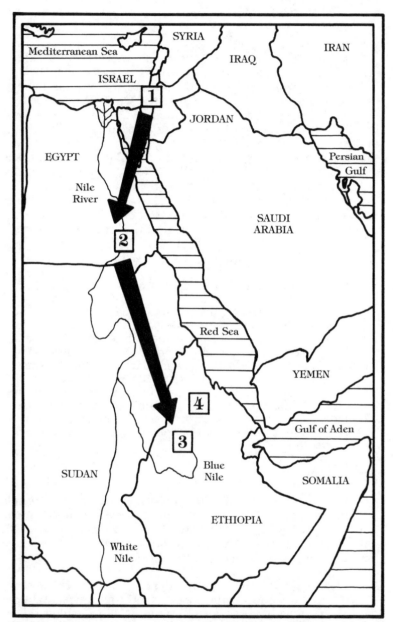

Route of the Ark's travels according to Graham Hancock.
Ark began at (1) Jerusalem moved to (2) Elephantine,
Egypt, then to (3) Tana Kirkos and finally arrived at (4) Axum

What Chronicles did not do, however, was give any indication at all that the Levites had complied with the king's order; indeed, far from the colorful ceremony that one might have expected to accompany any reinstallation of the Ark in the Temple, there was no follow up—either in this book or in any other part of the Bible to Josiah's strange command. On the contrary, it was clear that his words had fallen on deaf ears or on the ears of people who were not in a position to obey them.[10]

Hancock then coupled this reference to the prophecy given by Jeremiah that the Ark would no longer be missed (Jeremiah 3:16). He claimed this as final evidence that it had been taken out of the Holy of Holies some time previously. This, he believed, confirmed his theory that the Ark was taken out of the Temple during the time of Manasseh.

It is agreed by all that the Ark had been removed from the Temple sometime before Josiah ordered it returned. As we have seen, various theories have been given why this was so. But, contrary to Hancock, there is no hint that the order was not carried out. The natural assumption in the passage is that the Ark was restored upon the command of the king. To argue otherwise is not very convincing.

Experts Disagree

The experts have responded to Hancock's theory with universal disbelief. For example, Edward Ullendorff, retired professor of Ethiopian Studies of the University of London and preeminent expert on Ethiopia, said of Hancock's work:

"It's just a sad joke," he says, "I wasted a lot of time reading it."[11]

University of Toronto archaeologist John Holladay called the book:

"garbage and hogwash" with no "scientific merit whatsoever."[12]

Ullendorff told the Los Angeles *Times* that he had seen this "ark" that resides in Ethiopia.

"They have a wooden box, but it's empty . . . Middle to late medieval construction, when these were fabricated ad hoc." The mystery around it is "mostly to maintain the idea that it's a venerated object."

How does he know this? No one was permitted to see it, the monks said. Hancock had even tried to make a virtue out of this by arguing that it attested to the object's importance. For obviously, no mere mortal would be permitted to view something so divine. ("I . . . was never worthy enough," he wrote.)

Hogwash, Ullendorff says. "I've seen it. There was no problem getting access when I saw it in 1941," he says.

He isn't surprised that Hancock was denied permission, for he was nothing but a parvenu. "You need to be able to speak their language, classical Ge'ez," he said. "You need to be able to show that you're serious."[13]

Conclusion

The story of the Ark's journey to Ethiopia has too many "ifs" and conjectures to make it plausible. The Ethiopian tradition does not provide convincing evidence of the Ark's location. We must look elsewhere.

Endnotes for Chapter 24

1. Graham Hancock, *The Sign and the Seal: The Quest for the Lost Ark of the Covenant*, New York, Crown Publishers, Inc., 1992.

2. Sir E.A. Wallis Budge, *The Queen of Sheba and her Only Son Menelik*; being the *'Book of the Glory of Kings'* (*Kebra Nagast*), Oxford University Press, 1932, p. 29.

3. Budge, *Kebra Nagast*, ibid, pp. 77,78

4. Budge, Kebra Nagast, ibid., p. 29.

5. For example, the Bible says the Queen of Sheba gave Solomon 120 talents (9,000 lbs or 4 and one half tons) of gold. Allan Millard writes:

> The Queen of Sheba's gift of gold was probably drawn from the gold mines in western Arabia. Remains of extensive mine works dating back at least to Roman times have been explored there recently, and there are reports that considerable quantities of gold still await the miners pick (Allan Millard, Does the Bible Exaggerate King Solomon's Golden Wealth?, *Biblical Archaeology Review*, May/June, 1989, p. 34).

6. Hancock, ibid. pp. 131,132.

7. Expositors, Isaiah, p. 122.

8. Hancock, ibid. p. 436

9. Hancock, ibid. p. 409.

10. Hancock, ibid. p. 410.

11. Michael A. Hiltzik, Does Trail to Ark of Covenant End Behind Axum Curtain?, Los Angeles *Times*, Tuesday, June 9, 1992, H 6.

12. Hiltzik, ibid. p. H6.

13. Hiltzik, ibid. p. H6.

Note on Ethiopia and the Bible:

The late Bible teacher Arthur Bloomfield taught the novel theory that after Solomon's death, the kingdom divided into a three parts, Israel, Judah and Ethiopia. Though Ethiopia was the smallest of the three kingdoms Bloomfield contends they kept their faith in God and eventually came to possess the Ark of the Covenant. Through Solomon's son, Menelik, they also had a king of the house of David and the tribe of Judah. This is historically improbable and Biblically impossible.

Prophecy writer Grant Jeffrey has taken Bloomfield's theory (of the Ark going to Ethiopia) and made it popular in our day. He, like Bloomfield, accepts the unhistorical Ethiopian account as being the true story of what happened to the Ark. He believes the last mention of the Ark was during the time of Solomon.

> The last time we read that the Ark of the Covenant was still <u>unquestionably</u> in the hands of Israel is the report of the Second Book of Chronicles 8:11 in which Solomon asked his wife, the pagan daughter of the Egyptian Pharaoh, to leave the area where the Ark of the Covenant was stored because she was not a believer. Shortly after this event the most important and powerful religious object in history disappears from the scene of Israel's national life. In all of the Bible's subsequent accounts of battles, rebellions, invasions and the looting of the Temple by various armies, there is not one single word about this most sacred and powerful object (Grant R. Jeffrey, *Armageddon: Appointment with Destiny*, New York, Bantam Books, 1990, p. 112).

Jeffrey believes 2 Chronicles 35:3 does not refer to the Ark of the Covenant:

> There is one brief mention of an "ark" in 2 Chronicles 35:3 during the reign of King Josiah, when he ordered the priests to put this object back in the Temple, since it had been removed earlier by a wicked king to make room for idols. It is unlikely that this object referred to as an "ark" is, in fact, the true Ark of the Covenant because the Bible does not call it the "the Ark of the Covenant" (Jeffrey, ibid. pp. 112,113).

This is incorrect. Any good Bible commentary on 2 Chronicles, whether it be Christian or Jewish, will testify it was the genuine Ark that was placed in the Holy of Holies. As we have seen, the Bible uses over twenty designations for the Ark. It is called the Ark of the Your Strength, The Ark of God, the Ark of the Lord. The designation "Holy Ark" in 2 Chronicles 35:3 certainly speaks of the genuine Ark of the Covenant. The *International Standard Bible Encyclopedia* noted:

> Over twenty different designations appear with reference to the ark, and discerning any invariable pattern in usage is difficult (W. Lotz, M.G. Kyle, C.E. Armerding in the *International Standard Bible Encyclopedia,* Volume 1, Revised Edition, Grand Rapids, Wm. B. Eerdmans Publishing Company, 1979, p. 293).

Though popular among some Christians, the idea of the Ark going to Ethiopia has no Biblical or historical support.

Note: Has the Lost Ark actually been seen in Ethiopia?

The author has in his possession a book written in 1951 that makes the following claims about his drawing of the Ark:

> These original drawings were made from microfilm photographs of an exact replica or reproduction of the Ark of the Covenant, which reposes in the ancient Coptic Cathedral at Axum, Ethiopia . . . This is the first time any representation of this ark has ever been reproduced for publication in America.
>
> This micro-film was kindly provided by my personal friend Dr. J.O. Kinnaman, who spent fifty years in archaeological research and investigation in many parts of the world . . . He was called to Ethiopia and commissioned by Haile Selassie, Emperor of Abyssiania, now Ethiopia, to investigate, discover, and make records of all information available for the national archives, and to place in the national museum all objects to be found in Ethiopia of permanent archaeological value.
>
> As a mark of special respect and appreciation, Dr. Kinnaman was permitted to spend many hours in the immediate presence of the Ark of the Covenant in this national cathedral. His request to photograph it was denied; but he was permitted to make minutely exact measurements and sketches of certain of its details. On returning to America, a skilled sculptor fashioned a replica of the Ark from this data. This replica was photographed and from these photographs our artists drew the illustration [see illustration] . . . Dr. Kinnaman told the author that after many hours of silent contemplation in the presence of the ark at the temple in Axum, it was not difficult to accept the claims of the ecclesiastical authorities of the Coptic church in Ethiopia that they are, indeed, the custodians of the ORIGINAL

ARK OF THE COVENANT THAT FIRST WAS PLACED IN THE TABERNACLE IN THE WILDERNESS [emphasis his] (Bruce Corbin, *The Tabernacle in the Wilderness*, Enid, Oklahoma, Truth Publishing Company, 1951, p. 59).

On the following page is the drawing reproduced from Corbin's book. The possibility of this story being true seems remote. From all that is known about the sacredness of the "ark" in Ethiopia, it does not appear that the Ethiopians would allow anyone to make minute drawings of it.

CHAPTER 25

HAS THE ARK BEEN FOUND UNDER THE TEMPLE MOUNT?

Is it possible that the Ark of the Covenant has been hidden for over 2,600 years, directly below the place where Solomon's Temple stood? Has the Holy Ark been discovered in a secret passageway underneath the Temple Mount? Recent reports from Jerusalem have made such a claim.

We now arrive at a third possible resting place of the Ark: somewhere under Jerusalem's Temple Mount. If the Ark were hidden by the Jews sometime in their past, this would have been the most likely place.

Temple Mount

The Temple Mount in Jerusalem is the place where the First and Second Temples stood. It is located on Mount Moriah, which belongs to a mountain a range than runs through the city of Jerusalem. On the western side of the Temple Mount is the only physical remains of the Second Temple area. It is a one hundred and eighty-five foot wall known as the Western Wall or Wailing Wall. The Jews worship today at the Western Wall while the top of the Mount is off limits to Jewish worship.

The author believes the Temple Mount will find itself center-stage in momentous future events.[1] One of these events could possibly be the locating of the Ark of the Covenant. For centuries, stories have circulated that the Golden Ark was hidden underneath the Temple Mount to insure its safety. It is also believed the sacred object will be discovered in the "last days."

Solomon's Hiding Place

It has been theorized that when King Solomon built the Temple, he also ordered a secret underground vault to be built, to hide the Ark of the Covenant. If Jerusalem were ever put to siege by foreign invaders, the Ark could then be taken from the Holy of Holies and placed into this hiding place. Though the Bible does not speak of such a secret room, many Jewish authorities have argued for its existence.

This underground hiding place was supposedly put to use in the reign of King Josiah. We have already seen that Josiah ordered the Ark returned to the Temple after it had been previously removed:

> Then he said to the Levites who taught all Israel, who were holy to the Lord: 'Put the holy ark in the house which Solomon the son of David, king of Israel built. It shall no longer be a burden on your shoulders. Now serve the Lord your God and His people Israel' (2 Chronicles 35:3).

Many Jewish interpreters speculate that Josiah did not put the Ark back in the Holy of Holies at this time, but rather placed it in Solomon's secret hiding place.

He did this because he knew the treasures of the Temple were about to be plundered. King Josiah had been told by Huldah the Prophetess that the Temple would be destroyed soon after his death. Knowing this, he ordered the Ark to be put in this underground vault. Many Rabbinical interpreters believe that the Ark has remained hidden in that place ever since and shall only be manifested and brought out again in the days of the Messiah.

Hidden by an Angel

There is also the tradition that an angel hid the Ark. According to one Jewish apocryphal source, *The Vision of Baruch:* Baruch, the scribe of Jeremiah, saw an angel take the Ark and hide it beneath the sealed foundation stone on the Temple Mount known as the "Well of Souls."

And I saw that he descended in the Holy of Holies and that he took from there the veil, the holy ephod, the mercy seat, the two tables, the holy rainment of the priests, the altar of incense, the forty-eight precious stones with which the priest were clothed, and the holy vessels of the tabernacle. And he said to the earth with a loud voice:

Earth, earth, earth, hear the word of the mighty God,
and receive the things which I commit to you,
and guard them until the last times,
so that you may restore them when you are ordered,
so that strangers may not get possession of them.
For the time has arrived when Jerusalem will also be delivered up for a time,
until the moment that it will be said that it will be restored forever.
And the earth opened its mouth and swallowed them up.[2]

The angel then spoke to the earth saying, "hear the word of God and receive what I commit to your care until the last times."

Jeremiah

It has also been taught that the prophet Jeremiah hid the Ark before the destruction of the Temple. Rabbi Leibel Reznick writes:

Before the destruction of the First Temple . . . the prophet Jeremiah hid the national treasures of the Jews under the Holy Temple to prevent them from falling in the hands of the invading Nebuchadnezzar and his Babylonian troops. The treasures included the Holy Ark, the Two Tablets with the Ten Commandments carved upon them, the staff of Aaron, the oil for anointing compounded by Moses, and a container holding the last sample of the manna that sustained the Children of Israel during their forty years of wandering through the desert. After the seventy years of the Babylonian exile, the Jews returned to Zion, but, alas, the treasures were never found.[3]

Chamber of Wood

According to a late Jewish tradition, the Ark was buried under the Chamber of Wood in the Temple prior to the destruction of the First Temple by the Babylonians. Leibel Reznick writes:

> The Mishnah (Shekalim 6:1) records that the Holy Ark was hidden in a secret passageway that began beneath the Chamber of Wood, which was located in the northwestern corner of the Women's Courtyard. . . there is an underground room . . . in that corner. It is a chamber forty-four feet below ground level, and has a vaulted ceiling. It has never been explored.[4]

Could any of these places contain the lost Ark? There are several things keeping interested parties from thoroughly investigating these claims. First, it is impossible to do any excavating from the top of the Temple Mount because it is under Islamic control. No type of digging is allowed, certainly none to find the location of the most holy object to the Jews. William LaSor noted:

> Since the Six-Day War, the Israelis have done a lot of excavation and have gotten to what used to be the city of David . . . It's quite exciting. But if the ark was hidden down there, in a cave in the temple area, it would now be under the Moslem shrine (the Dome of the Rock), and you can't take of bunch of Jewish archaeologists in there to dig.[5]

Second, even if excavation were possible, the exact site in which to look remains a problem. The location of the First and Second Temples is a matter of debate. There are at least, three sites on the Temple Mount, where the Temple could possibly have resided. Determining the location of the Holy of Holies or the Chamber of Wood depends upon calculating where the Temple stood.[6]

Though the Jews cannot excavate from the top of the Temple Mount, they do have control of the area at its base. In recent years, a tunnel has been dug that runs the entire length of the Western Wall—some 1000 feet. Exploration has already occurred from this place known as the Rabbinical Tunnel.

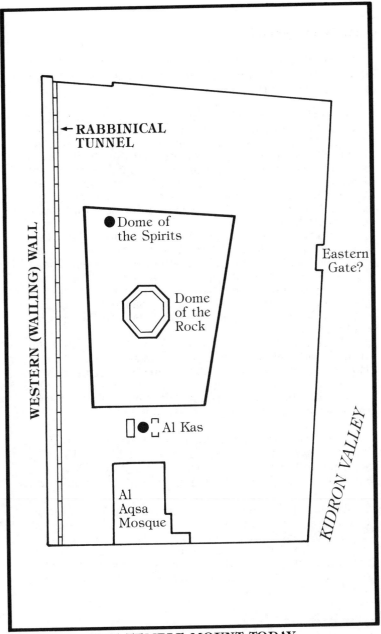

RABBINICAL TUNNEL

Dome of the Spirits

Dome of the Rock

WESTERN (WAILING) WALL

Eastern Gate?

KIDRON VALLEY

Al Kas

Al Aqsa Mosque

THE TEMPLE MOUNT TODAY

Secret Tunnel Found

Journalist Louis Rapoport reports on Chief Rabbi Shlomo Goren's claim, in 1982, to have found a secret tunnel concealing the Ark.

> Several months before *Raiders* appeared in Israel, at the height of the furor over the archaeological dig near the Temple Mount, Jerusalem's holiest site, Ashkenazi Chief Rabbi Shlomo Goren . . . announced dramatically that a recently discovered tunnel on the Temple Mount might lead to the Holy of Holies, in which the Ark of the Covenant and other Temple treasures were housed. . . The chief rabbi announced his revelation during an interview on Israeli television . . .
> The mysterious tunnel had been open late last summer by Religious Affairs Ministry workmen in an area north of the Western Wall—the Herodian remains of the wall around the Temple Mount. The subterranean discovery of the tunnel—which was first uncovered 100 years ago and then sealed up again—was kept secret over a month so as not to acerbate relations with the Moslem authorities . . .
> [Goren remarked] I had good reason to believe that the tunnel north of the Western Wall leads to the Holy of Holies . . . I believe I have found some trace, some way to find it . . .
> But the chief rabbi also said that he could reveal no more because of "secret and mystical reasons."[7]

Goren was the first person to make public the existence of what is now known as the "Rabbinical Tunnel." His claims to have found the way to the Holy of Holies and the Ark were met with skepticism as Louis Rapoport notes:

> Archaeologist and former deputy premier Yigael Yadin, when asked to comment on Goren's claim, called it "legend, fantasy . . . There is a vague reference to the fate of the ark in the Talmud, a late piece of information. [The ark may have disappeared 2,700 years ago, 700 years before the Talmud was composed.] I think he has attached too much importance to it."[8]

Encountering the Ark?

Since 1982 there has been much excavation in and around the Rabbinical Tunnel. Recent claims have been publicly made that the Ark has been discovered in a secret chamber underneath the Temple Mount.

Bible prophecy specialist David Lewis tells of a conversation with Rabbi Hacohen, one of the Jewish activists engaged in preparation for building a Third Temple. Speaking to Dr. Lewis and his tour group, Hacohen told about some of the excavations made underneath the Temple Mount. Lewis recalls Hacohen's story:

> He told of how he was working late at night with Rabbi Getz, a group of archaeologists, and rabbinical scholars. . . Hacohen told of how they were excavating along the lower level of the Western Wall. Passing through this doorway, the crew entered a fairly long tunnel. At the end of the tunnel, Rabbi Hacohen said, "I saw the golden ark that once stood in the holy Place of the Temple of the Almighty.
>
> It was covered with old, dried animal skins of some kind. However, one gold, gleaming end of the ark was visible. He could see the loops of gold through which the poles of acacia wood could be thrust so that the ark could be properly carried by the dedicated Levites.[9]

Hacohen and his friends went immediately to the home of then Chief Rabbi Shlomo Goren. The sleeping Rabbi was awakened to hear the news, the holy Ark of the Covenant had been discovered!

Goren told the excited group that preparations had already been made for such an event. The Ark would be carried out in triumph, by members of the tribe of Levi, the very next morning.

The next morning brought shock to the group as they went to the tunnel. Lewis explains:

> They found that during the night, the Moslems had erected a wooden frame and prepared a concrete wall, sealing off the tunnel that would give access to the ark of the covenant. I asked, "Why didn't you break through the concrete? It would have been so easy to do."
>
> He replied, "I begged Goren to give us permission to break through the wall, but Rabbi Goren replied, 'Every time we do anything around the Temple Mountain, it creates big problems for Israel with the Arabs, the United Nations, and the United States. It seems to make everybody upset, so we will not break through. We know where the holy object is and when we receive the word from the Almighty, we will go in and recover it. Don't worry, the Moslems revere the ark as much as we do and they would be afraid to touch it.[10]

The story that Hacohen had told Dr. Lewis and his tour group was never repeated to him as he notes:

> In years following, I talked to Rabbi Hacohen on a number of occasions about the previous discussion and each time I talked to him, he was more reluctant to have the subject brought up. Finally, in the presence of several people, he simply refused to talk about it at all. I suppose he got in trouble with his colleagues for talking to me and my tour group about their sighting of the ark of the covenant. I would like to point out, however, that we have a tape recording of his original discussion with our tour group on the very first occasion that he talked about the ark. It is our custom on our tours to record everything that every guide and every speaker has to say about any subject. So we have good records of everything that has been said. I have a colored slide showing Rabbi Hacohen holding a map and pointing to the tunnel as he is saying, "This is where we saw the golden ark of the Lord." Only time will tell what he and his friends actually saw.[11]

Rabbis Getz and Richman

A similar account is being told by the chief Rabbi of the Western Wall, Yehuda Getz. Appearing on a CBS television special concerning ancient mysteries of the Bible, aired in April of 1992, Getz claimed that the Ark had recently been discovered under the Temple Mount.

Earlier in the same year the author heard an identical claim being made. In February/March of 1992, the First Annual Temple conference was held in the city of Jerusalem. One of the speakers was Rabbi Chaim Richman of the Temple Institute. Richman told basically the same story as Hacohen and Getz: that the Ark had previously been discovered underneath the Temple Mount and that it was in a safe place. He, like the others, said it will be brought out "at the right time."

It is important to note that not all Israelies give credence to this story. Many, such as Dan Bahat chief archaeologist of Jerusalem, believe there are no buried treasures underneath the Temple Mount.

Conclusion

There have been several different Israelies telling the story that the Ark has been discovered underneath the Temple Mount. From their testimony it seems that some object does exist in one of the tunnels. Whether or not it is the Ark of the Covenant remains to be seen. If the Ark has been located somewhere underneath the Temple Mount, then its unveiling to the world could be just around the corner.

Endnotes for Chapter 25

1. Don Stewart and Chuck Missler,*The Coming Temple: Center Stage For the Final Countdown*, Orange, California, Dart Press, 1991.

2. 2 Baruch 6:4-8.

3. Leibel Reiznick, *The Holy Temple Revisited*, Northvale, New Jersey, Jason Aronson, Inc, 1990, 147.

4. Reiznick, ibid. p. 146.

The great Jewish scholar Maimonides wrote:

When Solomon built the Temple, he was aware it would ultimately be destroyed. He constructed a chamber in which the Ark could be entombed below the Temple in deep, maze-like vaults. King Josiah commanded that the Ark be entombed in the chamber built by Solomon . . . When it was entombed, Aaron's staff, the vial of manna, and the oil for anointing were entombed with it. All these sacred articles did not return to the Second Temple. (Maimonides, *The Laws of God's Chosen House*).

C.F. Keil comments on this ancient theory:

Some Rabbins regard it as a command to remove the Ark from its place in the Most Holy Place into some subterranean chamber of the Temple, so as to secure its safety in the event of a threatened destruction of the Temple taking place. But this hypothesis needs no refutation, since it in no way corresponds to the words used (C.F. Keil, *Biblical Commentary on the Old Testament*, Chronicles, C.F. Keil and F. Delitzsch, Grand Rapids, Eerdmans, reprinted 1971, p. 496).

5. William LaSor cited by Laurinda Keys, In Search of the Real Lost Ark, Associated Press, 1981.

Meir Ben-Dov tells the following story about archaeologist Benjamin Mazar desiring permission from the chief Ashkenazi Rabbi to dig near the Temple Mount:

The Ashkenazi chief Rabbi, Rabbi Unterman, agonized over the halakhic problems (questions of Jewish Law). What will happen, he mused aloud, if as a result of your archaeological excavation, you find the Ark of the Covenant, which Jewish tradition says is buried in the depths of the earth?" That would be wonderful! Professor

Mazar replied in all innocence. But the good Rabbi told the good professor that that was precisely what he feared. Since the children of Israel are not pure, from the viewpoint of Jewish religious law, they are forbidden to touch the Ark of the Covenant. Hence it is even unthinkable to excavate until the Messiah comes! (Meir Ben-Dov, *In The Shadow of the Temple*, New York, Harper and Row, 1982, p. 20).

6. For the various theories as to where the Temple was located see Don Stewart and Chuck Missler *The Coming Temple*, pp. 127-156.

7. Louis Rapoport, The Mystery of the Real Lost Ark, *Jewish Digest*, September, 1982, pp. 27,28.

8. Rapoport, ibid. p. 28,29.

9. David Lewis, *Prophecy 2000*, Green Forest, Ariz., New Leaf Press, 1990, pp. 175, 176.

10. Lewis, ibid. p. 176.

11. Lewis, ibid. pp. 176,177.

Note on Temple Mount excavations:

Since the fall of Jerusalem in A.D. 70, the Temple Mount has been explored only twice: First, a scientific survey took place in the 19th century led by British engineer Charles Warren. 2nd a very unscientific quest occurred the beginning of this century with Montague Parker. Parker, illegally digging for treasure on the Temple Mount in 1911, caused a riot in the city of Jerusalem. Reports of his excavating hit the headlines as the reproduction from the New York *Times* on the next page shows. Neither Warren nor Parker found any trace of the lost Ark.

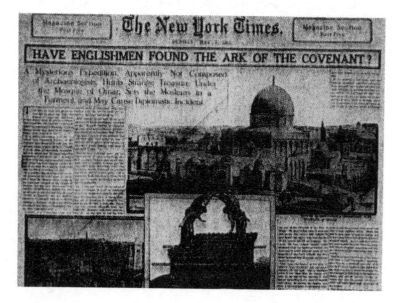

Has the Ark of the Covenant been forever lost or does it have a role in the future? Does the Bible say anything on this matter? Will the Ark be used in a Third Temple built by the Jews?

These and other issues will be the focus of our last section.

SECTION FOUR

DOES THE ARK HAVE A ROLE IN THE FUTURE?

CHAPTER 26

HAS THE ARK
BEEN FOREVER LOST?

We have examined the possibility that the Ark of the Covenant has been taken by a foreign invader or that it has been hidden by friendly hands. There is another possibility with regard to the mystery of the Ark's disappearance—the Ark may have been destroyed. A great number of people are of the opinion that this is exactly what happened.

William LaSor, late professor of Old Testament at Fuller Theological Seminary in Pasadena, California said:

> The very nature of the ark itself, made of wood manufactured in the 14th century B.C., would not lend a great deal of credence to the idea that it was preserved all that time, he said, "but the discovery of the Dead Sea scrolls changed our ideas of what is possible.[1]

The late Yigael Yadin, eminent archaeologist and former deputy premier of Israel, believed it was fruitless to search for the Ark. Before his death Yadin gave his thoughts on the lost Ark to journalist Louis Rapoport:

> Yadin himself is not tempted to search for the ark on anything else on the disputed Temple Mount . . . he believes that a search for the ark is like "trying to discover a mirage—it's not really archaeology." It is more a subject to be treated in fiction "because so little is known of it."[2]

The following view is typical of what many think happened to the Ark. Frank H. White says:

> When the Temple was burnt by Nebuchadnezzar, the Ark doubtless perished in the general conflagration (2 Chron. xxxvi. 19). Neither Ezra, Nehemiah, the Maccabees, nor Josephus make any mention of an Ark in connection with the second, or Zerubbabel's temple. The last authority expressly states that there was nothing in the Most Holy Place when the Temple was destroyed by Titus. Certainly no representation of such appears on the arch erected at Rome in honor of that conqueror, in which the spoils of the Temple are displayed.[3]

If the Ark had been destroyed the most probable time was during the sacking of Jerusalem by the armies of Babylon. As we have already noted, the Ark was in existence prior to this time, however, no mention of its existence is made after the Babylonian captivity. We know that Nebuchadnezzar plundered the holy vessels of the Temple:

> And he carried out from there all the treasures of the king's house, and he cut in pieces all the articles of gold which Solomon king of Israel had made in the temple of the Lord, as the Lord had said (2 Kings 24:13).

If the Ark were among the vessels taken, then the gold was possibly stripped off and the wooden container discarded. 18th century writer Humphrey Prideaux comments.

> What became of the old Ark on the destruction of the Temple by Nebuchadnezzar, is a dispute among the Rabbins. Had it been carried to Babylon with the other vessels of the Temple, it would have been brought back with them at the end of captivity. But that it is not so is agreed on all hands, and therefore it must follow, that it was destroyed with the Temple as were also the Altar of Incense, the Shew-bread Table, and the Golden Candlestick. For all these in the second Temple were made anew after the rebuilding of it.[4]

This line of reasoning does not necessarily follow. It is not required to assume the Ark was destroyed. The Temple vessels destroyed were the ones *made* by Solomon for Temple service. This would not include the Ark or the other furniture which was made by Moses and company at Mt. Sinai.

Ark Gone Earlier?

There are those who contend that the Ark was gone before the Babylonian captivity. Liberal scholar William Bennett writes:

> The Ark disappears from history after it is placed in Solomon's Temple, 1 Kings viii. 21. It was lost or fell to pieces some time before the Exile, and a prophetic oracle, Jer. iii. 16, forbade the construction of a substitute. Ps. cxxxii. seems to express the hope that God would in some way replace it.[5]

Jeremiah's Statement

There are those who see Jeremiah's statement as indicating the Ark was gone by his time (600 B.C.).

> 'Then it shall come to pass, when you are multiplied and increased in the land in those days,' says the Lord, 'that they will say no more, 'The ark of the covenant of the Lord.' It shall not come to mind, nor shall they remember it, nor shall they visit it, nor shall it be made anymore (Jeremiah 3:16).

C.J. Ball, commenting on this verse, writes:

> The reference to the Ark of the Covenant in verse 16 is remarkable upon several grounds. This sacred symbol is not mentioned among the spoils which Nebuzaradan took from the temple; nor is it specified among the treasures appropriated by Nebuchadnezzar at the surrender of Jechoniah. The words of Jeremiah prove that it cannot be included among "the vessels of gold" which the Babylonian conqueror "cut in pieces" (2 Kings xxiv. 13). We learn two facts about the ark from the present passage: (1) that it no longer existed in the days of the prophet; (2) that people remembered with regret, though they did not venture to replace the lost original by a new substitute. It may well have been destroyed by Manasseh, the king who did his utmost to abolish the religion of Iahvah [Jehovah].[6]

Jeremiah's statement has convinced many that the Ark had disappeared at the time of his writing.

Manasseh

It has been conjectured that the Ark was destroyed earlier by the evil King Manasseh. Menahem Haran writes:

> In actual fact, the disappearance of the inner sanctum objects from the Jerusalem temple does not seem connected with any external event, but with internal factors within the Judean kingdom—a unique religion-political constellation into which it passed only once in history. This was 'the sin of Manasseh . . .'
>
> Throughout the various changes that took place in the Kingdom of Judah, the Temple at Jerusalem never ceased to serve exclusively as the Temple of Yahweh . . . There was only one single period in its history when it was temporarily deprived of its original function and for a short while ceased to serve as a Temple for Yahweh . . . This occurred during the reign of Manasseh . . . who set up vessels for Baal . . . in the outer sanctum and introduced the image of Asherah into the inner sanctum of the Temple . . . This is the only happening which may explain the disappearance of the Ark and the cherubim. Some fifty years afterwards, when Josiah removed the Asherah from the Temple and burnt it in the Kidron Valley, beating it to dust and desecrating even the dust, the Ark and the cherubim were no longer there.[7]

No Record

There is, however, no historical account, whether it be in the Bible or elsewhere, that records the destruction of the Ark. Neither Daniel, Ezekiel, or Jeremiah record the Ark's destruction in Scripture. Furthermore, neither Flavius Josephus nor the Talmud give evidence that the sacred object had been demolished.

Some feel it would be unlikely that King Nebuchadnezzar would have deliberately destroyed such a prized trophy as the Ark. If he found the Ark, he would have kept it to display before his people.

Because there is no mention of the destruction of the Ark or its returning with the exiles, many have felt that another solution needs to be found to explain its disappearance. While it is possible that the Ark has been destroyed, the fact that the Scriptures are silent to its fate might weigh against this.

Endnotes for Chapter 26

1. Laurinda Keys, *In Search of the Real 'Lost Ark,'* Associated Press, 1981.

2. Louis Rapoport, The Mystery of the Real Lost Ark, *Jewish Digest,* September, 1982, p. 29.

3. Frank H. White, *Christ in the Tabernacle,* London, S.W. Partridge and Company, 1910, p. 147.

William Knight writes:

> What became of the Tabernacle vessels we know not: but we are told that, when Nebuchadnezzar took the Temple, he carried out the treasures of the Lord's House, and cut into pieces all the vessels of gold which Solomon had made for the Temple-service; that is the larger and more important implements. Many of the smaller ones were taken to Babylon, and after having been exhibited at Belshazzar's feast, were brought back on the return from the Captivity. Those that had been destroyed were restored by Ezra, in pursuance with the orders of the Persian kings (William Knight, *The Arch of Titus,* London, Religious Tract Society, 1896, p. 88).

4. Humphrey Prideaux, *Old and New Testament Connected,* Part 1, Vol. 1, 10th edition, 1729, p. 212.

5. William H. Bennett, *The Books of Chronicles,* London, Hodder & Stoughton,1989, p. 201

6. C.J. Ball, *The Prophecies of Jeremiah,* New York, A.C. Armstrong and Son, 1903, p. 124.

7. Menahem Haran, *Temples and Temple-Service in Ancient Israel,* Oxford, Claredon Press, 1978, p. 277.

We also have a reference that King Ahaz cut to pieces some of the holy vessels.

> So Ahaz gathered the articles of the house of God, cut in pieces the articles of the house of God, shut up the doors of the house of the Lord, and made for himself altars in every corner of Jerusalem (2 Chronicles 28:24).

There is also the fact that Ezekiel records the glory of God departing from the Temple in his time (600 B.C.)

> Then the glory of the Lord departed from the
> threshold of the temple and stood over the cherubim . . .
> And the glory of the Lord went up from the midst of the
> city and stood on the mountain which is east of the city.
> (Ezekiel 10:18:11:23).

Zev Vilnay records some Jewish legends concerning the
Ark.

> What became of the Holy Ark? After the Temple was
> destroyed some say it sank in its place on Mount Moriah,
> into the depths of the earth. . .
> In the course of his duties in the courtyard, a priest
> serving in the Second Temple perceived in the floor a slab
> which differed from all the others. He went to tell his
> friends about it, but before he finished speaking his soul
> departed from his body. Then the priests knew that the
> Holy Ark was hidden beneath this particular slab. . .
> The Ark was struck with a hammer until a flame was
> kindled and it was burnt (Zev Vilnay, *Legends of the
> Jerusalem,* (Sacred Land Vol 1) Philadelphia, Jewish
> Publication Society of America, 1973 p. 32).

CHAPTER 27

THE ARK AND THE
THIRD TEMPLE

If the Ark of the Covenant is eventually
located, it may play a decisive role in a future Temple to be
built in the city of Jerusalem. We have already seen that
Israel has had two Temples in its past. The First Temple
was built by Solomon and destroyed by the Babylonians.
The Second Temple was built by Zerubbabel, expanded by
Herod and then destroyed by the Romans.

Since the destruction of the Second Temple in A.D. 70, it
has been the desire of the Jewish people to see a Third
Temple built. Rabbi Leibel Reznick writes:

> The Holy Temple was the very heart and soul of the
> Jewish people. Before the First Temple was ever built,
> King David longed for it. In anticipation, he dedicated his
> royal treasures to the Temple building. He composed
> Psalms, liturgical works to be sung in the Temple service.
> After the Second Temple was destroyed, Jews yearned
> to rebuild it. It is now almost 2,000 years since the
> destruction of the Temple and still, three times each day,
> Jews express in their prayers their hopes for the
> rebuilding of their Temple. The Temple is not only a proud
> memory of the past, but represents the future of the
> Jewish nation.
> The future Temple, according to prophetic visions, will
> herald an era when no nation will raise up a sword
> against another, when war will not be taught, and when
> instruments of battle will be beaten into plowshares. The

Jewish Temple is the hope of mankind. The future Temple
will be God's palace on earth. God shall reign as King and
His subjects will be at peace with one another.[1]

This has been the hope of the Jewish people for almost
two thousand years.

Bible Prophecy

The hope of Christians is the Second Coming of Jesus
Christ. Certain things, however, still have to take place on
earth before Christ returns.[2] Many students of Scripture
believe that one of the necessary things is the building of a
Third Temple. This Temple will be built by the Jews in
unbelief. It will be defiled by a coming world leader who will
set himself up as world dictator. Though the Jews will
initially accept him as their Messiah, he will actually be an
impersonator—the Antichrist. This "Man of Sin" will be
judged at the Second Coming of Christ.

There are, however, good Christian Bible students who
do not believe the Scripture requires that a Third Temple be
built. They believe these prophecies have already been
fulfilled or will not be fulfilled literally. The author
respectively disagrees with this position and has
documented the reasons in another book.[3]

Where the Ark Fits in

It is possible that the Ark will never be found and a
Third Temple could still be built. We have already seen that
the Ark of the Covenant was not in the Second Temple—
which lasted from 515 B.C. to A.D. 70. Likewise, a Third
Temple could be constructed without the Ark.

The discovery of the Ark, however, could speed up this
process of the Temple's rebuilding by giving the Jews
incentive to begin. If the Ark is discovered, it may not be
possible to stop the building of a Third Temple. Too many
Jewish authorities in the past have spoken of the day
when the Ark will be discovered and the Third Temple built.
Louis Rapoport notes:

> Recently a noted (but unnamed) Israeli archaeologist
> told Ha'aretz that the discovery of the Temple treasure
> would be the crowing achievement for any archaeologist
> who has worked in Jerusalem. He might have added that
> such a discovery would have such an immense impact on
> the world; according to Jewish belief, it would portend the

advent of the Messiah and the building of the Third Temple.[4]

Former Chief Rabbi Shlomo Goren said that it is against Jewish belief to reveal the real story of where the Ark was hidden:

> The secret will be revealed just prior to building the Third Temple, he said, The ark will reveal the truth of accepting the Ten Commandments from heaven. This is the evidence that Moses brought to the Jews. It will be the greatest testimony of what we have followed because it contains both the broken tablets and the complete second tablets.[5]

One Israeli Rabbi put it this way:

> If we find the ark, it will force us to build the temple. After all the first temple was built to house the ark of the covenant. If we find the ark, what would we do with it? We couldn't store it in the prime minister's basement. It would demand the rebuilding of the temple. However, if we find the ark or not we are going to build the temple of Almighty God on the . . . temple mountain.[6]

Descend From Heaven or Built on Earth?

Part of the many controversies regarding a Third Temple revolves around how it will come about. Will it supernaturally descend from heaven or will the people here on earth construct it? This has been a source of debate amongst the Jews. Chief Rabbi Shlomo Riskin writes:

> What makes our generation unique is that the destruction of the first two Temples . . . has begun to evoke in us—the generation of Jerusalem's liberation—a hunger a curiosity about the building of the Third Temple. We know where, we know what, and some of us believe we even know why. When it comes to the how the Third Temple will be built, we find a controversy between the Sages, and this is fraught with implications for us today.
> Rashi, probably the greatest of the Ashkenazi commentators, makes a distinction between the first temples, that were built by human hands, and the future Temple, which he believed is to be built by God—a temple destined to "descend from heaven" whole and intact. While Rashi does not elaborate on this wondrous claim, he does provide a supporting verse: "The sanctuary, my

Lord, that your hands established" (Ex 15:17 cited in Succa 41a). . .

Maimonides, however, in his Book of Commandments, as well as the Mishne Tora, calls the building of the Temple, a positive commandment. In other words, it up to us to act. Maimonides cites the verse: "And let them make Me a sanctuary, that I may dwell among them" (Ex 25:8).

The text couldn't be clearer.

The difference of opinion is one of the most relevant issues in Jewish life today, given that for the first time in nearly 2,000 years the Temple Mount is in Jewish hands, and the rebuilding of the Temple has become a real possibility.[7]

The answer to this question may be resolved with the locating of the Ark. According to one Jewish tradition, when the Messiah comes he will perform seven miracles to prove his authenticity, one of them is discovering the Ark of the Covenant. Only time will tell, however, if the lost Ark will be found and placed in the Third Temple.

Endnotes for Chapter 27

1. Leibel Reiznik, *The Holy Temple Revisited*, Northvale, New Jersey, Jason Aronson, Inc, 1990.

2. This refers to the Second Coming of Christ, not the rapture of the church.

3. Don Stewart and Chuck Missler, *The Coming Temple: Center Stage For the Final Countdown*, Orange, California, Dart Press, 1991.

4. Louis Rapoport, The Mystery of the Real Lost Ark, *Jewish Digest*, September, 1982, p. 26.

5. Rapoport, ibid. p. 28.

6. Rabbi Hacohen cited by David Lewis, *Prophecy 2000*, Green Forest, Arizona, New Leaf Press, 1990, p. 178.

7. Jerusalem *Post*, International Edition, p. 23.

CHAPTER 28

WHAT DOES THE BIBLE SAY ABOUT THE FUTURE OF THE ARK?

In our search for the lost Ark we have looked at various theories as to what has happened to the sacred object in the past. We will now investigate what the Bible has to say about the Ark's future.

There is one passage in Scripture that speaks directly about this matter—Jeremiah 3:16.

'Then it shall come to pass, when you are multiplied and increased in the land in those days,' says the Lord, 'that they will say no more, 'The ark of the covenant of the Lord.' It shall not come to mind, nor shall they remember it, nor shall they visit it, nor shall it be made anymore (Jeremiah 3:16).

The people of Jeremiah's day attached too much importance to the Ark as the visible symbol of the Lord's presence. They needed to understand that this symbol was not made to last forever. Hence, Jeremiah spoke of a day when the Ark would no longer exist, would never be made again, and never even come to mind.

This was the first time in the history of Israel that such an announcement had been made, and it must have come as a shock to the Jews. Never had an Old Testament prophet made such a statement; it was unparalleled. Their entire worship was built around the Ark of the Covenant which symbolized God Himself. Now they were told it would disappear and no longer be missed.[1]

Many commentators feel that Jeremiah, writing before the destruction of the Temple, was predicting the soon loss of the Ark. They feel he was, in effect, preparing the people for what they were about to experience.

When Will This Occur?

It is clear that Jeremiah predicted that the Ark would be lost someday and never come to mind. The question before us now is, "When was this supposed to occur? Many commentators believe it was at the destruction of the First Temple in 587 B.C. They point to the fact that the Ark has been lost and not rebuilt as he predicted. Thus, Jeremiah's prophecy has been literally fulfilled.

There is, however, another way of looking at Jeremiah's prediction. First, he prefaces his remarks by saying it will occur when the people are "multiplied and increased in the land." It is difficult to find this part of the prophecy having been fulfilled. After the First Temple was destroyed, only a remnant of the people returned to Jerusalem. It seems that the blessings that Jeremiah said would come did not transpire in those days, nor in the entire period that the Second Temple existed. Therefore, it appears likely that the context he was speaking of is still in the future.

The next two verses give us a further clue that Jeremiah's prediction is for sometime still in the future:

> At that time Jerusalem shall be called the Throne of the Lord, and all the nations shall be gathered to it, to the name of the Lord, to Jerusalem; they shall walk no more after the stubbornness in their evil heart. In those days the house of Judah shall walk with the house of Israel and they shall come out of the land of the north to the land that I have given as an inheritance to your fathers (Jeremiah 3:17,18).

This future era will be a time when the Lord Himself, the One whom the Ark symbolized, is ruling from the city of Jerusalem— a time when Judah and Israel become one. In those days, they will not speak of the Ark. But those days have not yet come for all nations have not gathered in Jerusalem to worship the Lord, and the Jews have not stopped talking about the Ark. In fact, they have longed for it since the time of its disappearance. This part of the Jeremiah's prophecy is yet to be fulfilled.

The conditions that Jeremiah has predicted have not yet come upon the earth. Because these prophecies have not been completely fulfilled, it is possible that the Ark may indeed appear again in the future.[2]

We can, therefore, say that the prophet Jeremiah does not seem to rule out the Ark surfacing again.

Jeremiah 31

Jeremiah 3:16 is often linked with Jeremiah 31:31,33 which predicts a new Covenant that God would make with His people.

'Behold, the days are coming' says the Lord, 'when I will make a new covenant with the house of Israel and with the house of Judah' . . . But this is the covenant I will make with the house of Israel. After those days, says the Lord, I will put My law in their minds, and write it upon their hearts; and I will be their God, and they shall be My people (Jeremiah 31:31,33).

The old covenant, symbolized by the Ark, will be replaced by a new covenant written upon the heart. The Ark will not be restored because it will no longer be necessary as a symbol of the new covenant. The times of ceremonial emphasis will pass away for the actual glory of God will be in the midst of the people. This too has yet to be fully realized.

Revelation 11

The future of the Ark is thought by some to be found in a passage in the Book of Revelation.

Then the temple of God was opened in heaven, and the Ark of His covenant was seen in His temple. And there were lightnings, noises, thunderings, an earthquake, and great hail (Revelation 11:19).

Many commentators believe this statement teaches that the Ark was taken to heaven by God. This, it is argued, reveals that we will never find the Ark on earth because it is actually in Heaven. The Book of Revelation, however, is not speaking of the Ark of the Covenant that was built on earth, but rather the one that exists, and has always

existed, in Heaven. The Bible says that the Tabernacle and
its furniture were built after copies of things that are in
Heaven.

> For Christ has not entered the holy places made with
> hands, which are copies of the true, but into heaven itself,
> now to appear in the presence of God (Hebrews 9:24).

Though the eleventh chapter of Revelation speaks of
the Ark of the Covenant in heaven, this passage may have
some implications as to the lost Ark's discovery. The fact
that the Ark in heaven is mentioned in a chapter
(Revelation 11) dealing with the future Third Temple and
the coming "Man of Sin" may indeed indicate that the Ark
built on earth has been found and is used in this Third
Temple. The Book of Revelation, which deals with the
future, only mentions the coming Temple in chapter 11,
the same chapter where the Ark in heaven is mentioned.
This connection obviously has some significance, possibly
hinting at the previous rediscovery of the Ark. The Lord, by
revealing the heavenly Ark, may be contrasting the
original in heaven with the copy which was made on earth.

Though we do not know this for certain, it is entirely
possible, and can fit consistently into the Bible's end-time
scenario. This issue will be extensively dealt with in a
forthcoming book on the subject of this coming "Man of
Sin," and his appearance on the world scene.[3]

Conclusion

Jeremiah 3:16 speaks of a day when the Ark of the
Covenant will not exist, will not be constructed again, and
will be forgotten by the people. Many interpreters believe
this day has already come. Others think the time
Jeremiah spoke of is still future to our day. Revelation 11
may provide a hint about the future discovery of the Ark
seeing that it is connected with events surrounding the
Third Temple. There are no other passages that clearly
speak of the Ark's discovery.[4]

What we can say is this, until Jesus Christ comes back
and sets up His kingdom upon the earth, the Ark of the
Covenant will remain in the minds of people.

A Final Thought

After examining the possible solutions to the problem
of the lost Ark the only thing one can say for sure is that

the fate of the Ark is still a mystery. Although some have claimed to know the solution to this mystery, nothing has yet been brought forth to prove any particular case. William LaSor makes the observation:

> I don't think any archaeologist seriously considers finding it, . . . But there's always the happenstance that if things are buried properly, in the right kind of soil, they could survive.[5]

Whether it will ever be found no one knows for sure; the Scripture does not expressly state it one way or the other. We can only wait and see.

Endnotes for Chapter 28

1. These statements by Jeremiah that the Ark, containing God's eternal law, would be lost, have particularly perplexed Jewish commentators. Charles Feinberg notes:

> One of them, Abarbanel, expressed the opinion that the promise was bad since it uprooted the whole law and he wondered how the Scripture could refer to it as good. (Charles Feinberg, *The Expositors Bible Commentary*, Volume 6, General Editor Frank Gaebelein, Grand Rapids, Zondervan, 1986, p. 402).

It is also recognized that the Ark will not be found in the future Temple of Ezekiel (Ezekiel 40-48).

2. Some commentators assert that the Scriptures predict the discovery of the Ark. Grant Jeffrey writes:

> Only the passage of time and further research will conclusively prove the true location of the lost Ark. However, biblical prophecies clearly indicate that the Ark (wherever the Lord has preserved it) will be involved in the motivation of the Jews to build the Third Temple (Grant R. Jeffrey, *Messiah War in the Middle East & The Road To Armageddon*, Toronto, Canada, Frontier Research Publications, 1991, p. 247).

This statement is going too far. It is *not* true that the Bible unquestionably expresses the Ark will be found or will be involved in the Jewish desire to build a Third Temple. While this scenario is possible, it certainly isn't "clearly indicated."

3. The book is due to be released in Summer of 1993. It is tentatively titled *The Final Caesar: The Coming Antichrist*.

4. The late Bible commentator, Arthur Bloomfield, believed the Ark would be brought back from Ethiopia as a "sign" to the nations shortly before the coming of Christ. He argued that the word translated "banner" (Hebrew *Nes*) in several Old Testament passages was actually speaking of the Ark of the Covenant. His theory, which has been promoted by others, does not have any Biblical support.
  To begin with, this term (*Nes*) is never used of the Ark of the Covenant in any of the historical sections of the Old Testament. To assume it speaks of it prophetically has no basis in fact. K.H. Maahs explains what the term "banner" meant.

A banner was usually a flag, streamer, or wrought emblem affixed to the end of a standard. It was common in the ancient world for banners to be used for military, national or religious purposes in much the way they are today. The purpose of the banner was to indicate the rallying point for any group holding to a common cause. (K.H. Maahs, *International Standard Bible Encyclopedia*, Volume 1, Revised Edition, Grand Rapids, Wm. B. Eerdmans Publishing Company, 1979, p. 409).

Furthermore, the verses which Bloomfield and others use to support their argument are very weak. One example will be sufficient.

Isaiah chapter 18:1-7, are supposedly clear references to the Ark being brought from Ethiopia to Jerusalem before Christ returns. Grant R. Jeffrey writes:

In Isaiah 18, we find the clearest indication that the Ark of the Covenant will be brought from Ethiopia at the time of the end. God addresses the people of Ethiopia in the first two verses and tells them of the part they will play in the unfolding events of the last days (Grant R. Jeffrey, *Armageddon Appointment with Destiny*, New York, Bantam Books, 1990, p. 119)

A close examination of these verses will show this is not the case. The subject of the passage is "Ethiopia" or "Cush."

Woe to the land shadowed with buzzing wings which is beyond the rivers of Ethiopia, which send ambassadors by sea, even in vessels of reed on the waters, saying, "Go swift messengers, to a nation tall and smooth of skin to a people terrible from their beginning onward, a nation powerful and treading down whose land the rivers divide" (Isaiah 18:1,2).

The term Cush, which some Bible versions translate as Ethiopia, seemingly involves more than the modern country. Geoffrey Grogan writes:

Biblical Cush is usually translated Ethiopia," but the NIV has wisely chosen transliteration rather than translation; for the term designates a much larger area than present-day Ethiopia—an area including the Sudan and Somalia. This somewhat mysterious area, situated at the limits of the normal biblical world, had come right into the world in Isaiah's day. It was normally in Egypt's area of influence and, usually, of control; but for a period during the eighth century, Egypt was ruled by an Ethiopian dynasty (Geoffrey F. Grogan, *The Expositors*

Bible Commentary, Volume,6 Frank C. Gaebelein General Editor, Zondervan, Grand Rapids, 1986, p. 122).

Isaiah 18:3 reads:

> All the inhabitants of the world and dwellers on the earth when he lifts up a *banner* on the mountains, you see it; and when he blows a trumpet you hear it.

The word translated "banner" here is supposedly referring to the Ark. Yet this passage has been fulfilled long ago. It is *not* talking about a future time, nor is it speaking of the Ark. David F. Payne writes:

> Chapters 18 ff. are concerned with Egypt but ch. 18 names the people of Ethiopia (Cush), because it was an Ethiopians Dynasty which came to power in Egypt in 715 B.C. Evidently the Ethiopian King Piankhi, had sent ambassadors to the king of Judah, Hezekiah; we can be certain their purpose was to involve Judah in a coalition against the Assyrians. Isaiah warns Hezekiah against any such folly, by providing God's answer to the ambassadors. The are to go back home, to their land renowed for both its profusion of insects, and also for its tall and warlike people. For all their military prowess and their distance from Assyria, the people of Ethiopia are not safe; God Himself has spoken and it is a word of doom and destruction (David F. Payne, *The New Layman's Bible Commentary*, Editors G.C.D Howley, F. F. Bruce, H. L. Ellison, Grand Rapids, Zondervan, 1979, p. 784).

Verses 1-6 saw its fulfillment long ago at the fall of Assyria. It has nothing to do with the future as far as we are concerned. Geoffrey F. Grogan writes:

> Chapters 18-20 . . . all deal with Egypt and Cush, which were one at this time . . . the doom is really pictured as falling on Assyria . . .
> The message given to the messengers had universal application, for the whole world would reverberate at the trumpet blasting Assyria's fall (v.3). The banner and trumpet (addressing the eye and ear) represent the call to rally for battle (Grogan, ibid. pp. 122,123).

Isaiah 18:7 does speak of a future time when Ethiopians come and bear gifts. This is the age when Jerusalem is the city of the great King (the Millennium). Commenting on Isaiah 18:7 David F. Payne writes:

Verse 7 is addressed to the reader, not to the envoys; it looks beyond the immediate fate of the Ethiopian and Egyptian armies (defeated by the Assyrians in 701 B.C.). Ultimately, the prophet reminds his readers, God intends that even such a distant nation as the Ethiopians shall worship the Lord of hosts, bringing their offerings to the Jerusalem temple. God's final purposes in history are those of a worshipping people drawn from all nations; cf. 66:23 (David F. Payne, *The New Layman's Bible Commentary*, Editors G.C.D Howley, F. F. Bruce, H. L. Ellison, Grand Rapids, Zondervan, 1979, p. 784).

The "gift" the Ethiopians bring is possibly their own presence. Derek Kidner observes:

The final verse seems to look beyond the immediate crisis of Assyrian aggression which had brought the envoys to Jerusalem. Isaiah now sees the travelers in a new light, as the first of many who will come to Zion one day in homage (the Heb. lacking the word from in v. 7a suggests that they will be themselves the homage gift). It is the prospect already seen in 2:3; 11:10; it will be further developed in chs. 60-62 (Derek Kidner, *The New Bible Commentary Revised*, edited by D. Guthrie, J.A. Moyer, A.M. Stibbs, D.J. Wiseman, Third Edition, Leicester, England, Intervarsity Press, 1970, p. 601).

This will happen at a future time when the Messiah is ruling in Jerusalem through His Temple. Geoffrey W. Grogan comments:

The very people who, from their position of strength, had sent word to Judah to secure her cooperation in a military venture would come again with gifts for the true God in Zion. This picture (cf. 45:15 and also Pss 68:31; 87:4; Zeph 3:10) is a specific illustration of the general vision in passages like 2:1-4 and 60:1-14 of Zion as the religious center of the whole world (Grogan, ibid. p. 123).

In verse 7 Isaiah is speaking of a time when the Lord is ruling from Jerusalem and former enemies, from the area of Ethiopia and beyond, are bringing him *gifts* (plural).

Other passages often cited as predicting the return of the Ark (Ezekiel 39:21,22 Zephaniah 3:9,10, Jeremiah 4:6, Isaiah 11:11,12) are likewise unconvincing.

The idea, therefore, that the Ark still exists in Ethiopia seems highly unlikely, it is also unlikely that these passages are referring to its return to Israel in the last days.

5. Laurinda Keys, *In Search of the Real Lost Ark*, Associated Press, 1981.

CHAPTER 29

WHY THE ARK IS NO LONGER NECESSARY

The Ark of the Covenant, the most sacred object in Israel's history, disappeared some 2,600 years ago. Perhaps it will someday reappear. Maybe it is forever lost. Whatever the case may be, the Ark of the Covenant is no longer necessary for us today. This is because the promises that the Ark represented have been fulfilled in the person of Jesus Christ.

Promise

In the Old Testament, God made a promise that He would dwell among His people.

And let them make Me a sanctuary, that I may dwell among them (Exodus 25:8).

In the Tabernacle and later in the Temple, God's presence was manifested through the Ark of the Covenant which symbolized His presence in a special way.

Yet the Ark pointed to an even greater reality—the time when God would personally come down and visit our planet. The Bible testifies that God became a man in the person of Jesus Christ:

And the Word became flesh and dwelt among us, and we beheld his glory, the glory as of the only begotten of the Father, full of grace and truth (John 1:14).

True Bread From Heaven

The manna in the wilderness was gathered in the golden pot that was placed in the Ark. This spoke of Jesus Christ the "true bread from heaven."

Then Jesus said to them, "Most assuredly, I say to you, Moses did not give you the bread from heaven, but My Father gives you the true bread from heaven. For the bread of God is He who comes down from heaven and gives life to the world . . . I am the bread of life. He who comes to Me will never hunger and he who believes in Me will never thirst (John 6:32,33,36).

New Covenant

Jesus spoke of a new covenant between God and man.

Then He took the cup, and gave thanks, and gave it to them, saying, "Drink from it all of you. For this is My blood of the new covenant, which is shed for the remission of sins (Matthew 26:27,28).

The covenant between God and His people was to be made with blood. Once a year, on the Great Day of Atonement, blood was sprinkled upon the Mercy Seat—the Atonement Cover. The blood of bulls and goats could only cover up sin. The death of Christ *took away* the sins of the world. The Bible says:

Not with the blood of goats and calves, but with His own blood He entered the Most Holy Place once for all, having obtained eternal redemption (Hebrews 9:12).

Jesus Christ is the means of forgiveness of sins in the New Covenant sprinkled not with the blood of animals but with His own blood. At Calvary's cross, God made satisfaction for our sins:

And He Himself is the propitiation [satisfaction] for our sins, and not for ours only but also for the whole world (1 John 2:2).

When Christ died upon the cross, the veil of the Temple separating the Holy place from the Holy of Holies was torn in half:

And behold the veil of the Temple was torn in two from top to bottom; and the earth quaked and the rocks were split (Matthew 27:51).

This signified that mankind now had direct access to God, there was no longer a veil keeping Him out. The sins that previously had only been "covered up" could now be taken away.

One Door

The Tabernacle, as well as the Temple, had only one door by which a person could enter and have access to God. To enter into this new covenant, you must come through the door that God has provided. Jesus said He Himself was that door.

I am the door. If anyone enters by Me, he will be saved, and will go in and out and find pasture (John 10:9).

The Ark of the Covenant, made out of wood and covered with gold, is no longer necessary for humanity. The access to God has now been made complete through Jesus Christ.

We close our study of the Ark of the Covenant with the words of 19th century Bible commentator Samuel Ridout.

May Christ, the Ark of the Covenant, be increasingly dear, as the One who in Himself contains all our treasures, and who will keep them and us safe till the day of glory and of joy, to the praise of His grace.[1]

Endnotes for Chapter 29

1. Samuel Ridout, *Lectures on the Tabernacle*, New York, Loizeaux Publishers, 1914, p. 266.

Christ is the mediator of a better covenant—a covenant that will be kept because it is between God and Himself.

And for this reason He is the Mediator of the new covenant, by means of death, for the redemption of the transgressions under the first covenant, that those who are called may receive the promised of eternal inheritance (Hebrews 9:15).

The New Testament speaks of the one who makes the covenant:

For where there is as testament, there must also of necessity be the death of the testator. For a testament is in force after men are dead, since it has no power at all while the testator lives. Therefore not even the first covenant was dedicated without blood (Hebrews 9:16-18).

The promise that God would dwell with His people will be completely fulfilled when Christ returns:

And I heard a loud voice from heaven saying, "Behold, the tabernacle of God is with men, and He will dwell with them, and they shall be his people, and God Himself will be with them and be their God (Revelation 21:3).

APPENDIX 1

BIBLICAL REFERENCES TO THE ARK OF THE COVENANT

The following is a basic history of the Ark of the Covenant as recorded in the Bible.

Mt. Sinai

God gives directions for the Ark's construction.
Exodus 25:10-22

Ordered to be placed in the Holy of Holies.
Exodus 26:34; 40:3

Moses orders the Ark to be constructed.
Exodus 35:12

The Ark is constructed by Bezaleel.
Exodus 38:1-9

The Ark is brought to Moses by the Israelites.
Exodus 39:35

The Ten Commandments are placed inside the Ark by Moses.
Deuteronomy 10:1-5; Exodus 40:20

The Ark is placed in the Tabernacle by Moses.
Exodus 40:21

Ordained to be the meeting-place between God and Moses.
Numbers 7:89; Exodus 25:22

Ark to be anointed with the Holy Oil.
Exodus 30:26; 40:9

The Ark is anointed when the priests are consecrated.
Leviticus 8:10

Aaron is not able to approach the Ark whenever he wishes.
Leviticus 17:2

The blood is to be sprinkled on the Mercy Seat, and before the
Mercy Seat, once a year by the High Priest on the Great Day of
Atonement.
Leviticus 17:2

The Kohathite Levites are to be in charge of the Ark.
Numbers 3:31

The Ark is to be covered before marching.
Numbers 4:5,6

The usual place of the Ark in the procession.
Numbers 10:21

Wilderness Wanderings

The Ark leaves Mt. Sinai.
Numbers 10:33-36

The Ark remains in the camp of Israel.
Numbers 14:44

Aaron's Rod is placed before the Ark.
Numbers 17:10

The Ark was possibly taken to battle under Phineas.
Numbers 31:6

Moses orders the Levites to put the book of the Law in the Ark.
Deuteronomy 31:9-26

The Ark in the Promised Land

The waters of Jordan are divided by the Ark.
Joshua 3,4

The Ark leads the procession around the walls of Jericho.
Joshua 6

The walls fall down in the presence of the Ark.
Joshua 6

Israel loses battle with Ai. Joshua prostrates himself in the presence of the Ark.
Joshua 7

The Ark stands between Ebal and Gerizim as the blessings and cursings are read.
Joshua 8:30-35; Deuteronomy 26:11-26

Joshua camps at Gilgal where he directs the battles for the land of Canaan.
Joshua 9:6; 10:7-43

The Tabernacle and the Ark are brought to Shiloh.
Joshua 18

Joshua gathers all Israel and the Tabernacle to Shechem. The Ark may have remained behind in Shiloh.
Joshua 24:21-26

The Tabernacle and the Ark are at Shiloh during the days of Samuel and Eli.
Judges 20:18-26; 1 Samuel 3:3

The High Priest Phineas received counsel from the Lord concerning the civil war with the tribe of Benjamin.
(Judges 20:27)

The Ark is taken to battle and is captured by the Philistines.
1 Samuel 4; Psalm 78:60,61

The Ark is taken to the Philistine city of Ashdod. In the house of Dagon at Ashdod, the idol of Dagon falls before the Ark.
1 Samuel 5:1-8

The Ark is sent to Ekron where people are plagued.
1 Samuel 5:8-12;6:1-2

The Ark is placed in a new cart and goes by Beth-Shemesh. Men of Beth-Shemesh die after looking into the Ark.
1 Samuel 6:9-20

The Ark is taken to Kirjath Jearim and remains there 20 years.
1 Samuel 6:21; 7:1,2

Saul consults the Ark in Gibeah where it must have been moved.
1 Samuel 14:16-18

The Ark is back in Kirjath Jearim.
2 Samuel 6

Uzzah dies while touching the Ark.
2 Samuel 6:11

The Ark remains in the house of Obed-Edom for three months.
1 Chronicles 13:14

David prepares a place in Jerusalem for the Ark.
2 Samuel 6:12-23

David wishes to build a house for the Ark, but God does not allow it.
2 Samuel 7:2

David has an affair with Bathsheba. Her husband Uriah refuses to stay in his own house because Israel and the Ark are living in tents.
2 Samuel 11:11

David flees Jerusalem with the Ark because of the rebellion of his son Absalom. David sends the Ark back to Jerusalem.
2 Samuel 15:24,25

Solomon builds the Temple on Mt. Moriah to house the Ark.
2 Chronicles 3:1

The Ark is brought from Mt. Zion to permanent resting place on Mt. Moriah.
2 Chronicles 5

The Ark is placed in the Temple.
1 Kings 8

Solomon moved his pagan wife away from the area of the Ark.
2 Chronicles 8:11

Josiah orders the Ark to be returned to Temple. This is the last historical reference to the Ark.
2 Chronicles 35:3

Hebrews 8
The Ark is mentioned in reference with the Tabernacle.

Revelation 11
The Ark of the Covenant in Heaven is highlighted.

APPENDIX 2

OTHER THEORIES OF THE LOCATION OF THE ARK

We have mentioned three well-publicized theories as to the possible location of the Ark of the Covenant as well as other possible resting places for it. There have been other theories, apart from the ones mentioned, that have surfaced. They include the following:

1. **Ein-Gedi**

2. **Masada**

3. **Gordon's Calvary**

4. **The Vatican**

5. **Qumran**

6. **Old City of Jerusalem**

We will briefly examine each of these theories that have achieved some degree of notoriety.

Ein-Gedi

In 1958, Lawrence W. Blaser began his search for the Ark of the Covenant. Blaser read the words of Ellen G. White, founder of the Seventh Day Adventists, in Volume 4 of her book *Spiritual Gifts*. In a dream, the location of the Ark was supposedly revealed to Mrs. White.

> Because of Israel's transgression of the commandments of God, and their wicked acts, God suffered them to go into captivity to humble and punish them. Before the temple was destroyed, God made known to a few of his faithful servants the fate of the temple, which was the pride of Israel, and which they regarded with idolatry while they were sinning against God. He also revealed to them the captivity of Israel. These righteous men, just before the destruction of the temple, removed the sacred Ark containing the tables of stone, and with mourning and sadness, secreted it in a cave where it was to be hid from the people of Israel, because of their sins, and was to be no more restored to them. The sacred Ark is yet hid [sic]. It has never been disturbed since it has been secreted.

Elsewhere White wrote in her *Bible Commentary*:

> The precious record of the law was placed in the Ark of the testament and is still there, safely hidden from the human family. But in God's appointed time he will bring forth these tables of stone to be a testimony to all the world against the disregard of His commandments.

From these writings, Blaser assumed that the Ark was hidden in a cave somewhere near Jerusalem. He rejected the idea that the Ark could have been taken to Mt. Nebo because it was too far from Jerusalem, beyond the borders of Judah.

While attempting to reconstruct the situation during the time of the destruction of the Second Temple, Blaser concluded that the Ark could very well have been buried in Ein-Gedi, some forty miles from Jerusalem. Ein-Gedi is also the location of the cave where David hid from King Saul.

In 1975 Blaser decided to explore "David's Cave"—the one tourists are told that David hid himself from Saul. Blaser reckoned that the traditional site of the cave did not meet the biblical description. Therefore he started to look elsewhere but could not find "David's Cave." Believing that the entrance to the cave had been hidden, Blaser enlisted the help of two employees of the United States Bureau of Mines.

Returning in 1977, Blaser along with his experts, Frank Ruskey and Richard Burdick, conducted geophysical experiments of the area. A hidden "artificial wall" and underground caverns were soon discovered.

Thinking that he had discovered "David's Cave" where the Ark of the Covenant was hidden, Blaser started assembling a reputable team of archaeologists whom the Israel Department of Antiquities would permit to excavate. One of them was James F. Strange, Dean of the College of the Arts and Letters at the University of South Florida. Strange agreed to serve as field director of the project.

The expedition, however, showed that the seismic readings of the experts were misinterpreted. There was no hidden man-made cave. The magazine *Biblical Archaeology Review* wrote:

> The "artificial wall" was in fact a natural bedrock sea. The underground caverns were there all right, created by underground water activity that eroded the limestone. But the seal was bedrock and no man or animal had ever been inside.[1]

Disappointed, the group packed up the morning of the second day and went home.

Archaeologist James Strange commented on the expedition:

> We wasted a lot of money and certainly some valuable time, but there still may be caves that need opening out there in Ein Gedi. There is no reason to think that the Ark of the Covenant is there, but many other interesting things are likely to be found.[2]

Blaser was also disappointed by the results of the trip.

Larry Blaser is also disappointed. He admits that what he thought was the opening to the cave is in fact not the opening. But he thinks there may be an opening elsewhere that he hasn't found and that the cave may very well be David's cave. Although he speaks with less conviction now, he still believes this cave is the best site in the Middle East for hiding the Ark of the Covenant. However, he has no specific plans to pursue his quest further.[3]

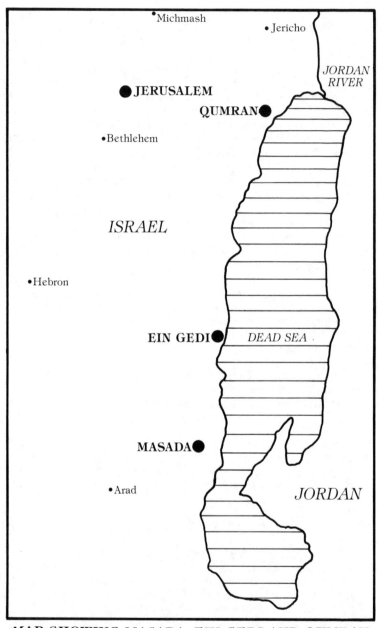

MAP SHOWING MASADA, EIN GEDI AND QUMRAN

Ein-Gedi, the place where David hid from the pursuing King Saul, did not yield the lost Ark of the Covenant.

Masada

The mountain of Masada has a very emotional place in the hearts of the Jews. In A.D. 73, a small band of Jewish rebels were attacked by the mighty Roman army who were attempting to scale this mountain fortress. After valiantly holding out, the people of Masada committed mass suicide rather than being taken captive by the Romans. Masada, the symbol for courage among the Israeli people, is also another possible location of the Ark.

Israeli journalist Abraham Rabinovich tells the story of a woman who came to him with a vision of the Ark's location. The woman, Frida Schlain, told him the story of her strange vision. She had come from her home in Argentina to Jerusalem, to follow the strange voice that was leading her. Rabinovich explains:

> First she saw events from her real life in which through accident or sickness she had come close to death. Then she heard a voice, the same authoritative voice she heard in the car. "This has all been conditioning for now, so that you will be ready to listen and to do what we ask."
>
> Then she saw herself flying high over a strange landscape. On one side was a large body of water; on the other, a lake. Near the lake, a flat mountaintop. In the center of the mountaintop was a circular wall of small stones surrounding a hole. Soldiers were digging in the hole as she alighted near them. They were pulling a box from the hole, a large box covered with dirt. From one end, the dirt fell away, revealing a golden metal. "This is . . . the Holy Ark," says the voice. "This is energy." Frida must go to the mountain and dig up the box, says the voice. The metal glows so powerfully that it knocked Frida back waking her up.[4]

Frida Schlain made a dozen different trips to Masada looking for the lost Ark. She was allowed to sleep on the mountain at night, yet she did not find any trace of the Ark she had seen in the vision. Soon thereafter, Frida Schlain died, her quest of finding the Holy Ark unfulfilled.

Gordon's Calvary

Another theory that has made the rounds is that the Ark was secretly buried under Gordon's Calvary, the place where many Protestants believe Jesus was crucified. The Ark was supposedly hidden there sometime in the distant past. When Jesus died upon the cross, according to this theory, His blood flowed down through the rocks and onto the Mercy Seat of the Ark of the Covenant. There is, however, no historical evidence whatsoever for this hypothesis.

Apart from the lack of historical evidence that the Ark was buried in the vicinity of Christ's crucifixion, the exact site of His execution is still a matter of debate. Gordon's Calvary is one possible location— as is the Church of the Holy Sepulchre. Other sites have also been suggested. This has not stopped some Americans from searching the area between Gordon's Calvary and the Garden Tomb for the lost Ark.

Vatican

In his booklet, *We Have Found the Ark of the Covenant*, Prophecy teacher J.R. Church theorizes that the Ark now resides in the underground vaults of the Vatican. Church says that he met a man who has supposedly seen the lost Ark. This man claimed he had served several years as a Benedictine monk in the Catholic church. He told Church that while working in the area of Rome, he was taken to a room some four stories below the ground where he saw the golden Ark. Church reports that the object the man described fits the Biblical description of the Ark.

There have been some ancient reports of the Ark being in Rome, but most are considered fanciful. William Knight explains:

> Adrichomius, a writer of the sixteenth century, in a work on the Geography of the Holy Land, gravely tells us that the Ark of the Covenant, the Tables of the Law, the Rods of Moses and Aaron and some portions even of the Shewbread were, in his days, in the church of St. John Lateran in Rome, . . . the Ark, the two Tables, and the Rods of Moses and Aaron . . . are admitted by the Jews to have been lost on the destruction of the First Temple.[5]

Similar reports of the Ark's presently residing in Rome have been brought to the author's attention. There is, however, no solid historical evidence that the Ark was ever brought to Rome though the idea of the Ark joining the rest of the Vatican treasures is certainly not out of the realm of possibility.

Qumran

The area of Qumran is the place where the Dead Sea Scrolls were discovered in 1948. Qumran is yet another location where people are searching for the lost Ark. One of the Dead Sea Scrolls called the "Copper Scroll" (discovered in May 1952 but not translated until 1961) contains a detailed list of instructions for finding hidden treasure.[6] Some believe these treasures could be the Temple vessels including the Ark of the Covenant. Unfortunately, the geographical references are so obscure that no one is certain where to look for these treasures, if they ever did exist. Yet this has not stopped some from looking for the Ark by using the Copper Scroll. Consider the headline that read:

Real -life 'Indiana' Jones Looking for Ark of the Covenant

This article, talks about the quest for Temple treasures including the Ark of the Covenant. Writer Dell Griffen states:

> A chemical analyst says he has positively identified a red powder found in a cove on the Kumran cliffs as the incense used in the Second Temple. And Vendyl Jones, the Texan Bible scholar and archaeologist leading the excavation says this means he will soon find a hidden cache of Temple treasure. . .
> The declaration was met with initial skepticism by the rabbinate and Israeli archeologists.[7]

The incense was found in a cave in 1989 by a volunteer with Jones's group. Jones, a former Baptist minister who has now denied the main beliefs of the Christian faith, claims that the character Indiana Jones in *Raiders of the Lost Ark* was loosely based upon his search for the Ashes of the Red Heifer. The article goes on to say:

> The former Baptist preacher . . . announced that he
> believes he is close to finding a burial stone concealing the
> entrance to a seventh chamber in a cave. If his wife Zahava
> Cohen's interpretation of the Copper Scroll is correct,
> this chamber may contain the desert-built tabernacle of
> Moses, and possibly the Ark of the Covenant.
> Jones said he believes these Temple artifacts were
> hidden initially by the prophet Jeremiah in a cave on
> Mount Nebo (Jordan) but were recovered by the priestly
> Zadokites who later lived in the area and had access to the
> writings of the Maccabees, which revealed where the
> objects were hidden. Jones said, adding that the
> discovery of a vial of . . . holy anointing oil nearby in 1988
> vindicated the scroll.[8]

The quest for these treasures has drawn skepticism
from Israeli archaeologists.

> Amos Kloner, an archaeology professor at Bar-Ilan
> University claims that Jones is wasting his time. "I'm
> sure the Temple treasures were destroyed," Kloner said,
> adding that the Copper Scroll has proven an unreliable
> guide.[9]

For the time being, Jones has not been granted a
permit by Israeli authorities to do any further
investigation. Others, not associated with him, are also
looking for Ark in the Qumran area. As with all the other
possible places the Ark may be, we will have to wait and see
what comes of the search.

Old City of Jerusalem

The Jewish Quarter of the Old City of Jerusalem is
another place where the Temple treasures were supposed
to have been buried. Louis Rapoport explains:

> The legend comes from a sixth century visitor to the
> Holy Land, Procopius, who said that when the Emperor
> Constantine built the Nea Church, between the Dung
> Gate and Zion Gate, he moved the Temple treasure there
> from Constantinople. " . . . the church was pillaged so
> many times that it would be a miracle if the ark were
> there," [Yigael] Yadin says.[10]

This has not stopped people from continuing to search
in the Old City of Jerusalem for the lost Ark.

Conclusion

None of these six theories has convincing evidence to substantiate them, but until the Ark of the Covenant is found, we should not shut ourselves off to any possible resting place for it.

Endnotes for Appendix 2

1. The author is aware of still other places the Ark is supposed to be located. Space does not permit us to deal with every conceivable theory. The ones examined in this book are listed because they have some possibility of being true or have become popular with different segments of people.

2. The Ark That Wasn't There, *Biblical Archaeological Review*, (BAR) July/August, 1983, p. 61.

3. BAR, ibid. p. 61.

4. Abraham Rabinovich, *Jerusalem on Earth*, New York, The Free Press, 1988, pp. 132,133.

5. William Knight, *The Arch of Titus*, London, Religious Tract Society, 1896, pp. 118,119. Knight also wrote:

> The same fabrication about the Ark is also repeated by Minutolius, Dissert, Roman Antiq. Illust. in Sallengre's Thesaurus, vol i. (Knight, ibid. p. 118).

6. The copper scroll was found in cave 3-Q-15 at Qumran. It is composed of three copper sheets riveted together. The eight foot long, one foot wide scroll contains sixty-four "secret locations" where treasures of gold and silver from the Temple were supposedly hidden. Archaeologists generally do not give the scroll much credence, particularly when the combined hidden treasure consists of forty-five hundred talents of gold and silver (a talent weights almost 100 pounds).

7. Dell Griffen, Jerusalem *Post*, International Edition, Week Ending May 23, 1992, p.13.

8. Dell Griffen, ibid. p. 13.

9. Dell Griffen, ibid. p. 13.

10. Louis Rapoport, The Mystery of the Real Lost Ark, *Jewish Digest*, February 1982, p. 29.

ABOUT THE AUTHOR

Don Stewart

Don Stewart is one of the most successful writers in the country having authored or co-authored over twenty books. These include *You Be The Judge, The Coming Temple* and *Ten Reasons To Trust the Bible.*

Don's writings have also achieved international success. Twenty-four of his titles have been translated into different languages including Chinese, Finnish, Polish, Spanish, German, and Portuguese.

He received his undergraduate degree at Biola University majoring in Bible. He received a masters degree from Talbot Theological Seminary graduating with the highest honors. He is also a member of the national honor society, Kappa Tau Epsilon.

Don is also an internationally known apologist, a defender of the historic Christian faith. In his defense of Christianity he has traveled to over thirty countries speaking at colleges, universities, churches, seminars, and retreats. His topics include the evidence for Christianity, the identity of Jesus Christ, the challenge of the cults, and the relationship of the Bible and science.

Because of his international success as an author and speaker, Don Stewart's various books have generated sales of over one million copies.

Other Books By Don Stewart

You Be The Judge: Is Christianity True?

Ten Reasons To Trust The Bible (formerly titled The Ten Wonders Of The Bible).

The Coming Temple (with Chuck Missler)

Basic Bible Study Series

* What Everyone Needs To Know About **God**

* What Everyone Needs To Know About **Jesus**

* What Everyone Needs To Know About **The Holy Spirit**

* What Everyone Needs To Know About **The Bible**

To order books call toll free
1-800-637-5177

**Dart Press
Box 6486
Orange, California
92613**